The Indian Face of God
in Latin America

FAITH AND CULTURES SERIES

An Orbis Series on Contextualizing Gospel and Church
General Editor: Robert J. Schreiter, C.PP.S.

The *Faith and Cultures Series* deals with questions that arise as Christian faith attempts to respond to its new global reality. For centuries Christianity and the church were identified with European cultures. Although the roots of Christian tradition lie deep in Semitic cultures and Africa, and although Asian influences on it are well documented, that original diversity was widely forgotten as the church took shape in the West.

Today, as the churches of the Americas, Asia, and Africa take their place alongside older churches of Mediterranean and North Atlantic cultures, they claim the right to express Christian faith in their own idioms, thought patterns, and cultures. To provide a forum for better understanding this process, the Orbis *Faith and Cultures Series* publishes books that illuminate the range of questions that arise from this global challenge.

Orbis and the *Faith and Cultures Series* General Editor invite the submission of manuscripts on relevant topics.

Also in the Series

Faces of Jesus in Africa, Robert J. Schreiter, C.PP.S., Editor
Hispanic Devotional Piety, C. Gilbert Romero
African Theology in Its Social Context, Bénézet Bujo
Models of Contextual Theology, Stephen B. Bevans, S.V.D.
Asian Faces of Jesus, R. S. Sugirtharajah, Editor
Evangelizing the Culture of Modernity, Hervé Carrier, S.J.
St. Martín de Porres: The Little Stories and the Semiotics of Culture, Alex García-Rivera

FAITH AND CULTURES SERIES

The Indian Face of God in Latin America

Manuel M. Marzal
Eugenio Maurer
Xavier Albó
Bartomeu Melià

Translated by
Penelope R. Hall

ORBIS BOOKS

Maryknoll New York 10545

The Catholic Foreign Mission Society of America (Maryknoll) recruits and trains people for overseas missionary service. Through Orbis Books, Maryknoll aims to foster the international dialogue that is essential to mission. The books published, however, reflect the opinions of their authors and are not meant to represent the official position of the society.

Library of Congress Cataloging in Publication Data

Rostro indio de Dios. English
    The Indian face of God in Latin America / Manuel M. Marzal . . . [et al.] : translated by Penelope R. Hall.
        p. cm. : (Faith and cultures series)
    Includes bibliographical references and index.
    ISBN 1-57075-054-8 (alk. paper)
    1. Indians of South America—Religion. 2. Indians of Mexico—Religion. 3. Syncretism (Religion)—Latin America.
    4. Christianity—Latin America. I. Marzal, Manuel M. (Manuel Maria), 1931- . II. Title. III. Series.
    F2230.1.R3R6713   1996
    261.2'98—dc20   96-17766
                                                                    CIP

Contents

PART TWO
THE RELIGION OF THE ANDEAN QUECHUA
IN SOUTHERN PERU
MANUEL M. MARZAL

PART THREE
THE AYMARA RELIGIOUS EXPERIENCE
XAVIER ALBÓ

Foreword

ROBERT J. SCHREITER, C.PP.S.

The language of the new evangelization, begun in Latin America and spread since to other continents, is informed especially by the idea of the evangelization of cultures. Of course, it is not cultures as such that are evangelized, but the people within those cultures; the point of emphasizing the importance of culture in the evangelization process has been to recognize how much culture shapes our very being in the world. Without addressing those powerful forces that make thought and expression possible, evangelization remains incomplete and, frequently, superficial.

What talk about the evangelization of cultures has led us to most recently is a deeper examination of the relation between faith and cultures. Christian faith is by its very definition transformative and liberative. That means, for faith to be inculturated in any given setting, it will necessarily provoke change in the culture. The intent of the evangelizer is that what is sinful or evil in the culture will be changed, and what is good will be upheld and even elevated. But is it all that easy? What if the good is swept away with the evil? Or, as has happened more frequently, what if the good is mistaken for evil? How much can fundamental aspects of a culture be changed without the culture itself disappearing?

From the side of the recipients of evangelization, how is one to find Good News in the fact that, after a first evangelization, a people is apparently worse off than before? Such experience prompted a group of native peoples in 1985 to urge Pope John Paul II to take back the Bible, for it had not been Good News to them in five hundred years of domination and subjugation. One may rue the fact that evangelization was undertaken under such violent and death-dealing circumstances as the *Conquista*, but that does not take away from having to deal now with the reality it has created.

The first step in dealing with the reality that was created out of the first evangelization is not to call for a second evangelization, but rather a close attending to what the peoples and their cultures have become. A second or new evangelization does not simply make some adjustments or fine-tuning, or press more emphatically points that have been ignored. It must begin by listening to what these peoples and cultures have become under the impact of the first evangelization, however imperfect that may have been. And, as the authors of these essays point out, it is not a matter of dismissing elements that we do not recognize in European forms of Christianity; it must also hold open the possibility that those unrecognizable forms of Christianity might be contributions to the larger Christian synthesis.

To attend closely to an evangelized people and culture in this way opens again the question of syncretism. Manuel Marzal, the editor and a contributor to this volume, has been one of the most sensitive and sympathetic students of the formation of religious identities that I know. His numerous works on the Quechua have shown him to be willing to understand these peoples on their own terms. What he has to say about syncretism in his Introduction to this volume is balanced and prudent. It is the "other face of inculturation," the effort by a people to understand the Christian message in terms of what they understand to be good and true in their own culture. If Christians do believe that the "seeds of the Word" have already been sown in cultures prior to their evangelization, then we must expect that goodness and truth to be present. This is not intended to condone anything and everything in a culture; it is meant to remind us that cultures being evangelized may indeed make a genuine contribution to the Christian synthesis.

If the new evangelization is to move us closer to God's Reign, then it will have to pay attention to where it begins. The essays in this volume look at those circumstances with an unblinking eye. One sees histories of persistence of faith in spite of long absences of the clergy; creative attempts to synthesize the Christian message with the local worldview; acts of resistance to a religious message too closely entwined with brutal repressive power; changes of context from rural to urban settings; the impact of market economies on traditional economies of exchange. One can trace the encounter of worlds built on harmony and balance colliding with a profoundly asymmetrical message of reversal of the current order in the Reign of God and the resurrection of the dead. One can wonder at what the cult of the Pachamama might mean for Christian ecological theology of the Guarani understanding of the word portends for Christian understanding of the Logos.

The authors of this volume do not provide a final evaluation of the quality of Christianity that has emerged among these four peoples of the Americas. What they do hold up for us is how God's face is seen—syncretism or synthesis or both—and remind us that the evangelization of cultures is not about an abstraction but about real people who try to live in God's ways.

Introduction

MANUEL M. MARZAL

This book was written as part of the events that commemorated the five-hundredth anniversary of the first evangelisation (of the Americas), with the express purpose of making a contribution to the church's ongoing discussion relating to the integral evangelisation of indigenous peoples and their cultures. An important part of this reflection is the image or images that the Native Americans of today have of God. Thus the title: *The Indian Face of God*.

Such an integral evangelisation insists, on one hand, on a knowledge of the mythical traditions, the indigenous rituals and all of the reinterpretation with which the Indians responded to the first evangelisation in order to bring about a second evangelisation that is *truly inculturated*; and, on the other hand, with the discovery of the liberating elements found in that Indian face of God, to bring about a second evangelisation that is *truly liberating*. Only in this way will the gospel be "good news" to the direct descendants of those who, almost five centuries ago, witnessed the arrival of Columbus's boats with the cross and the sword. In spite of the fact that they were the true owners of this new world, the majority of them today lead a difficult life, seeking refuge in the marginal areas of the continent.

THE TEACHINGS OF THE FIRST EVANGELISATION

It is well known that the Catholic church spent much effort reflecting on and preparing to celebrate the five-hundredth anniversary of the evangelisation of the Americas. John Paul II himself made an appeal in Santo Domingo in 1984, the beginning point of that process, that nine years be dedicated to the preparations for the great event. To this end the

1

studies, meetings and celebrations multiplied, all of which set in motion a record of the collective consciousness of the significance of an evangelisation that resulted in the conversion of the new world in its most numerically significant portion; for many, this is also a portion of the church for which there is much hope. Among such studies, one which I view as very important, is the coming together of the church and the cultures of Native American communities after almost half a millennium.

Such a coming together involves a double contradiction for the church: in the first place, the demonic character commonly attributed to the indigenous religions by the church is confronted with the difficulty that these religions permeate almost all aspects of life. Second, the close relationship of the church with the colonial state—which not only attempted to dominate the conquered peoples politically and change their culture, but also exploited them economically—is now deplored by all. For this reason, those in the church who were most perceptive tried to find a solution to this double contradiction in their theological reflections and in their pastoral practice.

Confronted with the imputation of a demonic character to the indigenous religions, which was a legacy from medieval theology and which had a certain Biblical basis (Bar 4:7; Ps 96:5), some clear-thinking missionaries argued that the indigenous religions had some valid points and that the Indians knew the true God by the light of their natural reason. Two examples of this attitude are seen in the Jesuits José de Acosta, a theologian of the Third Council of Lima (1582-1583) and the author of the first and the broadest treatment of pastoral America, the *De procuranda indorum salute* (1588), and Bernabé Cobo, who, in Volume XIII of his monumental *Historia del nuevo mundo* (1653), gathered together the most complete, though belated, synthesis of the religion of Tawantinsuyo.

Although José de Acosta thought that the formal similarities between the indigenous religions and Christianity were a feeble imitation on the part of the demons in order to fool the Indians, he was opposed to the radical method of evangelism which sought a *tabula rasa* approach as the basis of missionary work, destroying by blood and fire the idols and other elements of the Native American religions, just as was done in the beginning not only by certain conquerors but by many missionaries also. Therefore he declared: "To make an effort to get rid of idolatry by force first, before the Indians have spontaneously received the gospel, has always seemed to me, as it has to other very wise and sober men, to close, lock and bar the door of the gospel to those outside, rather than open it" (1954: 561). He also supported his argument by the authority of St. Augustine, who said, "It is necessary to take the idols from the hearts of the pagans before they are taken from their altars." Furthermore, he maintained that in evangelisation one must preserve all that is good in the indigenous culture:

> Our mission is to go, little by little, training the Indians in Christian customs and disciplines, and to cut off the superstitious, sacrilegious rites and the habits of savage wildness without making a fuss; furthermore, in those points in which their customs are not opposed to religion and justice, I do not believe it to be appropriate to change them; rather to the contrary, we should retain all that is paternal and civilised, so as not to move in opposition to reason . . .
>
> Therefore, there are many things that one should imitate, and others worthy of praise; and those aspects that are most deeply rooted and do the most harm, with skill and tact, one must substitute other similar good traits for them. In this we have the authority of the distinguished Pope Gregory, who, when asked by Augustine, Bishop of the Churches, wrote to Melito: "Tell Augustine that I have pondered much the situation of the churches, and I think that in no way is it prudent to destroy the temples where they have their idols, but just the idols themselves, so that when they see that these people have respect for their temples, they tear out the error from their hearts and, coming to know the true God, worship Him, meeting together in the places which are familiar to them" (1954: 502).

In this spirit Acosta wrote throughout his famous missiological text, which concluded with the wise warning that "to want to cut off by radical means all the bad habits at once is impossible; also, those who wish to climb the heights, gradually come down again, by steps and not by leaps."

As for Bernabé Cobo, he begins, in the first chapter of the above mentioned volume XIII, by repeating the theory of the demonic origin of the Andean religion ("the enemy of the human race . . . tried to usurp among these blinded peoples the worship which belonged solely to Him who created them"). This fact did not deter him from recognising that the Indians, enlightened by the light of reason, "came to reach and believe that there was only one God, universal Creator of all things and sovereign Lord, who was their Ruler" (1964, II: 145-155). This text, together with other similar writings of distinguished chroniclers, has been criticised by some ethno-historians (Urbano 1981, XVI; Rostworowski 1983: 29), stating that the chroniclers, in their zeal to find traces of the supreme God of the Hebrew and Christian traditions, forced the ethnographic information in order to make their preaching easier, and it is likely that these ethno-historians are correct in their assumptions. However, perhaps the text referred to above ought to be read, not so much from the empirical exactness of the good ethnographer who describes a social act just as it is, as from the interpretation of the theologian who judges that the Indians, by means of such cultural mediation, really believed in the true God, along the line of those who thought that the indigenous religions had an apostolic origin, as we shall see later. From Cobo's ethnography I cite one of the prayers to the Creator, a prayer of great beauty and transcendent content, which Cobo collected from Cristobal de Molina el Cusqueño (1574):

> Pachacutec, the Inca, composed these prayers, and although this people lacked the skill of writing, they have been preserved by tradition, by children learning them from their fathers. It seemed right to include some of them here so that the style and devotion that they evidence will be seen. When they sacrificed to Wiracocha for health and the common good of the people, they said the following prayer:
>
> "Oh Maker, who lives in the ends of the world without equal, who gave being and valour to men; saying: 'Be this man,' and to women: 'Be this woman.' You made them, formed them and gave them being so that they might live healthy and safe in peace without danger.
>
> Where are you?
>
> Do you live, by chance, in the height of heaven, or in the depths of the earth, or in the clouds and the storms?
>
> Hear me, answer me and grant me my petition, giving us eternal life and holding us by the hand, and receive now this offering, wheresoever you are, oh Maker" (1964, II: 205).

Another way to overcome the contradiction of the demonic character of the indigenous religions was found in doubting the original Christianisation of their adherents. Alongside the interpretation already described of the "diabolic origin" of these religions, a current of thought maintaining an "apostolic origin" began to emerge. The priest Miguel Cabello de Balboa (1586); the Indian chronicler Guaman Poma (1615); the Augustinian Alonso Ramos Gavilan (1621); the Cusco priest Francisco Avila (1648); and the bishop of Quito, Alonso de la Peña y Montenegro (1668) all participated in forwarding this thesis. However, the most distinguished representative of this school of thought, noted for the passion with which he defended the new interpretation, was the Augustinian Antonio de la Calancha, a Creole from Chuquisaca, who lived the majority of his life in Peru and wrote the *Crónica moralizada de la Orden de San Agustín en el Perú* (1639).[1]

In his discussion, Calancha commences with the similarities between the indigenous religions and Christianity, or as he says, certain "tidings" that the Indians had of the Trinity, the Eucharist, the worship of the cross, the oral confession of sins, etc. Later he suggests a double hypothesis: such beliefs and rites "had Catholic beginnings through evangelisation, though after the passing of years and the sowing of the seeds of demonic misinterpretation" brought about corruption and degeneration, or "the demon like an ape introduced them from the beginning in order to mimic God" (1639: 340). In his conclusion, Calancha passionately defends the former hypothesis, explaining the later distortion of indigenous Christianity by comparing it to that which occurred in India and Persia, places which reportedly had also been evangelised by the apostles. The alleged proofs supporting his hypothesis are of two kinds, some more philosophical and a priori:

> Those who are not persuaded that an apostle preached in this new world oppose the natural laws, divine and positive, and insult the mercy and justice of God. They oppose the divine mandate which Christ gave to his apostles: "Go and teach all people" . . . They oppose the positive law in that they do not wish to share the common good . . . They insult the justice of God in that they condemn those who do not believe in their faith, those who have not even heard their law, nor know anything about their gospel. They insult God's mercy, for although Christ died for every person in the whole world, their desire is that these lands which are greater than the other half of the world, should not know of His death nor should they have heard His law (1639: 313).

The other proofs are more ethnological and a posteriori. In this way Calancha gathers all of the available testimony concerning the arrival in the new world of a mysterious person who taught the true faith and performed miracles, who had to be one of the apostles. He thinks that the apostle in question is St. Thomas, even though he makes reference to the brotherhood which the mestizos from Cusco formed in honour of St. Bartholomew, following their belief that he had been the one to evangelise the new world. Although Calancha recognises the insufficiency of his testimony based on the oral tradition, he judges, with the pride of a Creole and with a clear confrontation with his peninsular reader,[2] that the existing testimony which proves that St. James preached in Spain is no more convincing (than those he refers to in support of St. Thomas preaching in the New World) (1639: 339).

We note here in passing that the hypothesis of a priori apostolic preaching appears to gain favour in the seventeenth century, when a national consciousness was being born. Such apostolic preaching allowed the Indians to reconcile themselves with their past; they were able to reckon that their culture had not been just a great diabolical lie, but that it had been founded on the revealed truth, even though it had later suffered distortion. This permitted the Creoles to go on believing in the truth of the Bible as a basis for their own culture and to accept the indigenous past, more and more, as their own, in the peculiar process of appropriation very characteristic of the American Creoles. Above all, it supplies the basis of the nineteeth-century movements for independence from Spain. With great erudition and insightful analysis, Lafaye develops these ideas for Mexico (1977) with relation to the Quetzalcoatl–St. Thomas myth.

However, it is not easy to know if the ideas of Acosta, Cobo and Calancha concerning the reevaluation of the indigenous religions influenced the majority of the doctrinaire priests and other pastoral agents in order to bring about an evangelisation that was more inculturated. Personally, I think that they would not have reached very far, because of the weight of theologico-pastoral Romanism, which was born in the Counter-Reformation, even though certain external adaptations continued, such as the story about the renowned Corpus Christi procession in Cusco which the Inca Garcilaso de la Vega relates (1944, III: 185). For this reason, I believe that the Indian face of God does not derive so much from the inculturation of the pastoral agents, as it does from the syncretism (which is, as it is known, the other face of inculturation) of the Indians, in their attempt to make the Christian God more comprehensible, or as it derives from their own beliefs concerning God.

The second contradiction which obscured evangelisation was its link with the colonial state, which considered itself a missionary-state. This contradiction is expressed well in the work of a first-generation missionary Pedro de Quiroga, a priest who returned from Peru to Spain and in 1563 wrote his *Coloquios de la verdad: causas e inconvenientes que impiden la conversión de las indios.*[3] In this work, which is presented in the form of a dialogue following classical Greco-Roman literary style, Tito the Indian gives this response to the priest who has spoken to him of the shortcomings of indigenous Christianity:

> Father, consider the patience with which I have listened to you and suffered . . . There is no way to satisfy you, nor to answer you in the same way in which you have spoken, because you do not hold with our ways . . .
>
> You have made the law which you preach to us odious by the things that you do to us, so contrary to that which you teach, that you rob the truth of its credibility . . . We are so resentful

towards you and we hold you in such hate and enmity, that we cannot persuade ourselves to believe anything that you preach or say to us because in everything you always have lied and deceived us.

Never in the whole time since we have known you has one word come out of your mouth but (that it is meant) to harm us; all has been theft and greed (1922: 115-118).

Thus Tito the Indian rightly concludes that "the first and foremost point (of evangelisation) must be to preach to them the liberty which God and the King imparts to them . . . , because there can be no doctrinal progress without this as a starting point" (1922: 125). However much the information revealed by the lengthy reasoning of Tito the Indian refers to the period of the conquest and the frenetic evangelisation of the first hour, now that things have improved, I believe he preserves for us a certain sense of reality, because the colonial system continued in force with its mission, its personal services, and among them the mining myth and the subjugation of the people. For this reason some missionaries with greater sensibilities and clearer insight have suggested how this contradiction may be overcome.

The first solution was one of prophetic protest. The prototype of this stance is found in the life of Bartolomé de las Casas (1484-1566), a Spanish colonial official who, as a result of a religious experience, was converted and dedicated himself to the defense of the Indians, initially from the pastoral pulpit of a doctrinaire, Dominican monk and bishop of Chiapas, and later from the intellectual position of an author of American history in the convent of Valladolid, and continuously as an agitator in the Spanish court against the horrors of the Conquest. Las Casas presented a passionate defense of human rights for the Indians in his memoirs and other polemic writings, the best-known example being the *Brevísima relación de la destrucción de Indias* (1552).[4] In addition, he offered a more objective defense of the American cultures in his historical works, such as *Apologética historia* (1559),[5] in which he endeavoured to show that the Indians had the capability of governing themselves by reason of the fact that they had produced such well-organised societies and cultures. Although the majority of the Dominican's works were not published during the entire Spanish colonial regime, his ideas about an evangelisation without colonial domination were spread abroad and nourished the ideal of the Native American. Furthermore, Las Casas himself organised two interesting Utopian, communitarian experiments, one on the Costa de Paria (Venezuela) and the other in Verapaz (Guatemala), which, despite their failure for many reasons and, above all, their failure to continue, inspired and reinforced the ideas put forth in his work *Del único modo de atraer a todos los pueblos a la verdadera religión* (1537).[6]

Las Casas had considerable influence on colonial politics through his polemical writings and by his action in the Spanish court, and by virtue of the fact that he was, for example, one of the architects of the "New Laws," which superseded the original missionary objectives. Above all, he was the initiator of a school of accusation, in which many clergy and lay people voiced to the king their alarm or their ethical judgements on the conquest and its accompaniying evangelisation. In the beginning it was a prolongation of the famous polemic of the "just titles" of the Conquest, so clearly presented by Vitoria in the University of Salamanca, but later moved on to discuss the legitimacy of certain colonial institutions, such as the original mission and the personal services, in the actual geographico-historical context within which they functioned.

The second solution was a Utopian one. Without doubt, those who best represent this position are the Mexican bishop Vasco de Quiroga and the Jesuits of Paraguay, creators of two Utopian modes which existed throughout a large part of the colonial period. Don Vasco was a veteran jurist who, at sixty years of age, was sent to Mexico as president of the second High Court and later was named first bishop of Michoacán. He organised Indian villages following the model of the ideal society ("the hospitals of Santa Fe") described by Thomas More in his *Utopia* (1516). Don Vasco's villages/hospitals were well-planned colonies, with communal agricultural land and family gardens, made up of patriarchal families who elected their own authorities, and who tended the agricultural activities, as well as all of the offices and necessary services to ensure their independence and their self-sufficiency, working a work-day of just six hours on a rotating system.

The reductions in Paraguay were considerably more complex, for, among other reasons, they managed to form thirty villages, inhabited by 150,000 Guarani Indians in a territory which now encompasses Paraguay, Argentina and Brasil. One of the builders of this Utopian scheme was the Peruvian Jesuit Antonio Ruiz de Montoya. In his book *La Conquista espiritual del Paraguay* (1639),[7] he describes the manner in which the Indians are "subdued" in self-ruling villages without the necessity of conquering them by weapons, in order to evangelise them and organise them into a free society, instead of through "diabolical personal service," as Ruiz de Montoya called the obligatory work that the Indians did for the Spanish (1892: 200), extracting the "Paraguayan grass" or *maté* (Paraguayan tea). The running of the settlements was founded on three principles: the breaking off of colonial relations, the good organisation of the society with equal distribution of tasks and wealth, and the instilling of a deep religiosity. In order to achieve this, the settlements had a system of mixed properties (plantations of *maté*, communal livestock and family gardens), with self-government (not only were the mayors and chiefs Indians, but the overseers as well), with a printing press where many Guarani books were published. This too was under their own jurisdiction, which was given authority by the king himself in response to a petition from the same Ruiz de Montoya who journeyed to Madrid to present it, in order to free the settlements from the invasions of the "Paulist fanatics." This formation of an "indigenous state" within the State was, without doubt, one of the reasons the Jesuits were expelled from all of the lands under Spanish dominion in the eighteenth century.

As has already been stated, one of the principles of the function of the reductions was the development of a deep religious experience. Ruiz de Montoya dedicated many pages to the description of personal religious experiences and even to the inclusion of some of the mystics among the Guarani. He probably did so in order to reinstate the Indians' Christianity, which had been so discredited in the eyes of many missionaries. If the Guarani, who had so recently left their tribal life of polygamy and ritual cannibalism, had religious and mystical experiences similar to those experienced by the Creoles (concerning which topic Ruiz de Montoya was surely a good judge, as can be deduced from a reading of his mystical treatise *Silex del divino amor*[8]), this was proof of the depth of the evangelisation process when it was carried out freely on the margin of the colonial rule.

However, neither the prophetic protest against the exploitation of the Indians nor the idealistic construction of free indigenous societies was the road most travelled by the evangelists; the greater majority opted for the more realistic solution of evangelising within the "Indian republics" or the "indigenous communities" which were instruments of the colonial domination, in turn becoming part of the "doctrine" under the pastoral control of priests. It is accepted fact that these communities became the crucible of the new cultural identity of the Indians and that in this long and complex process the doctrinaire priests played an important role.

To summarise, although certain more insightful sectors within the church during the first half of the colonial period tried in their theological reflection and by their pastoral practice, to overcome the double contradiction of the demonic character attributed to the indigenous religions and evangelisation bound to the colonial domination, it appears that the majority continued to evangelise within the confines of a narrow collaboration with the colonial regime without taking into account any indigenous religious roots. This resulted in resistance on the part of the indigenous peoples. In the beginning the Indians even resorted to rebellions in the name of the fallen gods (the Taquiy Onquy's movement in the southern Peruvian highlands around 1565 is a typical example) or, at least, concealing the old idols behind the Christian saints. As the years passed and the methods of evangelisation improved, religion among the Indians became increasingly more Christian and lent itself to a true religious transformation in the heart of the masses of the great Hispanic empires. In spite of such a religious transformation, indigenous Christianity was not simply a transplant of the Christianity of the missionaries; rather, there were indigenous religious elements that persisted together with Catholic religious elements, which were reinterpreted from the perspective of the people's traditional religion. Furthermore, especially during the nineteenth century with the decline of the number of clergy among the Indians, including those indigenous areas that had been truly Christianised, a noteworthy reactionary process to Christianity led to the consolidation of the syncretic religious worldview described in this volume.

The Latin American bishops, who met in Puebla, Mexico (1979) to study the present and future evangelisation of the continent, stated that "Latin America has its roots in the meeting of the Spanish-Portuguese race with the pre-Columbian and African cultures. The racial and cultural interchange has fundamentally left its mark on this process" (Puebla Final Document 409). Between the sixteenth and eighteenth centuries, "the foundation of the Latin American culture and its true Catholic substructure were formed. The evangelisation penetrated sufficiently in-depth to pass on the faith which became an integral component of its being and its identity" (Puebla Final Document 412). However, the bishops recognised that "this popular Catholic piety in Latin America still had not been implanted adequately, nor had it succeeded in evangelising some of the indigenous cultural groups" (here they seem to refer to the indigenous peoples who hold to a more syncretised Catholicism, rather than those dealt with in this volume, as well as referring to certain Amazonian groups who have yet to be baptised), even though there are some instances, according to the bishops, where "they possess the highest values and preserve 'seeds of the Word' as they wait for the living Word" (Puebla Final Document 450).

INDIGENOUS EVANGELISATION TODAY

When the Latin American church today tries to bring about an evangelisation of the indigenous peoples who have not yet been adequately evangelised, it has a different theological-pastoral starting point. Much water has passed under the bridge since the Council of Trent, which gave direction to the first evangelisation, and Vatican Council II with its post-concilium process, which sought to give direction to the second evangelisation. One characteristic sign of the change brought about by Vatican II is seen in its Constitution on the Sacred Liturgy, where it states:

> Even in the liturgy, the Church has no wish to impose a rigid uni-formity in matters which do not involve the faith or the good of the whole community. Rather she respects and fosters the spiritual adornments and gifts of the various races and peoples. Anything in their way of life that is not indissolubly bound up with superstition and error she studies with sympathy and, if possible, preserves in-tact. Sometimes in fact she admits such things into the liturgy itself, as long as they harmonize with its true and authentic spirit (SC 37).

Nevertheless this evangelization, which takes into account the cultural values of the target peoples, goes increasingly deeper into the modern teachings of the church and speaks of the evangelisation of the culture. Paul VI stated it clearly in his apostolic exhortation *Evangelii nuntiandi* (1975). After lamenting "the divide between the gospel and culture" evi-dent in modern civilisation, and describing this divide as "the drama of our times," he maintains that the evangelisation of cultures is to reach out and transform,

> through the power of the Gospel, mankind's criteria of judgment, determining values, points of interest, lines of thought, sources of inspiration and models of human life, which are in contrast with the Word of God and with the plan of salvation (EN 19).

Such an emphasis on the relationship between faith and culture, char-acteristic of the teaching of Paul VI, becomes even greater in the teaching of John Paul II. Indeed, in his letter to Cardinal Casaroli when the Pon-tifical Council for Culture was set up, the pope said that the "synthesis of culture and faith is not only demanded by the culture, but also by the faith." A faith which does not become part of the culture is not entirely accepted, not thoroughly understood, not faithfully translated into life (*L'Osservatore Romano*, No. 701, 6-July-1982). In addition, in his ad-dress to the bishops of Lombardy (Italy), the pope defined popular culture as "that which, together with principles and values, constitutes the ethos of a people" and reminded them that it was in Lombardy that "Chris-tianity gained an increasing penetration into the thinking of the people and into their customs, those areas which had gone into the makeup of this nucleus of essential values, in those which generation upon generation have provided the inspiration for his life" (*L'Osservatore Romano*, No. 685, 14-March-1982). It is not difficult to prove that these affirmations have much validity in the culture described in this book. Finally, I would like to refer to another more lengthy section of the address John Paul II delivered to the intellectual community in Cameroon, West Africa, where he interrelated inculturation to liberation and affirmed that the gospel ought to be expressed not only in the value system of each individual culture, but also must take a critical view of them:

> I understand the cry of certain Africans pleading for real freedom and just recognition of their dignity, apart from any racism and all the consequences of political, economic or cultural exploitation . . . In the first place, we must clearly understand that the liberation which is sought is the integral liberation of mankind, freedom from everything which enslaves whether from external or from internal sources . . . On the other hand, it is true that the Christian faith must be Good News for each and every people. For this reason it must respond to the most noble aspirations of the heart. It must be capable of being assimilated into the language, be relevant to the secular traditions which have gradually come into acceptance from the wisdom of the people in order to guarantee social cohesion, as well as a maintaining of both physical and moral health. Evangelisation cannot do less than take unto itself elements from the culture. The breach between culture and the Gospel is a serialised drama (EN 20). The positive elements, the spiritual values of the African people must be integrated, integrated even more so. Christ has come to bring completion. It is necessary, therefore, to bring into being an indefatigable effort for inculturation in order to achieve a faith that is not merely superficial. However, neither can we forget that the Gospel message comes not just to consolidate human values such as they are, but it must also play the role of prophet and critic. Everywhere in Europe just the same as in Africa, the Gospel comes to transform the criteria of discernment and the manner of life (EN 19). It is a call to conversion. It comes to regenerate. It screens out all that is ambiguous, tainted by weakness and sin. The Gospel must perform this function with relation to some practices which were introduced by foreigners together with the faith, as well as with regard to certain customs and institutions which you find among yourselves. The Gospel of God always comes as something apart to purify and to lift up, so that all that is good, noble, and true

might be saved, empowered and perfected, bearing the choicest fruit (*L'Osservatore Romano*, 1-September-1985).

If from the teaching of the universal church we move to that of the Latin American bishops, we can understand the importance that the Puebla document and conclusions (1979) gives to the evangelisation of the culture, which becomes one of the central themes for reflection on one of the principal pastoral options (Puebla Final Document 385-443). Here, however, it is necessary to take into account the teaching of the Latin American hierarchy in all of its particularities in order to study the evangelisation of the indigenous cultures. Above all these stand out Melgar (1968), Caracas (1969), Iquitos (1971), Ascunción (1972), Manaus (1977) and Tlaxcala (1978)—those which, coming into the decade of the seventies, mark the crisis of indigenisation and the birth of "Indianism." The first was the politico-cultural movement, which had arisen on the continent during the first thirty years of the twentieth century as a reaction to the ignorance in which the national governments that had come into power when independence was established had held the indigenous population, carried out under a pretext of equality for all before the law. The cornerstone of this indigenous movement on the continent was the Congress of Patzcuaro in 1940, where the goal was to integrate the Indians into the national social structure while maintaining their own cultural specificity. Since the movement for indigenisation was always in the hands of persons other than the Indians, and since the integration encouraged by this movement actually resulted in destroying the indigenous culture that it set out to preserve, "Indianism" emerged at the beginning of the decade of the seventies. This new movement placed the drive for indigenisation into the hands of the Indians themselves and set out to defend not only the preservation of cultural identity but also some form of political autonomy for Indian organisations. These ideas formed the basis for a series of meetings and consultations dealing with the pastoral ministry among the indigenous cultures mentioned above.

Perhaps the clearest expression of a new style of pastoral ministry among the Indians within the context of the Indian movement was the meeting of all the bishops responsible for the indigenous pastoral ministry sponsored by the Department of Missions of CELAM, held in the city of Bogota, September 9–13, 1985. At this meeting the bishops identified the indigenous peoples as "some 40 million brethren who identify themselves as members of an ethnic group. They are generally rural people, jungle inhabitants or emigrants who have settled in the slums which surround our cities, and who, structurally speaking, live outside of Westernised society or maintain their life by a process differentiated from integration in the same" (1987: 377). Later the bishops analysed the situation among the Indians and the pastoral ministry of the church to them in the various countries and arrived at a series of "pastoral options" to carry out a new thrust in evangelisation.

From among these pastoral options two are worthy of mention. First, the formation of autonomous indigenous churches:

> The Church should collaborate in the birth of particular indigenous churches, whose hierarchy and organisation is autonomous, with a theology, a liturgy and ecclesiastical expressions fitting a cultural life-style belonging to the faith, in communion with other distinct churches, and above all fundamentally in communion with the see of Peter (1987: 388).

Secondly, the defense of Indian territories and Indian organisations:

> . . . to defend the lands of the indigenous peoples and restore them to them, conscious of the fact that possession of such is an indispensable condition to their integral freedom; to support the existing indigenous organisations in their fight for defense of their territory and for self-determination for the people (1987: 390).

All of the documents and reports that underlie the discussion of the meeting of the bishops in Bogota sum up a perspective which is increasingly compelled to accept the autonomy of cultures in order to arrive at a true inculturation of the faith. Still I fear that, as is expressed in the syllogism that the greater will be much clearer than the lesser, it is even more important that pastoral agents in the indigenous regions of Latin America continue to discuss and contemplate the Indian face of God, so that such reflection can translate into clear and effective pastoral options.

CHARACTERISTICS OF THIS WORK

In order to understand the limits of this volume, it is well to keep before us some points that form part of the working document on which the authors were agreed when they committed themselves to writing their reflections:

1) With regard to the subject matter, every endeavour has been made to write about the indigenous peoples of the present day. We recognise that the term *Indian* is rather a colonial category, because the Spaniards who first arrived on this continent believed that they had arrived in India.

Under this name, however, there are many different ethnic groups. In the 1940s when the indigenous movement on the continent came into being, more suitable criteria to define the Indians were considered, such as race, language, culture, belonging to an indigenous community, and so on. The definition given by Alfonso Caso (1958) is a classic:

> The Indian is the one who feels that he or she belongs to an indigenous community, and an indigenous community is one in which somatic elements predominate and not European traits; where an indigenous language is spoken, which has a greater proportion of indigenous material and spiritual elements in its culture, and which, lastly, has social sense of being an isolated community in the midst of the other communities that surround it, which forces it to distinguish itself from white people of European origin and from those of mixed blood (1958: 15).

Such a definition is a combination of four criteria: race, culture, language and group consciousness. This definition neglects to mention, however, that the greater majority of the indigenous communities today are not only culturally different but also politically oppressed. For this reason, in a more recent work edited by Enrique Mayer and Elio Masferrer (1979), authors include within the "irreducible nucleus" of the American indigenous population, which is calculated to be some 28.5 million, together with the Indians from communities which have a self-sufficient economy and a tribal organisation, those rural Indians with an economy which is articulated within the national society and a rural organisation, as well as the Indians in the cities, whose economy is also based within the national structure but where "due to the process of conquest of urban territory the indigenous groups reaffirm at every level their place as a different culture, yet as participants in the national life" (1979: 238). From among American Indians, this volume refers only to the Tseltales of Chiapas, in the territory of the ancient Mayan empire; to the Quechua of the southern Peruvian highlands in the heart of the old Tawantinsuyo Inca Empire; to the Aymara who are established in Bolivia, Peru and Chile, inheritors of the Tiawanaco empire; and to the Guarani from the high Parana area of Paraguay and Uruguay. Although these five peoples are not representative of the total indigenous population, they provide good examples for the study of evangelism among the indigenous peoples in the present day.

2) With regard to the authors, all are Jesuit priests, none of whom was born within the culture whose religious experience he describes. Some are anthropologists and have many years of experience in the region.

Inevitably these are experiences seen from the outside. The very focus of the four articles is different: one is more in the form of an eye-witness account, without any critical apparatus, with the sole purpose of transmitting the religious life of a people to that which accompanies it pastorally; the others are more academic and analytical, and endeavour to understand the indigenous religious vision and the social processes that have spawned it. All reveal a deep respect for the Indian face of God.

3) With regard to the topic itself, it is a study of certain cases from the broad indigenous religious panorama of Latin America. This study deals only with religion but does not desist from making many references that take in the cultural and political challenges of today's indigenous peoples, recognizing the close connection between religion and politics in the entire indigenous social structure. Further, it deals only with the indigenous religion of the present day, not with that which greeted the Spanish almost half a millennium ago, though there are more than a few references to the past in the effort to understand the present. Lastly, it treats religion in the sense more universally accepted in the anthropology of religion and in the sense inspired by Durkheim (1912) as a system of beliefs, rites, forms of organisation and ethical norms by which a society endeavours to communicate with God and find a sense of transcendence in life.

4) This book does not present conclusions collectively, as was originally envisioned, because the authors, who have been working in different corners of a broad and distant continent, were unable to formulate such conclusions together. Perhaps this has been for the best, in order to avoid any possible manipulation of the facts. The distinct faces of God are here; and all of the pastoral agents who work in the areas where indigenous Christianity lives on discover the same music, even though the lyrics may differ. Nevertheless, in my position as editor of the volume, I would like to suggest some conclusions which come out of a reading of the texts:

a) Frequently there is rather passionate discussion about the nature of synthesis and syncretism shown in the religions that are presented here. For me, the answer lies mainly in the prior definitions, but it is true that this discussion may be more germane to anthropological studies, which are tied to the analysis of the social processes, than they are to the pastoral considerations, which are geared to an understanding of how a certain religious intervention can be appropriated in order to approach the God of "spirit and truth" (Jn 4:23). As I analyse in the second part of my work concerning the Quechua, when two religions are brought into contact with one another, in theory this can produce a juxtaposition (a simple superposition of both religions where each maintains its own identity), a synthesis (a perfect fusion of both religions to form a new one) or a syncretism (a formation of a new religion with elements taken from both religions). Nonetheless, if the contact has been over a prolonged period of time and if the religious specialists of both religions have managed to exercise real power for some time, the most frequent occurrence is the emergence of a true syncretism. In that analysis I define this as the result of the dialectic interaction of the elements (beliefs, rites, forms of organisation and ethical norms) of the two original religions, by which interaction certain elements persist in the new religion, others disappear altogether, still others synthesise with similar elements from the other religion or are reinterpreted and assume a new meaning. This is the case in the first two cases studied in this book.

As to the value of true religious intervention for those who are sincere in their practice, there is no doubt that, if Vatican II admits to the possibility of salvation outside of the church in certain circumstances (*Ad gentes* 7, *Lumen gentium* 16 and *Gaudium et spes* 22), how much more may we affirm the same of the syncretistic indigenous Christianity, so permeated with the values and sacraments taught by Jesus as the way to the Father? Though naturally the problem of the church's pastoral practice is not in the theological evaluation it must make of syncretistic Christianity, but rather in the studied societies which practice such a form of Christianity. The pastoral problem is to what point the pastoral agents of today can tolerate such syncretistic expressions and even defend them as real contributions from these local churches, as new "seeds of the Word" for evangelisation. Tolerance, patience and wisdom were the virtues the great theologian and pastor Acosta (1588), who recommended to missionaries, as mentioned previously: "There are many things that one should imitate, and others worthy of praise, and those aspects that are most deeply rooted and do the most harm, with skill and tact, one must substitute other similar good traits for them. In this we have the authority of the distinguished Pope Gregory" (1954: 504).

However, acceptance of indigenous marriages as part of the Christian sacrament, acceptance of the fertility rites of Mother Earth as worship of the providence of God, or acceptance of the indigenous religious experience, which is focused on communion with the whole universe in solidarity with others like oneself in the development of life to its fullest and in the balance of powers and shared resources—just to mention a few of the traces of traditional religion that appear in the monographs—is much more than a simple strategic form of tolerance. It not only signifies accepting that the Spirit of God continues working in the silence of the hearts of the baptised Indians, but it also lends credence to the cultural forms of their religious practice. This is the challenge that confronts the local churches in the more indigenous regions of the continent. And I do insist in dealing with the local churches, because I believe that the effort for inculturation must be made in a systematic and a collective manner, and not left to personal initiative on the part of priests. For were that the case it could cause confusion and even divisions among the Catholics of the region.

b) The second conclusion refers to the historical period in which the syncretistic indigenous Christianity of today took shape. In spite of the fact that the methods of evangelisation were not all the same, and that the evangelisation did not go through the same stages in the Indian societies here studied, still in these situations there was a long time in which the presence of the institutional church was very weak and almost nonexistent. This happened, due to the expulsion of the Jesuits, among the Tseltales, and the Quechua and the Aymara in the nineteenth century. In every instance there was a real regression in the evangelisation process and communication of Christianity. Aboriginal religious leaders were obliged to cling to their original religious tradition to redefine their Christianity. This freedom, which they did not have during the first evangelisation, came when these indigenous peoples had already been fundamentally Christianised. Thus the result was not the radical restoration of the original indigenous religions, but rather the "Indianisation" of Christianity. This seems to me to be the basic fact, although there are degrees of greater or lesser levels of Christianisation.

Therefore, as I have already observed, the Indian face of God does not come so much from the inculturation of the pastoral agents as from the syncretism of the Indians, in their efforts to make the Christian message more comprehensible and to conserve certain enduring traces of the aboriginal religion. It is this syncretism which I have called the other face of inculturation. If inculturation is the evangelists' systematic and conscientious effort to translate the universal message of the gospel into the religious categories of the target society, then syncretism is the inverse process by which those who have been evangelised try to retain vestiges of their own religion, not so much in opposition to the Christians as in reclothing the accepted tokens of Christianity in the appropriate aboriginal religious forms. Both processes, which are always difficult because of the profound change that they involve, become complicated because their real subject is a collective subject. And the second process, which is the only one that has actually taken place, was developed in a context of compulsory evangelisation.

c) The most important conclusion, however, and the one that is most difficult to synthesise, is the kind of challenge that these Indian faces of God signify for the present-day local churches in their search for a truly inculturated and truly liberated pastoral policy. I indicated some of this in the first conclusion, but this is not the whole story. I think that the local churches, under the illumination of the rich teaching of the church, to which I made reference in the second section of this introduction, must continue to search for the appropriate method to face the second evangelisation of indigenous societies today, bearing in mind the ambiguity of the indigenous syncretistic Christians as well as the contribution that these same individuals can make towards the Christian synthesis of the continent. I shall limit my development of these points, because I am trying to make a personal synthesis of the ideas that are presented in a much broader form and are explained more precisely at length in the monographs of this present volume.

In the first place, the indigenous forms of present-day Christianity emerged in an ambiguous way, both in the face of God that is revealed as well as in the level of personal freedom that is attached to them. We know that not only indigenous religious phenomena but all religious phenomena can be ambiguous because of their symbolic character, which does not lend itself to receive precise meanings from the distinct groups which use them as a means towards their own interests; more so, if such religious phenomena are a result of a syncretistic process. The same symbolism can lead to the God of life or to the god of death; the celebration of certain rites can be oriented to obtain divine favours and, at the same time, reinforce patterns of oppression. Some beliefs and religious practices are interpreted differently by various social classes. For this reason I believe that the challenge that confronts the pastoral agents is imparting symbolism appropriate to the indigenous societies that they feel is fitting in order to come to the God of "spirit and truth" (Jn 4:23).

On the other hand, is the indigenous Christianity of today—born of a evangelisation which arrived by means of conquest and colonial domination—really a proclamation of the "Good News"? In spite of their unquestionably good intentions, many evangelists destroyed indigenous religions, and with them the central base for resistance that the aboriginal societies had against invaders, thus facilitating the penetration of the colonial system. Although the base reductions were, as we saw in the first part, the cradle for a new cultural identity, and although the Christian God had been the motivating force behind certain indigenous freedom movements towards the end of the colonial period (the Tseltal rebellion of Maria Candelaria, which Maurer relates, is a typical example), is it possible to say that all of the weight of the domination by the original connection between evangelism and conquest has disappeared from the indigenous Christianities?

It is common knowledge that the Kerygma itself has definite repercussions and demands new formulations that are credible in a context that combines evangelism and subjugation on the part of those who are called

Christians. When the early church preached Christ dead, resurrected and as the bearer of salvation, it was clear to all that Christ was that man of flesh and blood who proclaimed the Good News and was killed by the powerful. This same preaching, however, delivered in the context of an invasion which imposed the Western order of Christianity by military force, has a totally different meaning and can become the myth of those who rule and impose even their gods on the conquered ones. A further example: Christian monotheism confronted with indigenous polytheism can result in a reformulation of another type; the margin of mere theological considerations, the monotheism of God, "the only One, monopolised by the dominant elite," can seem, when faced with the multiplicity of indigenous gods of protection, like another form of oppression. So I deem the challenge to the pastoral agents starts from an understanding of indigenous symbolism that is present, and that shows these sides (and many more which are related in the monographs), ultimately lead to the discovery of the God of true freedom.

Second, the indigenous Christians of the present day can make a contribution to the process of a Christian synthesis on the Latin Amemerican continent. Without a doubt the indigenous peoples at their various levels of articulation and conflict with the dominant society provide us with the principal encounter with "otherness" in Latin America, just as in the Asiatic world it may come from the great millennial religions or for the European milieu from postmodern agnostic humanism. How is it possible to re-evangelise these syncretistic Christians, all the while respecting this value of "otherness" and transforming it into a contribution towards a continental Christian synthesis? Among the contributions to this Christian synthesis that comes from indigenous Christianity I believe that mention should be made of the following:

- the sacred dimension of ecology (the Mother Earth and the spirits of the Aymara and Quechua cultures);
- the unity of the whole person (body and soul);
- the role of all the senses in religious experience;
- the images or "saints" as a pantheon of angelic beings;
- certain forms of animism, which horrify us from our perspective of one God but may be seen as symbols of the providence and transcendence of the one God;
- the logic of the physical and the sensual—without the domination by untouchable dogmas that respect the variety and harmony of every form of reality; and
- the varied ways of approaching the divinity (such as, for example, through dancing and certain kinds of fasting).

We must not forget that the negative value placed on these attributes of indigenous Christianity by some pastoral agents is not founded in the religion of spirit and truth which our Lord Jesus brought to us, and which is the only valid criterion, but rather comes from the cultural developments belonging to Western civilisation, which with a definite lack of scientific modesty is presented as valid for all societies. For this reason, I believe the church does well in openly approaching the indigenous Christians, not only with respect to those millions of baptised followers who, after nearly half a millennium since the first evangelisation, we cannot continue to consider as "new Christians," but also in recognition that these men and women are making a contribution to humanity in their different religious experiences of real worth and because they are filled with the Spirit of God who "blows where He will" (Jn 3:8).

One last word about this edition. This book is not a translation of the book which appeared under the title *O rostro indio de Deus* in Sao Paulo, 1989, published by Vozes as part of the series on Theology and Liberation. It is rather a book originally written in Spanish, which was scheduled to appear simultaneously with its Portuguese translation (and is now translated into English). Due to unforeseen circumstances the Portuguese edition appeared first, followed by editions published in Peru, Mexico, Bolivia and Ecuador.

PART ONE

TSELTAL CHRISTIANITY

Eugenio Maurer

1

Introduction

Historical Overview of the Maya

The Tseltal are one Mayan civilisation of twenty-some branches of people groups that spring from the Maya, whose arrival in middle America and establishment in Guatemala took place around five thousand years ago. The original group comprised some five thousand individuals. Through the centuries the various branches of the group were dispersed and emigrated as far as the highlands of Guatemala, the Yucatan peninsula, the highlands of Chiapas and the Huasteca of Veracruz. There is a basis for supposing that the Tseltalan (the ancestors of the Tseltal and Tsotsil of today) could have been participants in the classical Mayan civilisation in the environs of Peten (Guatemala) before they moved on to the high plains of Chiapas, where the division between these two cultures took place during about the sixth and seventh centuries A.D. approximately (Vogt 1971, 415-417).

When the Spanish arrived in this area, they found some cities on the Yucatan coast which were still flourishing (Lafay, 29), but the splendour of the great Mayan civilisation had, to all intents and purposes, vanished. There are various hypotheses put forward concerning the cause of the collapse, including epidemics, famines caused by the depletion of the land, and disagreements and wars both internal and with the Nahua people. In

23

any case it seems that the deciding factor was a peasant revolt. With respect to this we note that there was a marked cultural dichotomy in Mayan society:

> On one side . . . a select group of priests and leaders, entrusted with the task of safeguarding the wisdom: they understood astronomy, architecture, engineering and the arts . . . Owing to this fact they led lives of splendour (ibid., 20).

To the people of the lower classes fell the lot to maintain and clothe the upper classes and provide them with every luxury imaginable. In addition, the very heavy labour of building the grand palaces and ceremonial centres fell to them. Added to all this was the necessity to work to provide for themselves and their families. This enormous cultural dichotomy continued to increase more and more with the passage of the years, with the demands of the aristocracy becoming more intolerable until the situation erupted in rebellion. "Numerical superiority was the only weapon that [people of the lower classes] had. They probably strangled the majority of their masters" (ibid., 21, 36).

When the light of this culture was extinguished, or in some cases when the people fled from the theocratic class domination, their knowledge also was lost, since, as we have seen, those who upheld the culture were not the peasants but those of the aristocracy. In this respect, what Thompson suggests is interesting:

> Even before the arrival of the Spanish the state religion had been superseded by a popular peasant religion. This change can be explained by the disappearance of the ancient priesthood and the collapse of the centralised government of the autocracy. When the ceremonial centres fell . . . the peasantry was obliged to entrust themselves with delight to the propitiation of their own local gods of the land, a culture of hunters and the people, with local prayer leaders; a purely popular religion (206ff).

This is exactly what the Spanish found. Unfortunately for us, we cannot count on a Landa, who despite having destroyed all that he could of the objects and documents of the peninsular Maya of the Yucatan, partly redeemed his guilt by dedicating himself to learning from the Indians everything with relation to their employment, customs and culture in general. It is true that there were those who burned the documents of the Chiapas Indians, like Bishop Nuñez de la Vega at the end of the seventeenth century, but there was no one to gather first hand that which was relative to their culture. The data that this bishop and other authors, religious and lay, offer us is merely "by hearsay," as we shall see.

Thus, in order to analyze the present-day Tseltal culture, especially the religious domination, we have to make use of some documents from sister cultures, such as that of Landa, Popol Vuh, Chilam Balam, and others, which mention dates and elements similar to the those of the Tseltal. Consequently, it seems fair to use them to help us in our interpretations and analysis.

The Tseltal is the most numerous ethnic group in the State of Chiapas, numbering approximately some 150,000.

THE TSELTAL OF GUAQUITEPEC

I shall not analyze the religion of the Tseltal people in a general form, but rather I shall use as my base in particular the data from the population of Guaquitepec (that of the district of Chilon, State of Chiapas), situated in the foothills of the Chiapas highlands. The reason for having chosen this population, in which for two and a half years I carried out the fieldwork for my doctoral thesis in social anthropology, was precisely because it is one of the most traditional communities in which the cultural synthesis, which comes from pre-Columbian and Hispanic elements, has been subjected to the least Western influence in recent years, owing to its relative isolation from the "civilised" world. Actually it was not until around the 1950s that the government, along with the church, began to pay any attention to this and other population centres in the region.

With regard to the nurture of the religious life on the part of the church, this area was practically abandoned for more than a century as a result of the expulsion of the religious workers by the government of President Benito Juarez during the decade of the 1860s. During this time, once or twice a year the people received a visit from a self-sacrificing priest, who was the only one serving an area of thousands of square kilometres and whose ministry was reduced to celebrating Mass and baptising infants; he did not have time to do anything else. It was precisely during this century that, as I see it, the Indians perfected their synthesis of pre-Columbian and Spanish elements, which resulted in the observation made by Redfield with regard to the Maya of Yucatan:

Many cultural elements of the present day have parallels which are of European and Indian origin, and can be attributed to either one source or the other, or both.

The present culture is a perfectly integrated body of elements whose sources are Spanish and Indian (and which) have been totally remade and redefined, the one serving the other. Nothing is entirely Indian; nothing is entirely Spanish (1934, 48, 60).

To this body of elements I give the name *traditional religion*, which I consider to be a synthesis, precisely because the elements are found to be perfectly integrated into an ordered and harmonised whole. In my opinion, this traditional religion is Catholic, definitely not Western, but Mayan. My readers may form their own opinions with regard to the elements that are presented in this work.

As is natural, this traditional religion, which the Jesuits found on their arrival in the region in 1958, has continued to change, above all among the youth, owing to the intervention of religious workers and other pastoral agents. Despite this change, the adult sector, and in particular the elderly, have preserved the old ways and practice them almost exactly as they were.

2

The Cosmic Vision of the Traditional Religion

All of the attention which they gave to their gods was to no other end nor for any other reason than that these gods should grant them health, life and sustenance (Landa, 58).

HAPPINESS AND HARMONY

Not only for the pre-Hispanic Maya, but also for the Tseltal of our time, that which is truly essential in life is happiness here on earth. Happiness or misery in the other life is merely a logical consequence of life in this world: if the person was happy here, he will be so there also; if he was miserable here, there the same situation will prevail.

This is all very well, but happiness cannot exist in this world unless there is harmony, not only in relation to the world "above" (God and the saints, on whom depend all that is necessary for a happy life), but also in relation to the "image" of this community above, in other words, "the community on earth." And there will be no harmony in this community unless each member of the community has harmony within himself or herself.

If men within themselves are in accord with the rhythms of the superior forces, by that very fact they will be in accord with the fundamental order of all being (Berger, 69).

Harmony of the Subject within Oneself

With respect to physical attributes, health is the result of balance or harmony of the individual components of the organism. With respect to psychic attributes, harmony is also required. Thus, for example, of a person who is indecisive, worried or two-faced they say *cheb yo'tan*—two hearts; of a suspicious or distrustful person *ma'spisiluk yo'tan*—one who does not act with his or her whole heart; of a jealous person *ti'ti 'o'tantayel*—a biting heart, indicating thereby the uneasiness that another's welfare produces and the consequent lack of harmony.

On the other side of the coin, the person with self-control, maturity and calm is *nakal yo'tan*—his heart is at home or his heart is at rest, as when one has finished work and sits in the door of the house to enjoy the tranquillity of the surroundings.

Models of this personal harmony are the *Trensipaletik*—the community leaders—the elders who through long years of service on behalf of their community have acquired *sp'ijil yo'tan*—knowledge of the heart—that is to say wisdom or balance between the faculties of the intellect and the will.

Harmony with the Surrounding World

In the family: with a man's wife, whom he calls *snuhp' jti,' snuhp' ko'tan*—the other half of my mouth, the other half of my heart. The mouth indicates that there is not only a union in word but also in action, for in the Tseltal culture the value placed on the spoken word is so great that many times they use the term *utel*, which means "to say," to mean "to do." As for the heart, the union should be one of love, that perfectly joins one with another.

In the community: In order that harmony will reign there, its members should be *ch'abal*—respectful one towards the other, and above all towards the authorities, especially the community leaders, and revere the traditions. However, so that complete harmony reigns, it is not only necessary that there are no arguments, but that everyone be *jun pafal yo'tan*—of one equal heart.

This is seen very clearly in arriving at judgements in the resolution of conflicts, whose objective is not simply that the offender atones for the injury, but that harmony is reestablished between the two who are in dispute, so that these two remain in complete peace with each other. At the end of a judgement, the offender distributes a drink to each one in attendance beginning with the person whom he has offended, thereby signifying that once again harmony reigns in the community. One should note that especially in small groups this procedure is necessary, given the fact that all of the members of the community are continually in contact with one another and there is no way in which one can avoid another.

Harmony with the Spiritual World

We have already stated that if harmony does not exist among the members of the community there can be no harmony with the spiritual community. Furthermore, in order that complete harmony reigns between the two, it is essential that the community renders service to the spiritual dimension, particularly in festivals. On the other hand, if a misdeed has not received the appropriate penalty, harmony cannot hold full sway in the community; the delinquent must be punished, be it from the community authorities, or from God and the saints. (This topic will receive fuller amplification when we deal with the problem of evil.)

The Problem of Evil, or the Lack of Harmony

In the world of the Tseltal it can never be admitted that God or God's representatives, the saints, ever send any evil upon a just person. The reason is that if happiness on earth is regarded as vitally essential for humankind, then good and evil on earth are translated into absolutes. Yet, as is seen in the case of Job, there are just persons who suffer! Theology in traditional religion has found the solution: Just persons suffer because other spiritually powerful persons who are envious send unjust evil upon them by means of sorcery.

With this practical solution two ends are served: First, God is entirely exonerated from any suspicion that might suggest that God could act unjustly; and secondly, by this same reasoning the people can live more or less in peace. In effect, it would be intolerable to think that a being so powerful would be able to act in a capricious manner; the people would be living in a state of continuous anxiety. Of course there still exists the possibility that the sorcerer could send an unjust evil. Yes, but being a human being he or she can operate in a destructive manner only with the help of God. Furthermore, this falls within the bounds of healer's role, which will be examined later in connection with the sacrament for the restoration of harmony.

THE DIVINE PANTHEON OF THE TRADITIONAL RELIGION

God

They believe in one God only; this in spite of the fact that they call the saints *diosetik*, whom they consider to be God's ambassadors to the earth. God is the creator and giver of all: "By You we live," "God gives us everything that we ask." God grants the power to heal: "Medicine cannot, in any way, bring healing of its own power, but only by the power of Our Lord." He is Lord and Master of all: "The true master is God the Father; therefore, He himself is our protector in every village." "The hidden enemy [the sorcerer who has sent the sickness] is not the master of the body, but the Lord God is."

One of the most beloved concepts among the Tseltal is that of God the Father, and this is the invocation with which they begin their prayers and repeat as a refrain throughout them: *Anich'anon jTat, anich'anon Kajwal*—my Father, I am your son, my Lord, I am your child.

It is interesting to note that God (by analogy the saints also) is Father and Mother: *Ho'otkotik, awal-anich'anotkotik*—we, your children of woman, your children of man.[1]

It is not very clear whether God is eternal or whether God created the world, for they say: *k'alal chiknaj te bahlumilal, chiknaj ek te Diose!*—when the world appeared, God appeared also. As to God's knowledge, God sees us; however, it seems that God does not know absolutely everything. Thus, for example, God was not aware that some people having escaped the flood into the air, did not arrive in heaven. In the same way, as we shall see when we deal with evil, the sorcerer manages to make God believe that an "illegitimate" punishment that he or she is sending upon some person is justified; essentially, the task of the healer is to unmask the sorcerer before God.

They believe in the Trinity (three Persons)—*oxtohl*—*Dios Tatil, Dios Nich'a, Dios Ch'ul Espíritu.*

Jesus Christ

He is the one to whom they most often direct their prayers; it is him, God and man, whom they call "Father and Lord, Great Man, the True Father on the earthly plain, he who is raised up powerful in heaven." Is he Ladino (a white person) or Tseltal?[2] The spontaneous answer is: "*Ha'tseltal stukel, yu'un bats'il winik!*"—he is Tseltal, in that he is a real man. For a Tseltal (Tsotsil or Tojolabal or Ch'ol), the only real human beings are they themselves, never a Ladino, who was created by God from horse dung. However, after giving it some thought, they declare that Christ is Tseltal but is Ladino also, since he is the Saviour of everyone.

They call upon Jesus as *nichimalil schu,' nichimalil alajel ku' un*, which translated literally means "flowering bosom, flowering one who gives birth" to express his protection as tender as a mother's. (They also invoke the Virgin and saints using these terms, both men and women.) Jesus is *jManojel y jTojojel*—the one who buys and the one who pays— "Jesus Christ travelled throughout the world; he paid for our sins when he died at the hands of assassins . . . They killed him because he preached the Word of God. He was not guilty, not even of the tiniest sin, but we are guilty for our sins. All of us in the world are sinners, and Jesus Christ our Father, who really died on the cross and shed his blood gladly on the cross, freed us" (taken from an address or sermon, delivered on Good Friday by the head of the brotherhood, *cofradía*, the leader of the elders or community leaders).

The concept of original sin does not exist in traditional religion. Christ paid to free us from the sins we commit, and he redeemed us so that we might be happy. This is expressed clearly in the prayer that the midwife offers for the newborn child:

> You, my Lord Jesus Christ, came to buy it for me; You came to pay for it for me . . . You came to buy it with freedom, to pay for it with generosity. Receive as a present the gift of joy to the world! May this be a gift for all those whom He begets!

It may be useful to point out Christ's relation with the sun and the cross. Concerning the first, the Tseltal and the Tsotsil have a legend according to which Christ became tired of living on earth and decided to go up to heaven with his mother Mary. Since then he has been the sun, and the Virgin is the moon. To both they give the name *Jalalme'tik*—our Holy Mother. It seems that the source of this is found in the narrative of *Popol Vuh*, according to which twin heroes born of a virgin conquered their enemies, the lords of hell, and went up to heaven: one is the sun and the other the moon (48ff.). The Tseltal have baptised the narrative and applied it to Jesus and Mary. Perhaps there was also a basis for it in the gospel: Christ is the light (Jn 8:12)—in Tseltal, the same word *k'ahk'al* means both "light" and "sun." In the Book of the Apocalypse it is written that in heaven there is need for neither sun nor moon, because the glory of God illumines it and Christ is its lamp (Rv 21:23). In the same text it says of the Virgin Mary that the sun surrounds her and the moon is under her feet (Rv 12:1). In the event that these elements might have influenced each other, we meet another instance of synthesis between pre-Columbian and Christian elements.

Concerning the relationship of Christ and the cross, there are some authors (such as Vogt 1969, 374; Blom, 283ff.) who affirm that the cross that the Indians venerate today has nothing to do with Christ and the Christian cross, unless it comes from the *yak-che* or *(bobbax ceiba)*—the tree from which they plead for water in order to live, the water that is the source of every living being. Precisely, it is from these affirmations that one can clearly deduce the relationship between the pre-Hispanic Maya cross and the Christian cross, which is founded on a synthesis for the Tseltal and the Tsotsil of today: the Mayan cross was a symbol of life. So, the Christian cross is invoked as the tree which gives life (the liturgy for Good Friday). We find before us a marvellous synthesis: both are trees of life, the first is agricultural, the second is spiritual! For this reason, Medina and Sejourné are perfectly correct in affirming:

> [It is possible] to date its origin back before the arrival of the Christian missionaries, [who were] the only ones to introduce this symbol with an even greater significance (15).

The Virgin Mary and the Saints

God sent each one of them to the diverse peoples of the earth, where they act as delegates and their representatives. They report to God everything that happens among the people where they are patrons, and they ask for the necessary graces so that those under their protection may live in happiness. The Tseltal illustrate the mediation of the patron saint before God as like that of a translator who interprets the Indians' petitions to the government without knowing the Indians' language. Or like the overseer of a plantation: When an Indian wants a parcel of land, for example, the overseer writes to the owner (who lives far away in the city) who in turn sends a reply to the overseer to communicate it to the Indian.

We could say that between the patron saint and the people a kind of pact is struck. The community takes on the responsibility of honouring the saint, and in exchange the saint grants it special protection. For the Tseltal, it was the patron saint who chose the site for them where they should live. Thus, for example, the Guaquitepec say to the Virgin Mary, their patron saint: "It was you, Holy Virgin, who found my village for me so that I might dwell here." Each patron saint has appeared among the people to whom God sent him or her since the beginning of the world, and the saint pleads with the people in that place that they build a house in which he or she may live permanently among them. As we shall see later, for centuries past the saints have been "Tseltalised," in that they claim that it was the Virgin Mary herself who, in 1712, incited them to rebel against the Spanish and to kill them.

The patron of the village is the most powerful person there. Even though Christ and the Virgin are more powerful in themselves than are the saints, in any given village the patron saint is the one who wields the most power and is the one who is invoked and who is celebrated more than any others. The Tseltal say that the saints of the church are alive. They admit that they are made of wood by human hands, "but when the priest baptised them [that is to say that he blessed them and sprinkled them with holy water] God gave them intelligence so that they could represent God as they ought."

Each saint has his or her "double" in heaven, who relays the supplications and reports from the earth to God, and who sends God's answer to his or her "alter ego" on earth. In the same way, one who honours and serves the saint on earth, honours and serves the one in heaven at the same time. This beautiful symbolism does not stop here: The Indians treat the saints with the same courtesy with which they treat other persons; when they enter a church to pray, they go in passing before each one of the images of the other saints, addressing a short prayer to each one. To not do so would be like stopping to chat with someone in a group without even saying hello to the others.

We have something further: There are saints who are semi-clothed, like John the Baptist, St. Sebastian, etc. The Tseltal dress them. One of the reasons that they give, contrary to what we might think, is so the saints will not be embarrassed when the people come into the church fully clothed. They say: "We dress them so that we will not have to take our shirts off."

One of the most debated points concerning the worship that the Tseltal give to the saints is if this worship is directed to the Christian saints or to their ancient idols. There are those who affirm that behind the saints are hidden the pagan divinities (see Holland, 74, 79, 93; Vogt 1969, 460ff.). It seems to me that here again we are dealing with a synthesis. In effect, the role of the pre-Hispanic local divinities was to grant to their devotees "health and life, and preservation of them both" (Landa, 58). To achieve this, the most essential ingredients were "water and favourable weather" (Thompson, 264). In our region the conquest did not change the Indians' kind of agricultural life, and cultivating the land continued to be their main means of sustenance. Here again, we meet the situation where the function of the ancient divinities coincide, at least in some measure, with that of the Catholic saints. We have, for example, the rogation prayers, in which one asks God and the saints for "the rain and favourable weather for planting and harvesting." The meeting of the divinities of the Mayan pantheon and the Western saints does not pose any difficulty; the similarity of their roles is obvious (Lafaye, 47).

The Angels

The Tseltal do not seem to place much importance on the angels and traditional archangels (St. Michael, St. Gabriel, etc.), but they do give place to the angel who lives in the hill caves, who, though invisible, is the protector of life and of nature. At times they identify this angel with the mysterious *yajwal Ahaw*—lord of the cave, master of the mountain, the rain, and of the wild animals. He, together with the Virgin Mary, who lives in the caves in the hills too, tends the fields of corn.

They say that anyone who sees the Angel Yajwal-Ahaw will not live very long thereafter. I do not know whether it is possible to deduce from this supposition that the angel who guards the entrance into paradise and the angel who appears in the form of thunder and lightning (i.e., in Sinai, or at the resurrection of Christ) is the same angel who instills the fear of death.

The Demon Chopol Pukuj

Chopol Pukuj chopol—bad, perverse; *pukuj*—a perverse deity. This is the term that the missionaries used for the devil, and it is by this name that the devil is known today. In traditional religion it held little importance, and in one way we can say that he was considered to be "a poor devil," who could be vanquished relatively easily.

In Guaquitepec there is a legend that two valiant men from this village slew a devil who used to kill travellers. They received from the Virgin Mary (patron of the village) a small serpent, which entered into the devil by the anus and came out through the head, causing his instantaneous death. In another Tsotsil legend a man finished off a devil who was trying to kill him; he skinned him and then dressed himself in the devil's skin for the carnival [the celebration on the eve of Lent] (Laughlin, 1977, 30; Gossen, 310, 319).

It seems that this concept derives from the fact that they have always envisioned the devil as the cause of spiritual and future ills, which in the Tseltal cosmos has always held less importance than terrestrial and present good. For this reason a powerful sorcerer who can send sickness, disasters and even death is much more to be feared.

It is interesting to contrast the missionaries' continual insistence concerning the devil (in fifty Tseltal sermons which I analyzed, at least half of them dealt with the subject) and the little importance that the Tseltal concede him. We wonder what happened to this formidable demon of the missionaries, who has been reduced to a poor devil now. If he had been so important, is it possible that his influence could have been so toned down in just three centuries? Furthermore, as we shall see when we deal with witchcraft among the Tseltal, the devil has nothing to do with sorcery or witchcraft. It would be very strange if the concept of demons, which was so important to the missionaries, would have ceased to exist precisely when Christian influence was on the upsurge!

In my opinion, the devil was transformed into a "whirlwind" who wrestled with the missionaries, for whom, as Pitt-Rivers says, "Pagan religion ceased to exist . . . an error due to ignorance, in order to transform itself . . . into a sign of a privileged relationship with the demons" (1971, 19).

ESCHATOLOGY

Death

The Tseltal always think that death is due to the influence of witchcraft, even in the case of a 99-year-old man. This is clearly seen in the prayers that are recited for the dead in diverse circumstances, for example:

> May the person who brought harm to you [they say to
> the dead] not continue to live!
> May he in no way enjoy tranquillity, not with his wife
> nor with his children!
> May his sufferings be equal to those which he caused
> you! May his shame here on earth be equal to
> yours!
> May this be visited upon the one who brought this evil
> [death] upon you!

Another important aspect of the Tseltal vision of death is that the dead do not come back; if they did, they would cause problems and disturbances for the living. With this in mind, they bury the personal possessions with the corpse and, in addition, fifteen days after the death, the community leaders of the village perform a rite "to place the soul in the tomb." They go to the cemetery for three consecutive days and they fast all morning. After this they recite some prayers similar to the one above. Later, in the cemetery, they eat and drink to bid farewell to the one who has died.

November 2 is the official day for visiting the dead, when families visit the cemetery. I shall not take the time to describe the ceremony, because it is well known in its general aspects. I shall only emphasize the following: After the visit to the cemetery they celebrate with a feast in their homes at which their dead are in "attendance."

There is one point which is not clear, and that is whether they consider people to be happier here in this world than in the other. Actually, they say that the dead are "free" on the second of November so that they may visit the earth and "do whatever they like."

Heaven and Hell

Heaven is seldom mentioned. They say that those who have not sinned go there, but they add, "we do not know what happens there." Heaven is mentioned in a few prayers, but rather obliquely: *Xojobuk ta yutil gloria, xojobuk to yutil ch'ulchan*—There is splendour in glory, there is brightness in the heaven. They also think that their offerings enter heaven: "May my candles be placed today, one beside the other, on a table, on a chair inside heaven."

Hell is also seldom mentioned. When they are specifically questioned, they answer: "If a man has committed serious sins, he goes to hell. From that place he never departs, there he stays. Our ancestors told us so." I found only one legend on the subject: An adulterous woman died and was transformed into a mule in hell. Her husband went to visit her there, carried on a black horse by a Ladino dressed in black (most likely the devil). The husband was bidden to go for firewood and he was given the mule to carry it. As the mule did not want to move, he started to beat it. Then the animal began to talk. Lo! it was his wife! She said that they were both guilty; after all, he accepted the rich food that she received from her lover. After working there for a while, the man left by pulling a ruse. "Though we do not know whether he returned to the world or he was sent to another part." A little while later he died, "and we still do not know if he went to be reunited with his wife [as she had foretold] or if he was given entrance into the other world!"

Of the hell that the missionaries painted with hair-raising vividness, full of devils who tormented the people with all kinds of tortures, only a vague reference remains—a woman transformed into a mule and a man who had to carry on the tasks of daily life there. The food for both of them was worms (as a punishment for the luxury foods that they ate on earth, which were obtained by the adulterous activities of the woman).

This concept of heaven and hell comes entirely out of the cosmic vision of the traditional religion, according to which, as we have already seen, that which is essential in the life of a human being is happiness in this world and whatever happens in the other life is merely a consequence of what has happened here. To this we must add that the good and evil of heaven and hell are for some distant future and spiritualised, in contrast to the here-and-now and the tangible good and evil which bring happiness or shame in traditional religion.

3

The Tseltal Sacraments

Since that which is essential to life is "happiness here on earth," it is logical that the sacraments in the traditional religion are symbols of this happiness and a means to attain it. And as this happiness is founded on harmony, the goal of these sacraments lies in obtaining, increasing, or restoring harmony.

THE SACRAMENTS OF INITIATION INTO HARMONY

Baptism

Baptism is the beginning of a subject's harmony with the community. The aim of this Tseltal sacrament is not to erase original sin, because this concept does not exist among them. If a child were to have such sin, logically it would need to be punished here and now. On the other hand, we have already seen that Christ has atoned for our personal sins, but first of all so that we might be happy.

It seems that the role of baptism is to strengthen the unity of the community by reinforcing the social ties between the families through the system of godparents and, above all, through the system of *compadres* (the binding relationship between the godparents and the parents of the child). This latter is the recognition and consecration of the ties of friendship, which are already present and which prove to be even stronger among the Tseltal, so much so that usually the same godparents are chosen for all the children born to a couple.

For the Tseltal the ties of *compadre* are even stronger than blood ties. *Ta nadhil jbankilalat, yo" tik ini jkompadremjbahtik*—Before you were my older brother, but now we are *compadres*. These words were spoken by a Tseltal to his older brother (a person worthy of every respect). Of course this trait is not exclusively held by the Tseltal.

Marriage: Harmony of the Couple and the Community

From the decade of the 1870s, when all religious workers were expelled, just one priest remained in this area. He travelled the region covering countless villages, but only baptising and celebrating the Eucharist. The Tseltal, therefore, developed and perfected their own marriage rite and never concerned themselves with marriage in the church. This is understandable if we compare the Western rite, which is so plain, with the traditional rite, which I shall explain.

When a young man wants to marry, he tells his parents, who find an old man or an old woman to act as *monojel* (a coach or an appeaser) or, as we would say, a marriage arranger. This go-between begins a series of weekly discussions with the parents of the girl; a minimum of four sessions is required before they can accede to the petition for marriage, but they can prolong the process up to ten or more meetings.

Among the arguments that the *monojel* presents to convince the parents of the girl to hand her over, there is one which is very much in keeping with the Tseltal culture. If the parents persist in a negative reply, it could happen that the girl *ya xlok'ta ahnel*—flees, whereupon the worst possible things that could happen to anyone follow, *te k'exalal*—the shame! Another very important argument is also put forward: It was not man who initiated marriage but God who gave it to *sMe 'sTatik*—the ancestors. It is not right to depart even in the least from that which was instituted by them.

If the parents at last give their consent, once they have consulted with the daughter's wishes, they will strike a conditional agreement, for they must first assure themselves that the relatives are in accord. If the answer is in the affirmative, all are invited to a meeting, where the attendance of the suitor, his parents and the *monojel* are also required. They should come bearing *tut mahtanil*—the prescribed gift, bread, soft drinks, cigars, coffee, etc. The bride's father then asks each one of the couples present to give their opinion about the marriage. If everyone makes favourable comments, they accept the gift, but not before making the point, following the demands of etiquette, that they did not ask for the gift and that they really do not need it. Then it is time for the feast, made from food supplied by the bridegroom.

That is the moment for all those present to express in public what motivated and influenced them to accept the marriage. Among others, the following reason bears much weight: the boy is not insolent—*ma'ba ya stoy sbah*—rather he is *ch'abal*—respectful, especially towards his elders. This is a good indication that between him and his wife harmony should reign, because he knows how to grant to each one the proper place which corresponds to their status in the society.

This rite with some slight variations is celebrated again after some weeks, and, by means of much haggling, the date for the wedding is set for six months up to a year later. The *muk'ul mahtanil*—great gift is in essence a matrimonial contract. It consists of two pigs, many dozens of soft drinks, granulated cocoa, cigars, bread, salt and chile peppers. In attendance, in addition to the engaged couple and the marriage arrangers, are some of the community leaders—the highest civil-religious authorities—and married couples from among the bride's relatives. Part of the great gift will serve in the preparation of the banquet; the rest is divided in exactly equal parts and shared among all the families of the bride's relatives.

Here we can see clearly the communal character of the Tseltal wedding. In effect, each couple on the bride's side, by the very fact that they accept the gift, seal their promise to watch over the harmony of the newlyweds, first of all coming to the help of the woman, for in the Tseltal world the man is usually the cause of the majority of the conflicts that erupt in the community.

When the meal is finished, the bridegroom along with his parents and the *monojel* kneel before each couple in the bride's family in order to receive the *tsitsel*—advice. The couples exhort the young man to behave well, to work with constancy so that his wife will never be in need of clothing or food, and especially, to not get drunk. One rather moving piece of advice is the following: "That you never will get to the stage where your wife's face seems ugly to you." There are two expressions by which a husband refers to his wife that should be mentioned: *Te jmahtan*—my gift (from God), and *te snuhp' jti' te snuhp' ko'tan*—the other half of my mouth, the other half of my heart—with whom, therefore, perfect harmony reigns. When they have finished giving their advice to the young man, each one of the elders points out to him that should he fail to comply with his obligations, he will find himself once again standing in judgement before all the girl's family members.

To the parents and the marriage arranger fall the duty of watching over the harmony of the couple, as well as to continue to educate them in fulfilling their new tasks. The bride's mother-in-law is reminded that she should treat the bride affectionately and to go on teaching her the tasks of being the woman in charge of the house. (It is customary for the newlyweds to live for two or three years in the house of the young man's parents.)

What a difference between this ceremony, which is so human and solemn, and the barebones question, "Miss X, do you accept this man to be your husband? And Mr. X, do you accept Miss X as your lawful wife?," which has been preceded by warnings and perhaps the request for the hand of the bride. We realise why the Tseltal, even the catechists, consider marriage in the church before a priest as merely a complementary act that adds solemnity to the traditional rite. How could these people, who even make a ceremony out of purchasing an object, possibly contemplate a marriage contract that is so lacking in seriousness and so brief?

Furthermore, the essence of indigenous identity, the orientation towards the community, is seen only implicitly in the Spanish rite in the presence of the witnesses. However, in the Tseltal rite the presence of the community is obvious in the person of the community leaders, the highest authority in the village, entrusted to act in the name of the patron saint to watch over the harmony, along with the community of the bride's family as those in agreement that the marriage should take place. Those who give the bride to her new family are the same ones who remain ever ready to run to her aid.

When the Jesuits arrived in 1958, they began to celebrate two marriage rites, the Roman Catholic one in the church in the morning and later the traditional Tseltal one described.

It should be noted that the traditional ceremony is still considered to be the more important. No father would allow his daughter to live with the young man if they had only celebrated the Western rite. In the present day there is a strong tendency to move towards fusing traditional religion and Western Catholicism. In the case of marriage, the traditional rite could be an excellent pattern for the Indians to go on developing a rite in which the richness of their heritage complements those Western elements which more obviously portray for them the *ya'telimbeyej ya'tel Dios*— the sacrament, an effectual sign of the work of God in bringing perfect harmony to men and women.

THE SACRAMENT OF SPIRITUAL POWER AND THE RESTORATION OF HARMONY

The Priesthood

From the 1860s until 1958 the Tseltal had received extremely limited attention from Western Catholic priests. It was during this century that the burden to act as priest for the people was firmly placed upon the shoulders of the community leaders, who took over almost everything relating to worship and spiritual governing in the community.

As we shall see when we deal with the sacrament for antonomasia, the festival, a community leader is a person who has passed through all of the responsibilities involved in service to the patron saint on behalf of his community. This person, because of these tasks, has been in intimate contact with the world above and thereby has continued to receive an ever increasing level of spiritual power. To this is added the fact that he received a special soul from God, *lab* (that is to say, a powerful animal— a tiger, a nocturnal bird of prey, etc.), which is, as they say, the sacrament of power, both the sign and the condition of power (for more information with respect to this, see Maurer 1979 and 1983).

After passing through the various levels of civic and religious responsibilities, the person who has served well becomes a community leader and automatically enters as a member into the college of elders entrusted with governing the community in the religious realm as well as in civic affairs. To the elders also falls the lot of imparting justice, not only in the courts, but also in a mysterious form by means of their *lab*. This is often a nocturnal bird of prey who flies over the village for the purpose of gathering information as to whether anyone has committed a crime against harmony. The community leaders can send sickness and even death upon such a person.

This power, which is received from God, may be misused in selfish ways against the community; then it constitutes witchcraft (when a community leader, out of envy or because of some supposed offense, unjustly punishes a person). In order to get the power from God to punish, the community leader makes God believe that he is acting justly. We have seen that for these people God is far off, resulting in the possibility to deceive God in certain ways.

Restoration of Harmony

In keeping with the basic concept of happiness here on earth and the belief that God and the saints never send evil upon those who have not sinned, oral confession as understood in Western Catholicism does not make sense when the person has not committed any serious errors, namely, those that disrupt harmony. The only sure indication that such a disturbance has occurred is when misfortune falls (bad harvests, accidents, etc.), and above all, when sickness and death strike. Even then, it is still important to find out if the sick person disturbed harmony by committing a sin personally or if this disharmony is caused by a third party who is envious.

If harmony has been disturbed, how can it be restored? Let us look at the most common scenario, that of sickness which is not alleviated by ordinary treatment. In this case the *jpoxtaywanej*—healer—hears the patient's confession to ascertain that there has been no sin (theft, murder, assault, etc.) by which harmony within the person has been disrupted, resulting in the person becoming the object of just wrath from the one attacked and, in consequence, from the heavenly community also. The problem may lie with a neighbour, deprived perhaps of some object, health or life itself, or with the whole community, whose general harmony is seen to be upset by the crime, or the harmony of the celestial community, which may have been directly disturbed by, for example, the person not performing as he ought some civil-religious task in honour of the patron saint, who has therefore become angry with the community. In such an instance, harmony of the terrestrial community will be greatly affected, for the saint who has not received the worship that is due will not grant protection (good weather, good harvests, etc.).

If, following a detailed confession, the patient is found to be guilty, a punishment will be meted out, usually a whipping. By this means harmony is restored: for the sinner, who now needs fear no further punishment from God, and will be free from the sickness, which is the equivalent to disharmony; for the sinner's family, who were worried, fearful and at the same time angry with the person, because it was his or her fault that the ire of a superior being had fallen upon them, anger which was able to reach even the family; and lastly, for the one who was wronged or for his or her family, whose harmony is reestablished when peace is regained, knowing that the criminal has been punished.

I believe that all of this helps us to understand the adaptations of traditional religion, which only permit confession in the case of misfortune, especially sickness, and that such a confession takes place before the healer and the community leaders. If they are healthy, this means that no crime has been committed.

However, if during the confession no fault is uncovered, or if some days have passed after the punishment has been administered and the patient is not cured, the healer will realise that most likely he is dealing with a case of witchcraft, that is, an unjust punishment sent by a spiritually powerful person whose harmony was disturbed by something the patient did (but which was not sinful). Perhaps the patient had a much better harvest than the sorcerer, whose jealousy rose up, causing a loss of harmony. From the perspective of the sorcerer or his client, the punishment was justified.

If it has to do with a just person, *ch'abal kerem*, it was not God who sent the punishment, because God never does so when there is no sin. Rather, it will be necessary for the healer to prepare to struggle with the sorcerer; he will also have to demonstrate to God that this is a case of illegitimate punishment, so that God will help the healer to conquer the one who is misusing power. The healing of the patient will depend upon whether the healer is more powerful than the sorcerer.

What is noteworthy in this sacrament of healing is that the symbols are perfectly visualised by means of a social drama. Take the case of a healing of a fever: The healer is afraid, "I am dust . . . I am a mortal being; I am afraid!" but he trusts in Christ and in the saints, whom he invokes at length, asking for their help, "their cold mouth, their cold heart . . . the dew of a cold wind," and other cold things to refresh the feverish patient. In addition, every other moment he proclaims, "I am just!"—ch'abal keremon—and "My Father, I am your child; My Lord, I am your son!" Two reasons why God should listen to him and not to the sorcerer, who, in spite of the fact that "he is not master of the holy thought, nor is he master of the holy body, for the true master is the Lord," has performed as though he were the master and has disturbed harmony. Later, after having rebuked the sorcerer by this procedure, he adds:

Who will close his mouth in this moment?
Who can keep silent, since we are dealing with a just person (who is suffering unjustly)?

Against such iniquity the healer relies not only on the medicines which he administers to the sick one, medicines to which God grants the healing virtues, but he also makes use of the healing power of Christ Himself:

I shall put my foot in the midst of the vein, in the midst of the body, the word of Our Lord Jesus Christ!

While he is praying, he continually encourages the one who is sick so that he will not fall asleep, "Do not sleep, holy vein! Do not sleep, holy body!" and later on, "Now you are getting better, holy vein; already you are being healed, holy body!" The qualifying adjective "holy," applied to the body, reminds God that God is the master and not the sorcerer who unjustly has served his own end with his power.

No one has ever managed to grab this bull by the horns! The missionaries thought that if they preached the truth to the Indians, this error would disappear of its own accord. However, witchcraft still exists; it has even fallen to me in two or three cases to intervene in order to prevent the people from killing a poor person accused of being a sorcerer.

It is not that the Tseltal approve of witchcraft; on the contrary, they condemn it as an action against the community. The problem is that the Tseltal cosmic vision requires it. In effect, given the principle of happiness here on earth, anything that deprives the people of this happiness is not merely relatively but absolutely evil (except when God punishes a person to correct him or her and the person continues to live). On the other hand, since God is extremely good and just, God cannot send evil upon anyone who does not merit it. The solution is, therefore, that it was not God who sent the evil, but rather a third person who was envious, who managed to trick God into helping dispense the evil. Note this theory that God does not know very well what happens on earth. He is too far away. That is why God sent the saints to all the various communities. This solution exonerates God from any blame, and the anxiety of the Indians is lessened. If it is a human being who is dispensing evil, they can defeat and even kill the person. Conversely, what would happen to them if God were to act capriciously and send punishment upon them without cause?

THE SACRAMENT OF HARMONY PAR EXCELLENCE: THE FESTIVAL

"When we celebrate the festival for our brothers," the Tseltal say, "we give back to God part of what God has given to us; we honour our protector by having a festival for our brothers." The festival is the form of worship which the community renders to the patron saint through his or her representatives, the festival sponsors, delegated by the community leaders (who are the real priests of the village) in order to fulfil the obligation that they owe to the saint and thus obtain the whole blessing for the community, namely, harmony. As Redfield says:

> Between the saint and the community a kind of perpetual vow has been sworn which must be renewed every year . . . The people make the expected offerings, and the saint gives them health and good fortune. If the festival is not celebrated according to the traditional form, it is the equivalent to a rupture of the duty (1941, 217).

We have heard the words of the *cofradía*, the moral chief of the community leaders: "We, when we celebrate the festival for our brothers, give back to God part of what God has given to us." Here is a vividly clear expression of harmony, the union of the two communities, the earthly with the heavenly.

In the official prayers and greetings one can capture very well the aims of the festival:

> To honour you, my patron saint, to reverence you . . . and because you are watching me, oh my benefactor [I celebrate the festival]!
> By any chance have you ceased to watch over and observe me?
> Perhaps you have not contemplated [my service] attentively during the entire time, during the whole of the sacred period?

The saint, for his or her part, looks not only upon the deeds, but also on the underlying intentions themselves. "You know if our heart still beats [to serve you]."

We realise that not only is the saint petitioned for all that is necessary to maintain harmony, but the festival itself symbolises, reinforces and revives the community harmony. As Geertz says:

> The ritual ceremonies of the community are not just models of that which the participants believe, but models so that they can believe. By means of these malleable models the people develop their faith as they describe it [in visual terms] (29).

Here, with respect to harmony, we have the names that are given to the sponsors: first older brother, second older brother, first younger brother, second younger brother, indicative of the fraternal harmony that ought to hold sway among them. They also call the festival *kumpirali*—the relationship of *compadres*—to show the very intimate union in which all of the participants ought to work.

The sponsors cultivate harmony during their year of service, symbolising it by a monthly love feast. Each one supplies a gourd of *atole*,[3] a bowl containing a stew of pumpkin seeds and another with beans, along with a stack of tortillas. From each of the four stacks some tortillas are taken, and they make four new stacks; in each one of these latter stacks there are tortillas from each of the four sponsors. The gourds circulate continually among the participants. The pumpkin seed stew and beans are not distributed in individual bowls for each person; rather, two people share each bowl.

This rite constitutes an important part of the festival itself, and in it we discover many other signs of harmony. For example, the drink is not served in individual cups; rather, there is only one cup, which continues to circulate and from which each person serves himself in turn.

It is obvious that harmony must reign among the twenty to twenty-five persons who work in the homes of each of the four sponsors: those chop the firewood, carry the corn, shuck the maize, cook the food, serve the table, serve as masters of ceremony and sponsors, as well as the priests of the festival.

Thanks is given to the saint for the harmony that has reigned in their midst up to the present, and supplication is made against anyone disrupting it in the future:

> Your poor sponsors are gathered together to commence the holy matins we, your four sponsors, are all here, nobody has abandoned

his place, not your masters of ceremony, nor your precentor [the liturgical leader for the whole festival] have abandoned us or left us alone.

May neither the sponsors nor the other half of their mouth, the other half of their heart abandon the work.

May all the women [who work in the festival] act as if their hands and their feet were the same, as though it were only one woman preparing the food.

May all those who meet in my house [for the festival] have one equal heart.

The atmosphere of happiness, good humour and friendliness is extraordinary despite the fact that everyone's work is exhausting. The festival usually begins about six in the morning and finishes somewhere around one the following morning! And this goes on for six consecutive days! A feeling of joy is mentioned in the prayers:

> You, our patron saint, have given to us all who are
>   your children delightful happiness!
> The hearts of your sponsors are flourishing and happy!

After attending a Tseltal festival, one can understand that a Mass may seem insipid, and that it would only be a nonessential complement to the festival.

It is true that there is no comparison with that which has occurred in other domains within the colonial world where the Mass has become the sacrament of a sacrament: the bread and wine, Ladino elements instead of the tortillas and some drink from the region; the priest, a Ladino, who prays in a Ladino tongue, and causes a Ladino God to come down from the heavens.

The festival is the sacrament of life in the community; it is a symbol, since the community participates in it; it is an agent, because all the features of the community life are relived in a flexible context, the common work, the happiness, the participation, the conviviality, etc.

Geertz confirms this when he speaks of the religious ceremonies—in our case the festivals—that are not just presentations of one particular religious perspective, for in the midst of them the scene is set, they materialise and they become real . . . The festivals are not only the models of what the participants believe, but also the models in order that they can believe. In these plastic models the people develop their faith as they describe it in this creative and visible form (29).

Perhaps the reader finds it strange that among the Tseltal sacraments one cannot find the Eucharist, which Jesus Christ instituted as the sacrament of love and, by implication, of harmony also. The reason can be found in the answer that a Tseltal gave when he was asked the difference between the festival of the patron saint and the Mass: "In the Mass there is no participation."

Actually, in the Tseltal traditional liturgy the Mass still does not play a very important part. This is understandable, not only because of the absence of the priest for over a century, but also because some of the priests themselves during previous times disparaged this Indian form of worship and did not participate in it. Thus, a priest from Bachajon, in the 1830s, wrote in his report: "Once the Mass is finished they go off to their whistles, their flutes and their drinking sessions." This was a description of the sacrament of harmony! (cf. Documento).

Even today in a number of villages the Mass is not an essential element of the festival. The sponsors and the masters of ceremony attend the Mass and at the conclusion recite the prayers appropriate for the festival. The priest, in turn, honours the festival with his presence, though he remains almost completely passive. If the priest cannot attend, the Indians think less of him; the splendour of the festival, however, remains practically the same, with or without his presence.

On the other side of the picture, the celebration of the Eucharist, which was the symbol and agent of union among people and with God and which united all in a festive banquet, had ceased to exist. Even before the time of the Conquest, mere passive attendance at a rite where generally only the priest ate and drank was all that was usual; there was no real food, just a symbol in the form of the wafer, and a tiny drop of wine. In addition, another important element had been eliminated; the communication with God was not done directly by the people but through the priest.

Furthermore, the symbols used for the food and the drink, the bread made from wheat and the wine from grapes, were not known elements, nor did they bear any meaning for Amerindians; Christ-food and Christ-drink was signified by a food and a drink that was neither food nor drink for them.

This did not suffice for the Indians. For, as Landa said earlier, they were accustomed to worshiping their idols with "huge feasts, accompanied by alcoholic beverages, dances full of colour, and human sacrifices" (37).

For this reason the confraternities, imported from the Iberian Peninsula by the missionaries, had great success. Their objective was to render worship exclusively and visibly to the patron saint:

The festivals were occasions for public ceremonies, with ecclesiastical services, processions, food and drink, dances, floral decorations, fireworks, musical games . . . and precisely those open aspects of the Christian religion were those that the indigenous peoples most easily embraced (Gibson, 131, 103).

With very good reason, such features entered fully into their cultural patterns:

> With the introduction of the confraternities, the festive activities by means of which they had worshiped their idols in the past, were fully legitimised, only now they were directed to the worship of the saint. In this way they achieved a synthesis, for they combined the Christian rites with traditional forms of indigenous ritual . . . and they reconciled the Christian-Spanish world with that of the indigenous-pagan one (ibid., 131).

Everything was sanctified, even the rejoicing. This is clearly seen now among the Chamulas, for whom "the purpose of the festivals is that everybody should be happy and be able to enjoy themselves, though we all know that . . . we are doing it as a service to the supernatural world" (Gossen, 138). We draw to your attention the fact that this interpretation has a Pauline sense: "Whether you eat, or whether you drink, or whether you do any other thing, do all to the glory of God" (1 Cor 10:31).

There is yet another important characteristic in the indigenous worship of the saint—the concept of work. Not just that required for the festival itself, such as the preparation of the food and drink, along with that done by the musicians and the masters of ceremony, but the work done throughout the year previous to the festival, when the sponsors must fulfil their role so that they have maize and beans. These seeds must be planted by the sponsors, and even though they may have money, they are not permitted to purchase them. *Tak'in k'op ma'yuk stuk ta ich'el ta muk' Kajkanantik*—The language of money is useless when it comes to the honour of our protection. For this reason, those who do not own any land cannot function as sponsors, even though they may have money to buy everything that is necessary.

Thus we see that the festival is the sacrament of harmony, for it sanctifies all aspects of community life, and strengthens its unity and its identity at the same time.

4

Evangelisation and Its Results

The Ethnocentrism of the Missionaries

The Spanish were incapable of accepting the existence of another culture better than theirs, much less the culture of those "ignorant pagan Indians," who lived in the world the Spanish had recently discovered. It was necessary at all costs to rescue those people from the darkness of paganism and give them a civilisation that would pull them out of their barbarism. For the Spaniards, everything that belonged to the culture of the recently discovered countries was unacceptable, because it all was marred with the stain of idolatry and superstition.

> The obsession with idolatry became so dominant in some of the missionaries that it made them suspicious of everything that had to do with the civilisation of paganism (Ricard, 148).

Even the Indians' food appeared to be filthy to them, and they recommended that on the day when they would receive holy communion that they should eat clean things and white bread. Nothing in these cultures seemed good to them or in any way acceptable. As Ricard says:

> Instead of presenting Christianity as the completion and fullness of the indigenous religions, they proposed it as something altogether new that entailed a radical and absolute break with everything from the past . . .
>   They replaced the old with the new. They never amalgamated, nor continued, nor developed the old. In every area which did not touch anything religious from either far or near, they were determined to maintain the past . . . They did not pass that point; always reluctant to make any accommodation with regard to the spiritual and the dogmatic order, determined to destroy any customs that could barely be seen to have any religious character (112, 113ff.).

The missionaries not only brought new concepts from a culture radically different from that of the original people (a people unknown to them, and not even worthy of being studied), but these concepts seemed so clear to them that they assumed no person in his or her right mind could fail to grasp them just by hearing about them. They preached the "truth" to the Indians as if they found themselves standing before an audience of fellow Spaniards.

THE IMPACT OF EVANGELISATION ON THE INDIANS

It is only natural that the Indians should grasp the new concepts in their own cultural mindsets, which by the same token, take on a form and meaning distinct from that expressed by the preachers. A passage from a story which has been made into a novel by Madariaga illustrates what may have taken place in this area. An Indian is giving his wife a summary in Nahuatl of what he saw and heard from the missionaries:

> The most important God is the one that they raise up as soon as they get to a place. This God is made in two pieces of wood, one that goes straight from top to bottom, and the other which crosses it and is a little shorter. It represents a God-man-animal who was born of a woman and a spirit: all of a sudden he is a spirit; he walks in the clouds and on top of the water—this is when he is God; then all of a sudden they take him prisoner; they slap him about the face; they spit in his face and they put a crown of thorns on him . . . — this is when he is a man; and all of a sudden he turns himself into a little animal that they have in their land that is called a lamb . . .
>
> In the religious service . . . the priest eats and drinks very little. What he eats is a little piece of flour paste that does not even cover the palm of your hand, and so thin that you can see the light through it; what he drinks is a very small cup of a beverage that they make. But, everyone believes that what he is eating and drinking is the flesh and blood of God . . . (III, 15-16).

To the disdain many of the missionaries held for the indigenous cultures, in which everything was evil, abominable and in service to the devil, was added the prohibition by King Philip II against writing about the culture of the Indians, because of the danger represented there. With reference to a concrete case, that of the Dominicans who evangelised the Tseltal, we read the following disposition in an act of surrender in 1576:

> It is not legally permitted for any religious worker to seek to know anything of the Indians' business with regard to their idols and su-

perstitions, without first making application to our provincial Father (Ulloa, 230).

THE GULLIBILITY OF THE MISSIONARIES

The missionaries were disposed to believe the most amazing and aberrant stories about the Indians. The gullibility of the good bishop of Chiapas, Nuñez de la Vega, O.P., seems unlimited. Thus, for instance, he describes the method for training a sorcerer. After the person denies God and the saints and makes a pact with the devil, the following exercise is put to the disciple:

> On an ant hill . . . the teacher . . . calls a snake . . . , whom the ants address as mother: This one comes out . . . and other little snakes, and they enter into the joints of his hands, exiting through the nostrils, the ears and the joints of the right hand: and the big one, that is the snake, leaping around, enters and exits by the posterior . . . After . . . he goes out to meet a dragon . . . spewing fire . . . who swallows that disciple, and then throws him out of the lower part of the body; then the teacher says to him that he has now been taught (Pastoral IX, no. 8).
>
> By his declaration and confession he states and has stated to us, that he performed a carnal act with the demon . . . who was changed into the apparent form of his "nagual" [*lab* or soul-animal-companion]. There was also an Indian woman from the mountain who had been with the "nagual" demon for a whole week, sleeping with him as she could with her own male friend, a woman who was no longer a virgin (ibid., no. 12).

The low opinion of the Indians that the bishop held led him to swallow these tall tales. Even worse, he and the rest of the missionaries founded their teaching on these facts, obtained from the Indians "by their own confession." When we read the diatribes that he hurled at the Indians, we wonder what they possibly could have understood of all that he attributed to them and what a confusion of ideas all this presented. The missionaries not only brought a totally strange cosmic vision, but also transmitted different cultural patterns as well, which they did not translate into the Indian culture because they did not know it. Further, what the missionaries *did* know about the aboriginal cultures was based in many instances on falsehoods (as was the case with Nuñez de la Vega, bishop and inquisitor).

Therefore, the Indians had no starting point to allow them to integrate the new ideas and practices brought by the evangelists and went about taking from them whatever they could assimilate in some form or other, all the while preserving their own cosmic vision as a base. The Indians found themselves confronted with two cosmic visions and two worlds—not only different but in many ways contradictory. They could evade neither: not their own, which had made the universe in which they had lived for centuries intelligible; not that of the missionaries, with which they were incessantly hammered and which others were trying to impose upon them even by force.

In order to understand this process better, perhaps it will help to analyze what is happening today in Guaquitepec with respect to the *lab*. The catechists assure the Indians that they do not have a *lab*: "They have heard the word from the Fathers, who assert that there is no such thing." On the other hand, the community leaders "do have *lab*, because they have not heard the word of the Fathers yet." Thereby neither the Fathers nor the elders (whom they greatly respect) are lying: in the world of the fathers there is no *lab*, but in that of the community leaders—that is to say, in the domain of traditional religion—there definitely is! We are confronted with a process of syncretism here, an attempt to reconcile ideas from two opposing systems.[4]

We have, therefore, a situation in which, for the Indians of the colonies, the teachings of the evangelists are true for the world of the evangelists; and those of the pre-Hispanic religion are true for the Indian.

THE ASSIMILATION OF THE PREACHING

It seems that this question never occurred to the missionaries. It deals with a process of gradual assimilation of the Hispanic characteristics received into the indigenous cultural thought patterns (and, by consequence, in a different form), all the while preserving many pre-Hispanic features that made the world in which the Indians found themselves understandable. However, the majority of the evangelists put it all down to the hypocrisy of the Indians or to the influence of the devil:

According to this, those miserable Indians . . . want to appear to be Christians while being idolaters, in that it seems to them that they can both exist together: they take on many of the things in our holy faith, showing great reverence for them; but neither do they forget their old ways (Jacinto de la Serna, 449).

Bishop Nuñez de la Vega expresses his distress:

> The blindness of these poor deceived little lambs from Christ's fold
> . . . whom [Christ] by his just and inscrutable judgments has per-
> mitted to return voluntarily to his [Satan's] power and in whom,
> among the great selection of the truths of the faith, tares have been
> sown . . . [tares] of the false errors from their primitive Gentilism,
> impeding the fruit of the abundant harvest which has been culti-
> vated by the servants of the Lord by incessantly preaching his divine
> word for almost 200 years since they received the light of the Gos-
> pel . . .
>   However, the roots of their old Nagualism is kept in the hearts
> of those miserable Indians, by an explicit agreement with some of
> the teachers of this sect, and an implicit one with almost everyone,
> or at least with those who are beyond the hills, in whose provinces
> there is not one village where this sect has not been introduced, and
> their simple hearts infected with the contagious pestilence of its dia-
> bolic superstition (Pastoral IX, no. 13).

THE LACK OF ZEAL AND PREPARATION OF THE MISSIONARIES

To the missionaries' ethnocentrism is added their lack of zeal. According to Ricard, who is always so prudent in his judgements, towards the
end of the sixteenth century "the enthusiasm and the curiosity of the
beginning had died, and the mission had entered into a state that we
might say was in the process of becoming bourgeois" (149).
   Concerning the lack of preparation, I shall just cite two witnesses: the
first, from a pastoral report of Bishop Bravo de la Serna (of 1979):

> In the embassies that . . . the King of the Principalities of heaven
> sent . . . by the priests . . . How could they do anything without
> being sages and experts in the teachings of the faith and religion?
> How are they to understand what the Cross of Christ meant, when
> they did not know how to explain or help them understand the
> minister who has been sent . . . ? (Silbo II, 1).

The second bears considerable weight, for it is taken from one of the
reports of the Dominicans themselves in 1569:

> And so, the members of the orders, as soon as they donned the
> habit and studied a little, were put out among the Indians, because

of the great necessity for ministers that there was and still is. Many religious had entered the order . . . who were not very learned in the Indians' language. But since they were spiritual men . . . they bore much fruit among the natives, among whom it is not necessary to be very learned (Ulloa, 227).

To the lack of knowledge about the culture, add the evangelists' lack of preparation in the very truths of the Christian faith that they were going to transmit to the Indians. This is substantiated not only by testimonies but can be verified by reading some sermons from that time. For example, in one about the temptations of Christ in the desert, when the devil tells Jesus to throw himself down from the pinnacle of the Temple, Christ responds: "This cannot be because God cannot go down to earth." In another, on Luke 11, when Christ drives out a mute demon, the preacher adds that the man was blind, deaf and had a fever also. He further explains that the demon was in opposition to the man going to confess his sins: he covered his eyes so that he could not see the light that God sent to him; his ears so that he could not hear the exhortations urging him to be converted; he bound his feet so that he could not go to confession; and in the confessional itself, he filled him with shame so that he would be quiet about some of his sins.

The fifty sermons written in Tseltal that I have analyzed and some ten in Tsotsil are packed with ideas that are scarcely explained. And we are dealing with written sermons here, which suppose some effort on the part of the preacher.

EVANGELISATION, FEAR AND VIOLENCE

It seems that one of the most serious deficiencies in the preaching to the Indians was the insistence on fear and punishment, a theme which occupied a third or a fourth of many of the sermons. The motive for behaving properly is to gain entrance to heaven, but, above all, to avoid going to hell, which is described in hair-raising vividness.

In contrast, practically nothing is said about love. It is not mentioned except in passing, even when talking about the passion of Christ, the supreme work of love, or Adam and Eve, who were created in love. Certainly the missionaries never thought that these poor Indians needed to know and experience that somebody loved them or that they had a loving heavenly Father!

Another idea that goes against the grain in the theology of colonial times is that to a certain extent it tended to make the Indians more submissive towards their Spanish masters. "You are good Christians," says one of the sermons, "who fulfil the commandments and suffer with patience when you are maltreated!"

Not only did the missionaries transmit to the Indians a message of fear and not of love, but the form in which they delivered it caused great terror, because it was supported many times by physical violence. "Punishment and force played a much more important role in conversion in Mexico than is usually recognised" (Gibson, 119). "What is worse," complained the bishop of Yucatan, Fray Alfonso de Toral, to King Philip II, "is that they want to maintain (that is to say, hold as a basic tenet) that the Law of God cannot be preached without torments" (Landa, xii–xiii).

Landa, the provincial head of the Franciscans, was not only absolved of his actions in the "auto de fe" in Maní, in which "thousands of people were tormented, and 150 of them died" (Ruz Lhuillier 1963, 288), but His Royal Majesty made him a bishop of Yucatan, where he had carried out the "auto de fe" (ibid.). Canon Angel Maria Garibay tells us: "I wanted to make them Christians by force . . . Landa was no exception," (ibid.) thereby confirming the words of Toral to Philip II.

Fray Bartolomé de las Casas stood up against this violence with all his strength. He wrote a book about it, in which he maintained that not only did the missionaries have no right to use violence in their preaching, but that it was an obstacle to the conversion of the Indians. Furthermore, he demonstrated his assertions by bringing about the conversion of the Indians in Tierra de Guerra without any violence.

To deal with the violence and oppression on the part of the conquerors, of which the Indians were constantly victims, and which also had great influence in placing them into the situation in which they find themselves even up to the present day, goes beyond the limits of this work. However, I shall pause briefly to analyze the results of this violence. Naturally, such violence did not dispose the Indians to receive the message of the gospel, of "love and peace," which the Spanish had come to bring to them. As Cortes and Larraz observe:

> They regarded the Spaniards and Ladinos as aliens and usurpers of these territories, which cause them to look upon them with implacable hatred, and when they obeyed them, it was out of pure fear and subservience. They did not want anything from the Spaniards, not their religion, nor their teaching, nor their customs (I, 141).

According to the report of a Spanish landowner, the Indians became greatly weakened:

When the Spanish conquered these countries . . . the Indians were very warlike, possessed of a great gift for governing . . . and now they are cowards, crude and without talent, without government, discouraged, without art and full of malice (Fuentes and Guzman III, 431).

In spite of this situation, the Indians rallied their strength to rebel against the Spanish. As Klein contends:

They were tired of the terrible humiliations that they had been subjected to . . . and of the obstacles that these [intruders] . . . voiced about their religious expressions . . . They were victims of exploitation and excessive hostility from the clergy . . .

The spark which ignited the revolt on a grand scale was the announcement, delivered by bishop Alvarez de Toledo, in 1712, that there would be a second visit [the purpose being to collect money to perform the sacrament of confirmation] . . . The first . . . had turned out to be so excessively costly for the Indians, that the announcement of the second occasioned an intense hostility (ibid. 153, 158).

Thus the great Tseltal rebellion of 1712 was born. Twenty-eight Tseltal villages and some Tsotsil rose up, inspired by the Virgin Mary, who spoke to her people through the voice of an Indian girl. The leaders of these villages made a pact in which they promised to fight until they had exterminated the Spanish. On the tenth of August they launched the following proclamation:

That there is now neither God nor king, that they should only worship, believe and obey the Virgin who had come down from heaven . . . just to protect and govern the Indians and so for the same reason they should obey and respect the ministers, sponsors and officials that she had placed in the villages, expressly ordering them to kill all the priests, and the Spanish, the mestizos, the negroes and the mulattos so that only Indians remain in these parts in liberty of conscience without pressure to pay royal taxes, or ecclesiastical rights, and to extinguish totally the Catholic religion and the lordship of the king.

The leaders sent "soldiers of the Virgin" to confront the Spanish . . . In this way the whole Tseltal region was wiped clean of Spanish and Ladino men in a short time (ibid., 158, 160).[5]

After their triumph, the Indians did not return to their "idolatries," as one would have thought since the missionaries stated "that they were still idolaters and pagans." Sebastian Gómez, their leader—or bishop—went up into heaven and received his responsibility from the hands of St. Peter. He himself consecrated the mayors of the villages priests, who celebrated the Catholic liturgy, endeavouring to imitate the Spanish priests in everything, making use of their ornaments and instruments.

The Spaniards managed to reorganise and brought troops from various places in New Spain, even from Guatemala, and after some days of heavy fighting, Cancuc, the village chief, surrendered. By the beginning of 1713 peace had returned to all areas. Naturally, this peace was founded on oppression and the fear of the Spanish; the Indians, who for a moment had lifted up their head, returned to their previous situation, if not to a worse one, which we can plainly see from the description that the Dominican historian, Ximenez, gives of them eight years later:

> They appear so subdued under subjugation, that they are servants of the servants themselves; for there is no man, no matter how vile, though he be a slave, who is not insulted and mistreated, living in unspeakable servitude (I, 64).

5

The Birth of Tseltal Christianity

In their preaching, the missionaries insisted on the great good that the Catholic religion had come to bring to the Indians, "enslaved by sin and the devil," and how Christ had redeemed them with his blood so that they might be free. We do not know if the servitude in which, in the name of God, the conquerors had placed the Indians (many times with the assent of the evangelists themselves), was equal or worse than that in which they lived in pre-Hispanic times. However, the slavery and oppression in which the lower classes had previously found themselves, was, if I may say so, more "acceptable" because at least it fit the culture. In contrast, in the colonial era the message of Christ was preached, but the treatment that the Indians received and the way many of the Spaniards carried on seemed to come from a message totally opposite to Christianity.

No culture can survive if it does not have some comprehensible explanation, usually through religion, for the world in which the people live and if the same system does not offer the means to seek happiness.

The religion preached by the missionaries in many instances was heard by the Indians as an "anti-explanation" of the world. For their part, they went on taking from the Catholic religion those features which together with other pre-Hispanic elements helped them interpret the world in which the Conquest had placed them, and in this way, they developed their own traditional religion or Tseltal Christianity.

THEIR BELIEF SYSTEM

It is true that the Indians perceive God as a distant governor who is very busy, similar to Halach Uinik, the supreme lord of the ancient peninsular Mayans. However, although distant, God is a good father to them. Precisely for this reason God sent a protector saint as a representative to each one of the villages in the earthly plain.

We can affirm the fact that traditional religion is essentially "santo-centric"; its principal commandment would be: "Honour and serve your patron saint so that he or she will protect and favour you." This idea of "honour" embraces not only the festivals, but also the harmony that should reign in the village and which is necessary to please the saint.

Thus between the saint and the village a kind of agreement is established: the community takes on the responsibility of honouring the saint, and in exchange the saint concedes to them a special protection. This is evident in the greeting used among the participants at the festival:

No other people may come; no other village may honour and venerate our protector. It is necessary that we are the only ones who serve and worship him, and none other.

Naturally they have "Tseltalised" the saint, because if he were Spanish, not only would he not look after them, but he would exploit and punish them. Also it is natural that the saint should live in the community and form part of it, for according to the Indians' thinking, only a person in the community can really take an interest in them and help them. It is exactly for this affection in which they are held that the saint chose the village site so that they should have a place to live. "It was you, Virgin Saint, who sought this village for me that I might remain here and live and live in it . . . You did this so that I might live peaceably with them [the community]," according to the prayer of Guaquitepec to their patron saint. Let us hear what the Guaquitepec say about the love of their mother saint:

> Our patron saint watches us, she observes us attentively with her rainbow eyes, with her rainbow face [that is to say, she brings peace].
> Our patron, the Mother of heaven and Mother of glory, knows which part of our body is hurting; she makes the spot where it hurts disappear.
> You, my Holy Patron, you alone watch over me, you embrace me, you hold me in your arms day and night.

The Tseltal constantly insist to the saint that they have been faithful to their part of the contract, serving her well during the year and in the festival itself. They know that she watches over them and that she realises that they honour her as they ought.

> By any chance, Holy Patron, have you ceased to watch over and observe me? Have you not watched the whole time [of my service], during all of the holy period [the year of service of the sponsor]?
> Your work appears in glory; it appears in heaven. Your zeal and your concern [for the service towards the saint] does not end in darkness. Our patron saint knows our hearts still beat [with the desire to serve her].
> Whenever I am walking, every hour I am in your presence, my Holy Patron. My feet have not tired, nor have my hands.
> We, your poor sponsors, are gathered together now; we congregate to begin the holy matins.

> All your four sponsors are here; not one of them abandoned his place. Throughout the whole year the four have met with your official and with your music makers [to prepare for the festival].
> Neither your masters of ceremony nor your officials have abandoned their place nor left your poor sponsors alone.

Traditional religion is also centered on the saints in the sense that the social structure itself depends to some extent on the saint. Thus it is possible to apply to the patron saints what Max Weber says about ancestral gods:

> When their importance remains intact, it constitutes a natural whole, a very strong personal tie which exercises a profound influence over

the family and over the village, firmly unifying the members into one group whose cohesion becomes very great (Weber 1966, 15).

And what Gibson states about the confraternities of the colonial era is applicable to the festivals for the patron saints:

They offer security to the members, and a sense of collective identity which is lacking in the indigenous life . . . a long-lasting
institution which outlives its members, and this fact can inject a
feeling of stability into a population. The racism and distrust of the
Spanish [we would say Ladino now] are also characteristics of the
indigenous festivals, which usually are . . . institutions distinct from
the European festivals [in our case, of the Ladinos] with different
origins and ceremonies (Gibson 1975, 130).[6]

Actually the sense of security, stability and collective identity springs from the idea that the patron saint has always been, since the beginning of the world, the one who cares for them; the saint is exclusive protector of the village, which she will never abandon so long as they faithfully serve her.

The main features of indigenous identity are community spirit and a sense of belonging to a definite group. The festivals are community undertakings and reenforce the sense of community spirit and sense of belonging. We are reminded also that precisely in service to the saint for the benefit of the community, the sectors of civil-religious organisation are formed and receive renewed vigour.

The sense of identity, freedom and autonomy from the Ladino world is also strengthened. The Ladinos have nothing to do with the worship that the indigenous community renders to its saintly protector.

The sacrament of harmony, the festival, is "a communal liberation and an act of self-protection; a propitiation of the supernatural forces and a demonstration of the existence of the community" (ibid., 135).

THEIR SACRAMENT SYSTEM

We have seen that sacraments are perceptible symbols of harmony as well as factors in achieving it (in that they initiate it, restore it and cause it to grow).

The sacraments, especially the festival, were instituted by the *jMe* "*jTatik*—our mothers and our fathers (the ancestors)—who are regarded as legislators and founders of the holy traditions. Everything that is important is considered to have been initiated by them, *hich laj yal te jMe "jTatik*—as our ancestors said (or ordained it).

However, the ancestors acted as delegates of the saint: "Our patron saint, our holy Mother from heaven, was the one who arranged everything to remain forever." All of this received the approval of Christ: "Our protector saint, the great purchaser Jesus Christ, who shed his blood for us, and who paid for our sins, looked upon our festival."

A RELIGION OF FEAR

The insistence before the saint that they have served him or her well is due to the fear that if they do not fulfil their part of the contract as they ought, the protector will become angry and will not bestow grace upon them, especially good harvests. One year when they did not manage to persuade those who were designated as sponsors to accept the responsibility, great fear reigned in the village: the saint would be angry and would punish them!

They believe also that the Virgin, their patron, is somewhat angry with them because for many years the village elders did not take care of her image and it was lost. They implore her:

Holy Mary, Ancient Refuge [benefactor and protector]! Do not be angry with me! Because I am not to blame that you are now living in the place where you are! This is no fault of mine, but rather of my ancestors. Why do you still not give me your green shirts; why do you still not give me your green clothes [the maize, which does not grow as well as it did previously]?

In some form this fear may have its origins in pre-Columbian religion, in which even the gods, who were generally good, sometimes sent punishments without cause. Probably there are also traces springing from the missionaries' preaching, which they thundered continually from the pulpit, proclaiming the wrath of God who punished sinners with hell. The Indians, for whom evils are found in this life, translated these punishments as a "lack of that which is necessary for life, health and happiness."

Another fear with which they continually live is fear of witchcraft. The person who practices the role of healer can, for one cause or another, feel offended and act as a sorcerer by sending an unjust punishment.

6

Present-Day Evangelisation

THE CATECHISTS[7]

When the Jesuits arrived in the area in 1958, there were already groups of catechists in several main villages. These young people had been taught by the missionary emeritus P. Mandujano, on whose shoulders the responsibility for this vast area had rested for years. The catechism that they passed on was the old traditional one, memorisation of the prayers and the principal truths.

The process was evolving based on reflection on the word of God, and later passed to the reflection and analysis of reality in the light of the word of God, since, as Jesus said, "The truth shall make you free." Gradually the method called *tijwanej* (*tijel* means to move or stir, as to stir the water in order to dissolve sugar in it) was improved. It was the job of the *jtijwanej*—the catechist—to promote the reflection by asking questions.

Every year, semester or trimester, the *jtijwanejetik* meet for a few days, and with the priest acting as a consultant for the catechists, they study and analyze the themes selected for the year or the semester, for example, confession, the Eucharist, and so on. They always base the discussion on scripture and especially on the New Testament. The reflective study is done in small groups, and after each session they gather the conclusions from each group. The consultant corrects or makes additions as necessary.

The *jtijwanejetik* repeat the process, acting as consultants to the small groups in their respective communities each Sunday, and also gathering it all together at the end. This is a method that fits very well into Tseltal culture, in which, strictly speaking, there is not teaching but rather learning. The desired result has not yet been achieved though, for there are still catechists who do not act as *jtijwanejetik*, but who delight in giving grand and boring speeches. However, with perseverance and practice they are moving forward.

THE BIBLE

A little more than fourteen years ago, two priests (Nacho and Mardonio Morales) began the translation of the Bible, because the Protestant version done by the Summer Institute of Linguistics contained intentional pernicious errors. What is also very important about the Morales work is that bilingual catechists did the translation, with the Morales priests simply serving as theological consultants. Another merit of this work is that several different communities, whose Tseltal dialects differ somewhat from each other, collaborated in the work, and the language was enriched by contributions of words and idiomatic phrases from the various communities.

In 1983 the volume containing the gospels and Acts of the Apostles came off the press, and shortly the second volume will appear with the rest of the New Testament. Work on the Old Testament is in process. Bishop D. Samuel Ruiz considers this work to be one of the most important projects in his diocese of San Cristobal de Las Casas.

THE LITURGY

The texts of the new post-conciliar liturgy had barely appeared in Latin when Father Mardonio Morales exerted pressure to have them translated into Tseltal. The resulting Tseltal version was ready even before the Spanish one. This translation was literal, as was required at the beginning, and for that reason it was Tseltal "in Spanish," because the text did not lend itself to the nature of the language. Presently the team is working on the "Tseltalisation" of the Roman liturgy, and at the same time reevaluating the Tseltal cosmic vision and the Tseltal sacraments with the view to arriving at a synthesis in which the indigenous elements will be enriched by Western features.

It was supposed to be a question of the Tseltal themselves doing this work, but for the present, because for so many years the idea was hammered in that Tseltal culture was worthless, idolatrous and superstitious, it is still very difficult to get them to take the initiative. The missionaries continue to guide them in the hope that eventually their work will be merely that of consultants.

THE INDIGENOUS CLERGY

More than ten years ago as a result of several days of reflection, anxiety arose concerning what would happen if the non-indigenous priests and pastoral agents had to leave. "Everything would come to an end," remarked some Tseltal, "because you have not allowed the Spirit to speak to us in our own language." A search was begun then and culminated with the institution of the predeaconate. Each community that wished to do so chose a man who was wise and had sufficient knowledge of the most important theological elements. The elders from each community presented the candidates to the bishop, who then solemnly conferred the responsibility to baptise, to assist in matrimony, to distribute communion when the priest could not be present, and to pray for the sick. The responsibility was entrusted to the candidate for a period of three years, after which there would be an evaluation of his work. If the advisors as well as the community served by the candidate were satisfied, the bishop would confirm him and ordain him "deacon," whose significance in Tseltal is also "server": *jtuhunel.*[8] We should note that one or more advisors or counsellors are assigned to the pre-deacon or the deacon. This fits very well with Tseltal culture, in that nobody ever carries a responsibility alone; either there are two who are responsible or they assign advisors.

The aim of all this is not simply to provide deacons to help the priests. Above all, it is the beginning of the formation of an indigenous priesthood, whose members will be taken from among the Indians, and who will exercise their priesthood for the Indians, according to the idea of St. Paul.

THE ROAD AHEAD

It is very important to arrive at a synthesis of the traditional religion and Western Catholicism, especially with regard to the sacraments, among which, it seems to me, the most important thing is the joining of the festival and the Mass. The festival is an event that is drawn out during the days of celebration, with the Mass as the culminating point. It seems equally essential to bring about the transformation of the patron saint into a "liberator" of the people rather than the person with whom a dual contract is celebrated each year: "I give to you so that you will give to me!"

The other feature is that of witchcraft. With respect to this, the first thing that is needed is an understanding of it, the deepest possible understanding through reflection with them on all their symbolism. It cannot simply be declared that "all this about witchcraft is lies." I state this for two reasons: 1) I believe that one cannot deny some effects of sorcery, attributable, for example, to parapsychology. 2) To accuse this phenomenon of lies undermines, by the same token, the social structure that is founded on the service to the saint, from whom they, and in particular the community leaders, receive spiritual power. In such a case, there would be nobody to replace them—neither the civil authorities, because they have no value in the eyes of the Indians, nor the priest, because that is not his office, "His duty is to preach the word of God, and not to govern the community in general." On the other hand, to deny the existence of the *lab* (soul-animal-companion) is to proceed recklessly, because we do not know its symbolism in depth.

It seems that what must be stressed, especially while we have yet to discuss the problem in depth with the Tseltal, is that sorcery in itself is evil, because it is a misuse, selfish and vengeful, of a good power God has bestowed upon authorities for the good of the community. In principle, all are in agreement with this view.

Conclusion

The Christianity of Traditional Religion

The reader will have formed an opinion about whether the Tseltal traditional religion is Christian or not. For me, it certainly is, although it does not have a Western form; I believe we can qualify it as Mayan-Christian.

This is not a unique case, for commencing with the most ancient branches, we meet a Christianity which we could call Greek or Latin. Furthermore, it is clear that there are several types of liturgy depending on the country in question. Just to mention two extremes: the worship the Andalusians render to Christ, to the Virgin and to the saints is very different from the manner in which they are venerated in Nordic countries.

Many accuse indigenous religions of being syncretistic just because they are indigenous; they are not fully understood, and so it is thought that their elements are a confused mixture of pre-Hispanic and Western features. It is precisely this lack of knowledge that leads some to think that these religions are full of superstitions. One such superstition is that the Indians think the saints of the church are alive. "The saints of the church are wooden and made by a carpenter; but when the priest baptises them, that is to say, he blesses them and sprinkles them with holy water, God gives them intelligence so that they know our needs and can help us." For many, this most beautiful and poetic way to explain the protection of the saints is a superstition, because the Indians think that such saints are alive. However, it is *not* considered superstition when non-Indians say that the saints "watch over us" from heaven. Despite their lack of bodies, they are given eyes!

All this adds up to the fact that we have a tendency to accuse persons of superstition whose religious thinking is different from ours. Therefore, when I am asked if the Tseltal are superstitious, I respond with the question: "And you, do you have any superstitions?" If the person says no, I deny that the Tseltal have any; if the person answers in the affirmative, I admit that the Tseltal have a few superstitions.

I have already mentioned the main defects of traditional religion from which the Indians must be freed. This task, however, does not fall to the Ladino pastoral agents but to the Indians themselves. Otherwise we would fall into the error of wanting to "transculturize" them—that is, impose another culture on them—the very thing we criticise the Hispanic missionaries for doing.

To the Ladino pastoral agents falls the office of advisors, or better still, "encouragers." In Tseltal such persons are called *jtijwanejetil*—literally "stirrers." The advisors should stir up the Indians, so that they themselves will form a critical judgement of their religion, in which not only the shortcomings are considered but the elements reevaluated.

Ricard very tactfully proposes what should be the attitude of the pastoral agents:

If the Christian ideas present themselves . . . dressed in foreign garb, most likely it is because they continue in the Indian mind as something that is perpetually foreign. "It is necessary (says Allier, 435) that our ideas take on an indigenous direction, are expressed in an indigenous manner; if this is not so, they will remain on the surface; we will have nothing more than a 'superimposed' civilisation." Not only will the Christian ideas be badly assimilated or totally foreign, but also the whole work of Christianisation will take on the appearance of a foreign religion . . . The history of missions has abundantly proved that there is nothing more fatal or unwise a mistake (Ricard 1947, 144ff.).

Let us now hear the voice of the church in Vatican II:

[The church] does not try to impose a rigid uniformity on that which does not affect the good of the faith or the good of the whole community; on the contrary, she respects and encourages the genius and particular qualities of the different races and peoples (*Constitution on the Sacred Liturgy*, no. 37).

Concerning the work of the non-indigenous pastoral agents the same Council says:

To reform and promote the Sacred Liturgy it is necessary to take
into careful consideration . . . the full and active participation of all
the people (ibid., no. 14).

In short, we are not talking about a *transculturation* or an imposition
of an alien culture, but rather an *inculturation*, that is, to take the message of the gospel in the most appropriate form possible to their culture
so that they will be truly able to understand and assimilate it. Theirs will
be the task of cultivating this seed in their own fields, cleaning out the
noxious weeds, watering it, and fertilising it with elements that belong to
their culture so that the flowers and fruits will be Christian, but Tseltal-
Christian.

PART TWO

THE RELIGION OF THE ANDEAN QUECHUA IN SOUTHERN PERU

Manuel M. Marzal

1

Introduction

These pages, which tell the story of the religious world of the Quechua, are not written as the personal testimony of the religious experience of a member of this culture. Neither are they the testimony of a priest dedicated to pastoral ministry in an Andean parish who relates his experiences, reflections and strategies for his work, as did José Ma. García in his fascinating diary (1983). Rather, they are the result of a systematic study of the religion of the Andean Quechua in southern Peru, done from the perspective of the social sciences, though not neglecting the theological and pastoral concerns involved. I began this study with some anthropological monographs about religious world among the rural people around Cusco and Puno (1971 and 1977), and continued with studies of Peruvian religious change (1983), the technological and theological dimension of Spanish American syncretism (1985), and the religious ways of the immigrants to metropolitan Lima (1988). I have tried to nourish my reflection on these subjects by participating in various national and international meetings and by reading the published writings of my fellow anthropologists, especially those of the Andean Pastoral Institute of Cusco, which has made an enormous contribution in spreading the knowledge of Quechua religion since its foundation in 1969 (Gallego 1984).

I begin with certain definitions and clarifications to define more precisely the limits of my investigation. First, I call religion the symbolic system comprising beliefs, rites, forms of organisation and ethical norms that pertains to a certain society or culture and by which its members endeavour to communicate with God and meet with the transcendent in their life. Although all religious systems have the four dimensions indicated here, they do not develop them to the same degree. Thus, for example, we often find a greater emphasis on the ritual dimension among the popular religions.

Second, I direct my attention solely to the Quechua population in the five southern Andean regions in Peru, which together form the so-called Andean Trapezoid. In 1981 these departments of Apurimac, Ayacucho, Cusco, Huancavelica and Puno had almost three million inhabitants and constituted approximately 17 percent of the total population of the country. Although the same Peruvian census calculated the Quechua-speaking portion of the whole to be 21.8 percent (two-thirds of whom also speak Spanish), we must not forget that in Peru there are three regions of Quechua-speaking people: the Ancashino of the northern sierra, the Huanca of the central sierra and the Cusqueño of the southern sierra. The rural area of the five regions in the Andean Trapezoid, including the highland provinces of Arequipa and excluding the Aymara provinces of Chucuito and Huancané in Puno, constitute a true linguistic and cultural unity. This region, which was the nucleus of the ancient Tawantinsuyo Inca Empire, in the present day is inhabited by farmers organised into rural communities, in other kinds of group associations which have sprung up as a result of agrarian reform, and by small landowners. These three groups often augment their meagre earnings by working as labourers or resorting to temporary migration. In general, we are dealing with a region that is economically very poor, as can be deduced from the negative migrant wages (the difference between the earnings of the emigrants and the immigrants). In the last two censuses (1981 and 1972), the regions of Apurimac, Ayacucho and Huancavelica showed the highest net rate of migration (in excess of 30 percent), and the regions of Puno and Cusco were not very far behind (Peru: Demographic Facts and Figures, 1984, chart 26). Another confirmation of the depressed economic situation and explanation for the high proportion of the population leaving these areas is the fact that terrorism from the Sendero Luminoso (Shining Path) has taken root in the three departments first mentioned above.

In spite of the impact of modernisation, which first arrived by the new highways, through the channels of mass communication and by the return of the migrant workers, the rural Quechua culture seems to preserve many of the traits of the ancient Andean culture, as it was redefined during the colonial period: cultivation of the soil and raising cattle as the basic economic activities; vertical control of the ground to safeguard its use by the various ecological levels; reciprocity as a fundamental norm for coexistence in this environment; kinship and the *compadre* system as the basis for social organisation; dualistic criteria in the conceptualisation of social life; use of the Quechua language as the basic means of communication; communion with nature through the deification of the earth and the hills that mark the boundaries of the dwelling place of each community; celebration of the patron saint's day as the most important religious rite, which carries with it certain implications about the distribution of the communal power and wealth; and so on. As we can see, some of these traits are religious in nature and manifest the role that religion plays in the configuration and maintenance of the rural Quechua culture. There is much agreement among the studies of the Andean world concerning the designation of these traits; for example, Rodrigo Montoya (1987) speaks of a Quechua cultural matrix with three basic traits: reciprocity, competition and the collective self.[1]

Montoya, however, considers the Quechua language, art and religion, that of the Wamanis as well as that of the "humanized" Christian saints, to be the traits of this culture (1987, 50). Nevertheless, he believes that the Quechua culture in the city is destined to disappear among the migrants from the second or third generation onwards (ibid., 18).

Continuing with these clarifications, there is more than one religion among the Quechua of the southern Andes; in fact, there are several. Such variety is owing to the impact of local traditions and to the relative autonomy of the various small isolated regions, which became stronger when, because of the growing decline in the numbers of clergy in the rural areas during the second half of the nineteenth century and the first half of the twentieth, the religious control of the institutional church diminished. Thus, the peasant religion of Urcos (Cusco) is not exactly the same as that of Orurillo or Coaza (Puno), to mention only the first two anthropological monographs of the Andean Pastoral Institute (Marzal 1971 and Garr 1972). Nor is the religious practice in the villages and communities among the more agricultural Cusqueño peoples in the valleys the same as that of the pastoral communities in the desolate highlands. From this last mentioned group, the Q'ero (Paucatambo) religion is known as a result of the studies of their oral tradition done by the Müllers (1984) and by Flores (1984), though the latter study includes the religion of the neighbouring community of Lauramarca. Despite these differences, however, there is a fundamental uniformity which permits us to speak of a rural Quechua religion in the Andean Trapezoid.

In the following chapters I will explain patterns of Quechua religious world, its historical formation, and its transformation as a result of the emigration of the rural people to the city. It seems to me that such a projection of the Quechua religion from its Andean past and colonial roots to a possible future in a society that is increasingly more urbanised can give us a clearer understanding of the whole.

2

Patterns of Quechua Religion

Although Quechua religion is an integrated system of beliefs, rites, forms of organisation and ethical norms by means of which the rural Quechua of the southern Andes communicate with God and find a transcendent sense in their life, not all of these symbolic elements hold the same degree of importance. It can be said that Quechua religion has two directions, vectors or nuclei: one, of Catholic origin, is built around the celebration of the patron saint, which is the most significant religious rite for all of the villages judging from the numbers of people that gather for the fiesta and from the energies that are mobilised in the celebration; and the second, of Andean origin, is the "payment to Pachamama," a significant religious rite for every extended family whereby Mother Earth is appeased and offered thanks so that she will go on nourishing her children. In spite of their different origins, I think that both rites are most important in Quechua Christianity in the present day. Consequently they constitute the key to understanding how the Quechua celebrate their faith.

THE RELIGIOUS RITES

All religion begins with a mysterious vision of the sacred. Human beings, freed from secular experience by the appropriate forces, discover in each mysterious vision a door leading to the different world of the sacred, through which they try to reach beyond themselves or avail themselves of the divine forces in order to satisfy their own needs. The rural Quechua learn from the early years of their Andean socialisation that the "saints" in the church of their village or community are alive in some way, that they hear the prayers that are directed to them, that they are pleased with the "fiestas," that they perform "miracles," and that they send "punishments." Thus saints, fiestas, miracles and punishments are key words which summarize a fundamental religious experience for the majority of the rural Quechua. At the same time, these people, from the time they are children, also learn that the earth is alive, that her name is Pachamama, that she nourishes humankind, and that it is essential to offer her a "payment" at the beginning of each new agricultural year during the first days of August. To the rural Quechua, the saint and the earth are two basic forms of the realm of the mysterious, the opening to the sacred domain.

The Celebration of the Patron Saint

There is one day that is set apart for all of the Quechua villages and communities, the day of the fiesta in honour of the patron saint. On this day, which is seldom confined to just one day but rather includes a sequence of three or four days with the eve, the principal day and the leave-taking or farewell, the majority of the rural people, along with many of the emigrants who are visiting their village to participate in the celebration, gather at the church, take part in the procession and participate in the feast, the abundant alcoholic drinks and in the rest of the activities those who carry the responsibility have organised in order to celebrate their patron saint.

Such a celebration provides a unique vantage point from which to view the saints. According to Catholic theology, the saints are those Christians who, for having lived a life full of virtue, have been canonized by the church and have thus become models and intercessors for all Christians. On the other hand, according to the theology of the rural Quechua, the saints are first and foremost visible representations of the intermediaries of the invisible God (the canonized saints, the Virgin Mary and Jesus Christ himself), about whose historical reality there is a paucity of information owing to the lack of proper catechizing of the Quechua Christians. However, there is a real experience of the power of their intervention, strengthened each time the patron saint heeds the petitions of the devout and supplies their needs. In the Quechua religion the saint, in his or her visible character, fulfils the role of bringing God closer to the people, of making God, therefore, more comprehensible to a society that moves within the parameters of concrete thought patterns. The Andean saint, however, cannot, by his or her historical character, fulfil the function of model, in that the devout know nothing of the saint's concrete virtuous actions. Nevertheless, since certain extraordinary facts about the life of the saint, more or less true from the perspective of historical science, are passed on orally, the saint often is transformed into a myth and, as such, becomes a force and a motivation for the behaviour of the rural religious person. Finally, Andean saints, in their role as intercessors, maintain a presence that is continually at work in the Quechua religion, and although in theory the saints are inferior to God, in practice it seems to be the saints who grant the petitioned favour.

Many of the saints that belong to the Quechua world are connected in some way to a mysterious vision. Sometimes they speak of a real appearance of the Lord, the Virgin Mary or some saint who is represented by a statue. Other times they tell of a statue that becomes heavily weighed down at a certain moment in order to make known its desire to remain in that place. Others relate how a cross or the face of a saint was discovered on a certain stone or tree trunk. Such visions, accompanied later by miracles and punishments, can even happen in connection with the saints venerated in one village only, though soon visits occur in the neighbouring villages. Such seems to be the case of the Lord of Achajrapi, a painting of the crucified Christ that is worshiped in a side chapel in the beautiful colonial church of Andahuaylillas (Cusco). An elderly informant, promoter of piety in the village, told me the story of the vision of one of the promoters of popular piety as follows:

> The Lord of Achajrapi is very miraculous. He even performed a miracle for me; he brought me back to life. Many years ago, after giving birth (I have had twelve children, although now there are only four living), I was in very poor health. I was dying, yet I felt as if I were being beaten with a sword and someone was telling me to return to life, that there was yet much that I must do in this life. I believe it was the Lord of Achajrapi who healed me.
>
> The story of this Lord is very ancient, coming from the time of my grandfather, José del Valle, who had purchased a small ranch here in Andahuaylillas. My grandfather had a brother who was a priest, serving in the parish of Azangaro where there was a painting of Christ on canvas. Sometime later there was a famine in Azangaro and many people died. But one day an "akarapi" rain (a light snow or hoarfrost) fell on the canvas of the Christ; it fell only on the painting. The people went out to see if it had rained anywhere else. Men from the four *ayllus* of the village went out with their horses and returned saying that it had not rained. Then the priest of Azangaro wanted to come and live with his brother in Andahuaylillas, bringing seven orphans with him (children from seven different families who had been orphaned during the famine and whom the priest had taken in), and bringing the painting of Christ as well, but he could not. Because the people did not want him to take away the Christ, and because he was trying to do so, they

poisoned the priest. The orphans, however, were able to escape with the painting. They came to the ranch, where they began to work as labourers. Much later, my mother brought the painting from the ranch to the church, where Father Gonzalez, the priest, received it, ringing the bells and placing it between candles. Since 1930, more or less, it has been venerated in that place. Now the Christ painting has a glass-covered frame and its own chapel. Many Masses are said in that place. They come from many other parts too, because the Lord of Achajrapi performs many miracles (Marzal 1971, 323-324).

In this myth of the origin of the Lord of Achajrapi, although there are dates and numbers that give it a certain veneer of historicity, there are still a number of unlikely elements, such as the people poisoning the priest of Azangaro, indicating that this act may be a later elaboration, a characteristic typical of the whole popular narrative tradition. What is really important about this myth is the narration of the vision, the fall of dew on the painting of Christ, which imparted power from on high and made it miraculous, something confirmed by the healing of the informant as well as by the many favours the devout people of the village and other parts receive. Power from on high and the multiplication of miracles seem to be essential traits which accompany every vision.

It is not necessary to describe the Quechua patron saint festival in detail, because it is substantially the same as patronal fiestas of popular Catholicism. In addition to the elements that are specifically religious, such as vespers, Mass, the procession and certain dances in honour of the saint, the festival includes other elements that are more appropriately deemed secular, such as the food, drink, dances, bull fight, procession, tree-cutting rite, and so on, but which, when occurring in the context of the patronal festival, often take on a religious meaning for the devout. With regard to organisation, the Quechua patronal festival in many communities continues to be celebrated by a system of responsibilities according to which members of the community in turn take on the responsibility for the preparation, direction and financing of the festival. As the festival is costly, especially in terms of the true earnings of the rural Quechua, it is necessary to bring together funds from various sources, such as family savings, sale of animals, temporary migration to areas where work is dominated by market trade (like the mines and plantations), and help of other members in the community based on the system of reciprocity (*ayni*).

Lastly, the Quechua patronal festival fulfils a number of social functions in the community and adapts itself with great flexibility to new circumstances, all of which explain its unflagging vitality and persistence despite the fact that in recent decades many priests and other pastoral agents have not been great supporters of the festivals. In the first place, these celebrations fulfil the specific function of venerating the saints and satisfying religious needs as well as bringing a sense of the transcendence of life to the rural Quechua. Second, they act as a promotional mechanism for the person of social prestige, even though now the majority of the communities do not adhere to a ranking of the responsibilities, by which the members of the community should ascend throughout their ceremonial career. Third, the festivals function as a means of integrating the participants into the life of the community, bringing together those who habitually lead quite individualised lives because of their type of small, self-sufficient properties, the community members with the emigrants, and all the participants with the dead of the community, those who initiated the celebrations and throughout the centuries maintained them. Fourth, the fiestas also serve as means of collective relaxation in the midst of an austere and difficult rural life, even a return to the "beginning of time" in the world is preserved in a real sense in the celebration. Lastly, the festivals provide a way of levelling out wealth, because, with regard to the system of responsibilities carried out by the sponsors, those who are more able spend large amounts on the food, drink and other goods and services which are distributed among everybody; at the very least, the festivals are a way of justifying social differences, for all those who have benefitted from what has been dispensed at the festival are going to tolerate more easily the greater wealth of those who carry the responsibility.

Everything that I have stated about the Quechua patronal festival can in some ways be repeated concerning the pilgrimages to the great regional shrines, such as the Lord of the Temblores[2] (Cusco), the Lord of Huanca (Calca), the Lord of Qoyllur Riti (Quispicanchi), the Virgin of Cocharcas (Andahuaylas), the Virgin Candelaria (Puno), and others. The festival procession is longer in pilgrimages to shrines, and the sacred time of the festival is celebrated within the sacred confines of the shrine. If some of the patron saints have their myths of origin, all of those to whom shrines have been dedicated have theirs too, and here also the two characteristic traits of a myth of origin of a patron saint are present—the power from on high and the multiplication of miracles. For example, here is the myth of origin of the Lord of Huanca:

Long ago in the year 1675, an Indian from Chinchero, Diego Quispe, was finishing his shift in the Yanantin mines belonging to the Marquis of Valle Umbroso. Fearing the punishment that he might be subjected to because of an error he had committed, he decided to run away to his own land one night. From the gorge of Quispicanchi he passed into the upper reaches of the Vilcanota valley and there he took refuge in a cave during the day in order to continue his journey by night. When he was about to set out on his journey, he saw the Lord, who was naked except for a linen cloth wrapped around his waist; his body was full of sores caused by a lash; he bore a sad expression on his face. The Lord told Diego Quispe that he had chosen that place to demonstrate his love and mercy, and he asked him to return after he had presented himself to the priest at Chinchero for his first communion. Some weeks later, Diego Quispe returned, actually accompanied by the priest of Chinchero, Urioste de las Borda, along with his relatives, and all witnessed the presence of the Lord. When the Fathers of Mercy, who were the owners of the land on which the apparition, the "Huanca Rumi," had appeared were informed, the priest in charge of Cusco had a small chapel built on the spot. He commissioned an artist from the Cusqueño school to paint a fresco, which is venerated to this day. In the fresco the painter tried to represent the Lord exactly in the manner in which he manifested himself, according to the details supplied by Diego Quispe.

A century later a rich miner from the Potosi region, Pedro de Valero, who lived in Cochabamba, fell victim to an incurable disease. About that time a doctor, unknown in the community, arrived in the city and healed the man who was sick with a little water. He then invited Pedro to make a return visit to his home: "If you wish to do something nice for me, visit me in my home. I live in Huanca in Cusco and my name is Emmanuel." Pedro de Valero could not set out on his journey to Cusco until 1778. He arrived in the city and had spent several months there, yet still nobody could give him any information about the famous doctor. At last some Indians who delivered firewood to the house told him of their land of Huanca. So Pedro set out for the inhospitable region. He arrived at the small abandoned chapel, and in the undergrowth he discovered the fresco which was a true likeness of the doctor. It was the fourteenth of September, which is the feast day of the Lord of Huanca. When the bishop of Cusco, Monsignor Juan Manuel Moscoso y Peralta, was informed, he appointed a commission to study the occurrence and officially granted permission for the veneration of the saint, which began to spread among the people (Marzal 1971, 226-227).

This myth of origin has a threefold structure, like other foundational myths associated with the great Christian shrines in the Andean area, for example, that of the Lord of Qoyllur Riti (Gow and Condori 1976, 87-89; Marzal 1971, 231-233). There is a problem of human limitation (a persecuted accountant in charge of records for forced labor and a man with an incurable disease in Huanca; an abandoned Indian boy about to commit suicide in Qoyllur Riti). There is a visitation of Jesus Christ who saves the person. Finally, Jesus' image becomes a centre of salvation for the people when they are in extreme situations. Therefore, one of the main reasons to make a pilgrimage to shrines such as these is that "the Lord is very miraculous."

However, there is one important difference between the myths of these two neighbouring shrines: Qoyllur Riti is a place of pilgrimage primarily for the indigenous population and the myth has as protagonist an Indian boy; in contrast, Huanca is also a place of pilgrimage for the mestizo people and the myth has two protagonists, one a Quechua accountant and the other a Creole miner. In a sense it seems that in Huanca the great contradiction in the colonial system that fostered obligatory manual labour from the Indians in the most dire conditions is ritually surmounted; there is equality in the opportunity for salvation for both the persecuted accountant and for the sick miner. The myth does not justify a system of inequality, but it affirms the fundamental equality of all in spite of the system. This fact is seen repeatedly in the myths and rites of the great interethnic shrines of the country, even though some see them as a negation of the faith which works in favour of the exploited, thus delaying the building of an egalitarian society. The very fact that these are ritually celebrated, however, leads me to believe that these myths and rites are the first steps in establishing an equal society, because in the celebration, at least, when faced with a higher court of appeal, there is truly equality of opportunity.

I cannot present here the complex ritual of the great Christian shrines in the Andean region, but it is necessary to note that together with the guidelines for the rituals, which are clearly the same as those given for other Christian shrines, such as the confession and communion of many pilgrims, the participation of confraternities or brotherhoods from the various villages, the presence of water fountains to which are attributed powers of healing, the abundance of different forms of penitence (walking barefoot, wearing crowns of thorns, beating the flesh itself, etc.), the emotive atmosphere that is expressed in the preaching and in the singing, and the organisation of a regional fair that takes advantage of the great numbers of rural people who have come together, there are also guidelines for rituals that are more Andean in nature. For example, in the shrine of Qoyllur Riti, situated in the heights of Ocongate (Quispicanchi, Cusco) some 4,500 metres above sea level, a Christ engraved on a rock is venerated. There are religious dances; a ritual building of huts; paper money or other objects the supplicants want to receive from the Lord; and offerings of blocks of snow that, together with the cross, are carried to the shrine from the snowcapped mountain of Ausangate, a place the Quechua associate with Apu, the protector.[3] There are, then, in some of the Andean shrines certain ritual characteristics which belong to the Andean cosmic vision and are not simply transplants of the Spanish Catholic tradition. This brings us to the other great rite of Quechua Christianity.

The Payment to Pachamama

In spite of the rapid acceptance of baptism on the part of the conquered Quechua population, and despite all the "stamping out of the idolatries" to which I shall make reference later, the majority of the rural people of the Andean Trapezoid continue to celebrate the *pago a la tierra* (sacrificial offering) every year. For them the earth is a sacred reality, known as Pachamama. Rosalind Gow (1976) collected the following myth in the community of Pinchimuro (Quispicanchi):

From the dawn of the universe, Pachamama said:
I am the Holy Earth. I am she who raises you, she who suckles you. I am Pacha Tierra, Pacha Ñusta, Pacha Virgin. (Therefore from the creation of the world I am worthy of respect.) You are going to call me, you are going to whisper to me, for the three persons: Pacha Tierra, Pacha Ñusta, Pacha Virgin. This I shall speak to you. Do not touch the Sacred Earth.
Thus said Pachamama:
Beneath the holy earth, in her interior, live three persons, Pacha Tierra, Pacha Mama, Pacha Ñusta. This earth is alive and in her we all live together . . . Like our mother, she is suckling us and raising us. But our mother, in any case, dies, the earth never dies. At death we disappear into the earth, she absorbs us. Like her own child she is rearing us. Her hair grows: it is the pasture land, it is wool for the animals. With this pasture she feed the animals.
In ancient times Pacha Tierra could speak. There lived wise ones (*altomisa*) who knew how to speak with the holy places and with the Apus. God had given them a star to talk with the Apus . . .
The earth feels it if work is continued during her day of rest. She gets angry, she very sadly rejects you, if you work this day. She resents it if you touch her. On St. John's Day and the first of Au-

gust, the earth makes everyone ill. In the same way, she does not hear you during Holy Week. How will Jesus Christ be? For this reason she becomes deaf . . .

Pachamama knows how to give birth, the potatoes give birth, we give her the seeds and these give birth. With supplications to God, we hand over our seed to her . . . In August, from the first she lives unto herself . . . Of course she receives gifts. Wine and drink for her blessing, this is what Pachamama wants . . . The gift must contain huiaracoya, tallow, cane, incense, sugar, a vicuña foetus, a viscacha foetus, wrapped in vicuña wool.

Offer me this. Then I shall rear you, I shall give you whatever you ask—said Pachamama—do not forget me, but live, thus saying what Pachamama had said.

They offer gifts to Pachamama for produce and for animals; so that the young ones will not get sick, so that they will have good produce (Gow and Condori 1976, 10-12).

It is important to point out, as Rosalind Gow does, that in this myth the three Pachas "all are only one Pachamama. They symbolize the unity of time and space" (1976, 6) and that the earth exists in three distinct forms: during most of the year it is an active and a generating principle; some days of the year (for example, the first and sixth of August) it is passive, receives nourishment from the gifts, and punishes if it is violated; and once a year, during Holy Week, the earth dies, symbolizing the death of Christ and a time of danger because at that time the earth cannot control the evil spirits or the soq'a (1976, 5). Although the myth reflects the Andean vision, it contains certain symbolic elements of Christian origin, such as the allusion to the suffering of Christ in Holy Week and the identification of the earth as a virgin in the sense of sacred reality.

The rest of the ethnographic details are also important, like the listing of the elements used in the offerings and the ability of the wise ones to speak with the Apus. Above all, however, it is important that the earth is considered to be a living reality, that they attribute to it the characteristics of a mother who nourishes and protects, and that it is judged to be capable of ritual communication. In addition to having a physical reality, it symbolizes a spiritual reality. For this reason, the Quechua use the word allpa to refer to the chemico-physical components that make up the earth, and the word Pachamama to refer to its function as sacred mother or God's intermediary who nourishes humankind. This knowledge that the rural Quechua have concerning the earth as a sacred reality is not scientific in nature but mythical. They are not interested in the knowledge of the things themselves but in their significance, which is not supported by rational and positive knowledge typical of the modern world, which classifies every object in some way. They seek traditional knowledge, more symbolic and emotive, by which they participate in some way in the object. This mythical knowledge of the earth allows the peasant to understand reality in a different way and in some ways experience that which is really real.

I am not going to describe the *pago a la tierra* ritual here, in spite of its aesthetic beauty. We are dealing with a rite that is quite fixed, though there are certain local variants or individual preferences of the religious specialists (*altomisayo* or simply *paq*) who perform the rites. During the night, in the presence of all the members of the extended family who have requested the service, the ceremonial specialist prepares the recognised offering as a "dispatch," an "approach," or a "gift," constituted of elements from the Andean agricultural reality. Later he offers it to Mother Earth, and lastly he burns it or buries it, concluding a ceremony that has lasted several hours, during which everyone in attendance has not only remained respectfully silent and devout, but also has responded to the prayers and forgiven one another. The rite in itself signifies a payment, a giving back to the earth something of what she gives to them, within the logic of reciprocity that permeates all rural organisation. The offerings are presented "because the earth is hungry," "because the earth can punish them" and "to say thank you for all that the earth, on God's behalf, apportions them," according to the more important reasons which are usually given when the peasants are questioned.

However, concerning Andean Christianity one important question remains for this work: Is the payment to the earth a Christian rite or, at least, can it be Christianized? Is this fertility rite which the Quechua have observed for hundreds and even thousands of years a simple remnant of Andean religion, or has it been transformed by its contact with Christianity? The answer is difficult and may not be identical for all of the areas or for all of the rural peoples who live in the Andean Trapezoid. In order to respond to the question, it is necessary to take as a starting point the tenacious persistence of the cult of the earth. Already Eliade (1954), when explaining the sacred character of agricultural activity "because it is carried out on the body of the Mother Earth, because she sets in motion the sacred forces of the vegetation and because she introduces the labourer into a realm that some sense is under the control of the dead," concludes that "the religion of the earth does not die easily. Once its form has been established firmly, millenniums can pass over it" (1954, 314 and 239). Effectively, the cult of the earth is pre-Inca and, in spite of the profound religious transformation wrought by the evangelisation and the campaigns to eradicate it during the seventeenth century (carried out on a large scale in the diocese under the archbishop of Lima and to a lesser degree in the other colonial dioceses), it continues to exert a holding power up to the present day among the majority of the Quechua who live in the Andean Trapezoid.

Another starting point is to view the rites from an ethnological perspective. Although they remain substantially unaltered in form, they may be reinterpreted, acquiring different meanings, or at least, additional significance. Have the Andean agricultural rites been Christianized? We do know that Inca Garcilaso de la Vega, in his efforts to rid the Andean world of idolatry, the great disgrace of his era, interpreted the mountain-worship cult as a form of worship to God, who causes those who climb the mountain to carry the burden. This interpretation was based on his analysis of the Quechua word *apachep-ta* (which is the dative form of the present participle of the verb *apachep*, thus meaning "he who causes to carry"), which is what the Spanish, if they were listening, heard when the Indians who were carrying burdens deposited their offerings in the mountains. Even Pope John Paul II, in 1985, when speaking to the Cusqueño peasants who gathered together in Sacsawaman, said: "When your ancestors paid tribute to the earth (Mama Pacha), they did so recognising the goodness of God and his beneficent presence that provided food for them through the earth which they cultivated." If is as if the pope were inviting them to make a Christian reinterpretation of the ancient rite. With regard to the real significance that the payment to the earth has for today's Quechua, I quote a catechist who spoke to me when I had the occasion to analyze the meaning of the ritual with a group of rural catechists from Puno: "The earth is like a virgin saint who says to God, I am going to feed your children." Since the expression "virgin saint" means a sacred reality to the Quechua—for they use the expression to refer to the Virgin Mary as well as to Mary Magdalene or St. Anne, whom they recognise were not virgins in the true sense of the word—undoubtedly the Pachamama is not an indigenous Andean divinity for them but rather a symbol of the providence of God, whom they may worship according to the most orthodox interpretation of the faith. However, I do not know how far this Christian reinterpretation of Pachamama voiced by the catechist from Puno extends. I think that many continue to consider her an indigenous Andean divinity, although in so doing they consider her to be an indigenous Andean divinity who is under the control of the supreme God.

THE RELIGIOUS WORLDVIEW

These Quechua Indians who faithfully celebrate the festivals and the *pago a la tierra* rituals have their own religious worldview with roots submerged in the two traditions, Christian and Andean.

God, Saints and Andean Intermediaries

In the present day, God holds the most important place in the Andean divine pantheon, even though the most complex and meaningful rituals are directed to the intermediaries, both the Christian saints venerated in the church and the Andean ones who are Mother Earth (Pachamama) and the spirits of the mountains (Apus or Wamanis). In practice, atheism does not appear as a cultural phenomenon, a situation which repeats itself when the Quechua move to the city, according to surveys carried out in the suburbs of Lima. Probably this is due more to the fact that God is a key person in a sacralized society without competing claims than because God is the object of a deep personal relationship. Although God has created the world and will reward each person after death accordingly, this Andean God is, above all, a God for the here and now, a providential God close at hand, who rewards and punishes in daily life. The Quechua experience the nearness of God especially in the difficulties and the limited situations of life, in the cults of the great shrines, and in their dreams, which take on the significance of revelations. Furthermore, in the oral Quechua tradition, of which we have a firsthand account from Avila (1987), God is manifest at a festival in the form of a poor old man and punishes by means of a flood those who do not receive him; this is the explanation for the origin of many Andean lakes. The Quechua think that God rewards and punishes men and women during the present life. This idea is the result of a certain kind of preaching in the church, which serves as a mechanism for social control and, in particular, enables a "religious" reading of history, uncovering new meanings in the course of human events. Such a belief in God as punisher may serve to rationalise pain as a punishment in a culture noted for the historical domination of whites over the Indians, even though the majority of the Quechua do not attribute socioeconomic inequality to God.

Some Quechua do not easily identify their God with the Holy Trinity, even though they speak of "Dios Yaya, Dios Churi and Dios Espiritu Santo" (God the Father, God the Son and God the Holy Spirit) and repeat the trinitarian formula in the rituals associated with their popular religion and in the official Catholic liturgy. Some do not identify totally their God with the historical Jesus of the gospels due to a lack of adequate catechesis and because the Jesus cult is communicated through different images or representations of the various mysteries in his life, which may cause them to think that the Lord of Accha and the Lord of Qoyllur Riti, who are worshiped in two separate shrines in the region, are brothers. However, although Jesus is revealed to them more as a saint associated with a certain invocation than in the books of the gospel, as we shall analyze more carefully later, the majority of the Quechua know that Jesus is the Son of God, even though this is not the central tenet of their spirituality.

This importance given to the saint leads us to another theme in this section about the Andean pantheon. The second highest rank belongs to the saints, who are images symbolizing the sacred beings (Jesus, Mary, and the canonized saints). As I have already stated, the saint as mediator between them and God carries much more importance for the Quechua than the saint as a model to follow in life, for they do not know about the real life of the saints. However, many saints have entered into the Andean oral tradition and function as actual myths; although they have lost their historical setting in time and space, they are beings who maintain their real existence and even have enhanced it through the process of becoming a myth. This process frequently begins with an apparition, is strengthened with miracles and is nourished by the multiple social relationships which are established between the saint and his or her followers. In effect, the patron saint becomes the symbol of the village. The saint provides the occasion for the consolidation of many unifying ties among the members of the village, and in his or her honour selected persons within the community take on the costly venture of shouldering the responsibility for paying homage to them.

The Andean intermediaries must be placed in the pantheon together with the Christian saints, for these too grant favours to the people, though to obtain these favours the peasants perform rituals different from those observed for the saints. Pachamama is a kind being without concrete form, although they think of her as a vigorous woman to whom it is necessary to offer payments in the month of August and with whom one must always share one's drink by observing the *tinka* (ritual offering), which consists in pouring a little of the drink on the ground before partaking of it. The Apus (Lords, in Quechua) of the Cusco region and the Wamanis of the Ayacucho area are the spirits of the mountains (which rise above every community). They have been created by God and they must watch over and protect the peasants, although they also can punish them with sickness and the loss of cattle that graze in the mountain pastureland. For this reason, the people must make suitable offerings to them by means of the payments, performed principally by the wise men or *altomisa*, who have the ability to talk personally with the Apus. Ansion describes and analyses the Ayacucho Wamanis from his material on the oral tradition and in the logic of the search for the Andean worldview (1987, 115-144).

There are other Andean intermediaries who seem to have more validity in more traditional communities. In reference to Q'ero and Lauramarca, Flores (1984) lists Estrella (the Apu who is a personal protector), Quya

Ñusta (a feminine divinity who always accompanies the Apus, who are considered to be masculine, though she is much less important than the Apus and sometimes seems to be confused with Pachamama), Mujurumi (a stone which protects the cattle, and other stones who are guardians over the fertility of various species), and so on. Flores also lists the various evil spirits or *sok'a*: Sok'a Wayra, Sok'a Machu, and Sok'a Paya (spirits who live in caves, in abandoned buildings or in ancient tombs, who can bring harm to people, causing them to get thinner and thinner until they die), Ñak'aq (the Beheader), Uma Pureq (spirits of the dead who appear to people in order to frighten them), Pukio (spirit of springs, who can bring harm to those who carelessly use the water sources), Kuychi (spirit of the rainbow, who can bring sickness to those who pass under the bow or point a finger at it), and others (Flores 1984, 261-265). The information about evil spirits which Ansion collected in Ayacucho (1987, 145-179) is not very different from the above. One ought to take note in passing that in spite of the emphasis placed upon the devil in missionary preaching and the recognition of the same by the Quechua, giving him the name Supay, this does not fully symbolize all the evil spirits in the religious worlds of Cusco and Ayacucho.

The Cosmos and History

The Quechua believe that the universe is the work of God, and they explain this belief through the myths of their oral tradition. The myths collected by Rosalind Gow in the community of Pinchimuro allow us to divide history into five periods: the primordial time of creation, the time of the Ñaupa Machulas, the time of the Incas and the Conquest, the modern time and the future, all of which are also described as the time of God the Father (the first two eras), the time of God the Son (the following two) and the time of the Holy Spirit (the last one). According to Gow, we are dealing with cycles which can be represented by intersecting circles, for each cycle has something in common with the previous one and likewise with the following; thus we are dealing with "a vision of history that is both cyclical, in that a catastrophe brings one cycle to a close and inaugurates the next, and cumulative, in that the previous cycle has not been destroyed but rather incorporated into the next and continues to exercise a powerful influence through its frequent appearances in present life, as well as through the rituals and the myths" (Gow 1976, 20). The conception of time that we find in Thomas and Helga Müller (1984b) in the community of Q'ero is very similar. The same holds true for Flores (1984) in the same community and in Lauramarca, with certain colouring to which I shall later make reference. In my own study of the Urcos I collected the following myth in the community of Qoñamuro:

God created the world in three stages or different eras. First, the era of the Father. God created the world in six days, resting on Sunday, which is why we do not work on Sunday. The first day of creation everything was mixed up, in that one could not distinguish the rivers, the trees, the light or the darkness. When God saw this, he separated them and put each in its place.

The moon was not created by God because it always existed, and during the days of creation God just assigned it another place. In the beginning God created some beings that lived by the light of the moon, the Machus. They were provided with great power because they built big cities and fortresses, and they lived a long life, 150 to 200 years. The Machus dressed and built their houses in similar fashion to that of the present day, but they did not worship God, nor did they pray, but rather they lived like animals. To punish them God made three suns appear, melting the rocks with their heat and burning the Machus, obliging them to take refuge in the caves where they still live and whence they come when there is an eclipse of the moon to dance to the flute and drum.

In the second stage, God created the world of Jesus Christ, which is the present age and which will one day come to an end. God created three categories as part of the present generation. First, the Colla who live at the edge of a big lake. They always come into our territories in search of food, for the Colla were sinners. Second, he created the Incas, who lived in the great city of Cusco. They possessed great power and accomplished great things, such as cities, roads and fortresses, because God made them like that, but he did not give them the great power of knowing how to read. When the Mistis or Spaniards arrived, the Incas went to Taita Paytiti and escaped into the mountains, hiding themselves with their wives on the high plateaus where the Mistis could not reach them. For this reason they live in the more isolated and inhospitable areas, as punishment from God for the sins that they committed. Third, he created the Mystics, the last sons of God, the *chanas* of creation, and so they do whatever they fancy and God puts up with their sins; furthermore, they know how to read.

This world is going to end in the year 2,000. In connection with this there will be many signs: Mules who have never produced will give birth. There will be volcanoes of fire, wind, stones and water. There will also be portents: men with two heads, animals with five feet and many other things. Antichrists will also appear, who are the sons of the priests. Large stars will be seen passing close to us. The wandering Jews will appear and will return, but they will never reach the earth. And Cosipata, the mountain of fire, will kill all the men.

After this, the third stage will come, that of the third person, God the Holy Spirit, and other beings will inhabit the earth (Marzal 1971, 62-69).

From this myth and similar ones collected by Gow (1976), the Müllers (1984b) and Flores (1984), I think that the vision of the cosmos and of southern Andean history can be reduced to the following points:

a) Athough God is spoken of as creator of heaven and earth according to the formulation of the Christian creed, creation is understood not in the more philosophical sense of making a world out of nothing, but in the more restricted idea of bringing order to the world, which is especially necessary in a cyclical history when one world is ended by destruction (*pachacuti*) and another begins;

b) There is a close connection between space and time, expressed in the word *kaypacha*, which means "here" and "now," and corresponds to the idea of one cycle enclosed within itself and within a space that is in some way permanent. As the Müllers observed, "According to the original Andean worldview, time developed in cycles . . . Down through the centuries of encounter with Christianity, whose concept of time is linear and progressive, the Andean concept has gradually undergone a transformation which has caused it to represent time as a spiral kind of movement" (1984b, 165). In a further observation they state that "the idea of the cyclical development of time is based on the experiences of a people who are farmers and shepherds who are experiencing the reality of the cycle in their daily lives: sowing and reaping, a dry season and the rains, fertilisation and birth, etc. And this continues despite the influence of Western culture" (1984b, 165). Although *kaypacha* is a basic reality where the Andean spirits and people coexist, under Christian influence more and more it is taking on the image of Hanaqpacha as the dwelling place of God and the place where good people will go finally, including adopting the image of Ukhupacha as a definite place of punishment for evildoers. However, this process has not been identical in the various regions. In some there has been a real reaction to Christianity, and therein lies the difficulty in knowing how representative is this idea of a tripartite division as it appears in the oral tradition from Q'ero, which has been studied more than most.

c) Another concept of the Andean worldview is asymmetric dualism, which they call *yanantin*. According to this idea there are two poles, masculine (*phaña*) and feminine (*lloq'e*), of which the former is stronger, thus producing an asymmetrical worldview. The Müllers state:

Everything that lives, man as well as the animals, the Apus and their supernatural beings, living beings, and everything that is subject to a life cycle, lives with its *yana*, with its companion of the opposite sex. Only together do they form a unified entity which is capable of survival. As the peasants say: the worm in the soil has its *yana* also, even the spun textile is of two threads . . .

This concept of *yanantin* is found in Andean mythology, as well as in their songs and ceremonial texts (e.g., the *wamichakuy*). In addition it explains the traditional man-woman relationship, which is expressed in the myth of Maria Angola and Mariano Angola, for example (1984b, 164).

Flores found a remnant of this idea in the chants for livestock or *ch'uru taki*, where the patron saint for livestock appears, San Marcos and his feminine mate Santa Marcela (1984, 135).

d) This myth is another version of the myth of the three eras of creation collected in Moya (Huancavelica) in 1965, which has already been cited by Fuenzalida, who thinks that it is a "pan-Andean myth of colonial origin," probably inspired by the ideas put forward by the Cistercian Joaquin de Fiore concerning the three successive ages of history presided over by the three persons of the Trinity. These ideas were spread by the Franciscans (Fuenzalida 1977, 60). Ansion, however, says that his material does not permit him to make such a generalisation for Ayacucho (1987, 183).

e) This myth gathers many of the elements of the Andean worldview and its history, such as the idea that history is not linear but cyclical; the description of the Machus, inhabitants of the world during the first age; the classification of the three great empires in Peruvian history (the Colla of Tiawanaco, the Inca of Cusco and the Misti of Lima); the flight of the Incas to the pristine Utopian land of Paititi, led by Inkarri in other versions of the same myth; the Indians' occupancy of the desolate highlands as the Mistis during the colonial years and after independence take possession of the valleys; the allusion to man as the reason for the periodic dry spells, suffered by the peasants from Puno; the same criticism levelled at the priests in a region where they play a somewhat ambiguous role because of their connection and membership in the world of the Mistis, and so on. In spite of its richness, however, the myth leaves out certain elements with regard to the Andean worldview, such as the absence of any comment about the Inkarri myth.[4]

f) An important aspect of this myth is that it permits the Andean person to find a religious meaning to life, knowing that God creates the world and humankind and governs human history. Thus the Andean man or woman is placed in the universe and does not feel like an unknown inhabitant of a planet governed by unknown forces. It is true that, in order to express the action of God, the language of the myth suggests an immediate divine action and manifests a vision that is not only religious but ritualistic, one in which there is little room for human autonomy. Therefore, the punishment of the Machus, the Colla and the Incas, or, in spite of their sins, the impunity of the Mistis as the last sons with God's sympathy, or the grandeur of the Incas who have power "because God made them so," are hardly understood in the secular vision of God appropriate for the modern world. However, in interpreting these expressions we must not forget that the myth has its own meaning, because it is not a exact formulation of reality but an analogous one.

Eschatology and Death

One of the themes in the myth that has not been analyzed is in its eschatology. In the myth we see that this world is to end in the year 2,000, a date that recurs in other versions (Müller 1984a, 133). The language used in the myth (the birth of the mules, the animals with two heads, the eruption of volcanoes, etc.) implies the end of the cosmos and the outbreak of chaos, including certain elements of Christian eschatology (like the antichrists) confirm the syncretistic nature of the myth in question.

Even if the imminence of the end is clear in the Andean world, which explains the success among the Quechua of the preaching of the fundamentalist churches (as we shall see below), the acceptance of the Christian concepts of heaven and hell on the part of the Quechua is not so clear, even though the Quechua words *hanaqpacha* and *ukhupacha* have been translated as such. Naturally the paucity of surveys about religious opinion among the Quechua yields a high incidence of scepticism about heaven, and even more so about hell. Although this scepticism may be due in some degree to methodological reasons because of the difficulty in asking the question properly, it seems absolutely certain to me that many Quechua do not believe in either the Christian heaven or hell even though they do believe in God and practice with sincerity many of the Andean Christian rituals. This lack of belief may be due to the fact that although life after death was accepted in the pre-Hispanic religion, the dimension of moral sanction had not been developed to the same extent as it is in Christianity. Perhaps it was because of the insufficiency of colonial evangelisation that Andean eschatology, remained unchanged, or perhaps, even though it might have changed, from the nineteenth century onwards a real realignment of the Christian religious belief system occurred.

Although there is a certain degree of scepticism, many truly accept the Christian view of eschatology and everyone participates in the beliefs and funeral rites of today's Quechua culture. In the greater part of the Andean Trapezoid, the people believe that the human being is made up of body, soul and spirit. The spirit is not the vital principle in Aristotelian terms, but the basis for health. Thus, they believe that the spirit abandons the body in sickness, especially when it is related to a frightful experience (*mancharisqa*), which is more frequent among children. Although every human being has one soul, in contrast he or she has several spirits; in the community of Capacchica, this number is four for the men and seven for the women, which expresses a greater moral fortitude in life and in difficulty in women. However, in Q'ero they call spirit that part of the human being that is alive, and the soul the spiritual reality that separates from the body at death (Flores 1984, 108).

Once the soul has left the body, it must give an account of the person's actions before God. The road that it must travel is narrow and is blocked by a river, which for many is the River Jordan. The soul must be helped across the river by a dog, which must be black; white dogs will not help because they do not want to dirty themselves. This belief explains why in some Andean villages, when a person dies the relatives sacrifice a dog with the corpse. However, with regard to those who have committed serious sins, such as incest, God can punish them, making their souls wander about the earth in the form of different animals. In Q'ero, a person can fall into the category of the condemned through a sexual sin, sorcery or lack of compassion for those less fortunate. The condemnation is to roam the glaciers of the cordillera (some come down from Ausagate and ask for forgiveness from the Lord of Qoyllur Riti) or some roam the volcanoes and are changed into women who eat children, or riding mounts for the demons (Flores 1984, 114 and 133).

Death is announced by definite omens. Certain dreams (such as dreaming that a tooth falls out), the behaviour of certain animals (the hoot of the owl, the howling of dogs or the grunting of foxes) and other strange signs (a light that goes out all of a sudden or the doors of the house open and close on their own) presage death. In these portents the Andean and Spanish traditions seem to converge, and even some potentially universal symbols (Roheim 1973, 647), which may better be explained by the hypothesis of the collective subconscious. Lastly, they believe that before the soul finally departs for the life beyond, it prowls for eight days around the corpse. During this time it goes to bid farewell to the places where it had been in this life to "pick up its footprints," or it can appear to relatives to ensure that they follow through on specified obligations, such as the payment of debts the person owed. These beliefs express two forms of reconciliation with the universe itself.

More persistent than the beliefs concerning death are the funeral rites. Among these the following stand out: symbolic objects, defined and differentiated by age and sex, which are buried with the dead for use in the other life; the funeral cortege in which each godchild of the deceased carries a banner; the purification of the "bad wind" from the corpse (*qayqa*) by rubbing the body, especially in the case of children, with specified plants which are thrown into the open grave; the ceremonial wailing of the women who are present when the tomb is closed, so that the deceased will "pass through the critical point of life"; the washing of the clothing of the deceased (a ritual that is carried out in a river near the community, usually performed on the fifth day; the purpose is to be able to use the clothing again, purify the dead person and free the relatives from pain and sickness); and finally, the placing of offerings of food when the funeral Mass is celebrated or on the day of the dead during the celebration of the *punchay* soul, so that "the souls can smell the flavour of the food" (Flores 1984, 131).

THE RELIGIOUS GROUP

This is the third element of the Quechua religious pattern. Although the majority of the southern Andean Quechua in Peru are considered part of the Catholic church, their sense of belonging, their religious and their values are a result of syncretistic reinterpretation, as are the other elements of the religious pattern that has produced Andean Christianity.

The Church Community and the Cultural Community

Independent of the mysterious bond of the body of Christ, which unites all of the Quechua who have been baptised in the church, their sense of a psycho-social belonging exists as part of their culture and the mechanics of socialisation in the same. In spite of the persistent proselytizing of the newer churches, the majority are still Catholic for the same reason that they are Quechua. This explains why the conversion of a Quechua to an evangelical denomination means not only a religious change but also a breaking away from his or her own cultural world. This sense of belonging to the church does not refer to the universal Catholic community, of which they have no immediate experience,[5] nor does it refer to the parochial community represented by the priest of the parish to which they belong, in relation to which the Quechua feel like clients who solicit certain services (baptisms, Masses, blessings, etc.). This feeling of belonging refers to their own local community as a cult community, because on this level the Quechua peasants form a real religious group with norms, shared values and interaction for the performance of the common rituals.

Entrance into the religious-cultural community is baptism, a rite of passage or transition in life. The children are baptised during the first months of life "in order to become Christians" and "to be people and not mountain pigs" (jungle savages). Baptism has been changed into a necessary feature of the Quechua culture; certain mechanisms in the cultural collective subconscious seem to function to confirm its place. For example, they believe a beam follows children who have not been baptised, and that if these children die they become elves who cannot see God, because when they arrive at the gate of heaven "they cannot find the rope for the bell" to ring and gain entrance.

Baptism is the occasion when one of the most important relationships within the broad spectrum of ritual relationships is established, the selection of godparents. This relationship, although it refers principally to the two chosen godparents, in a way also includes everybody who attends the ceremony. For this reason, the mother of the child usually does not attend the ceremony, because then she would become a *comadre* of her own husband, and because of the taboo against incest, she would not be able to carry on a normal sexual relationship with her husband; however, the explanation given is that "to attend will bring bad luck."

Although baptism is fully accepted among the Quechua, the same does not hold true for the rest of the sacraments. Confession is seldom practised today, in spite of its roots in the pre-Hispanic Andean world, when oral confession before the religious was an important part of the traditional fasts in honour of the Wakas (religious images and sacred places), and in spite of the institutionalisation during the colonial period of the Lenten confession for pardon, which is confirmed in many ecclesiastical documents, such as the reports of the 137 priests in the bishopric of Cusco in 1689 (see Villanueva 1982). Neither is communion received regularly, not even during Easter, although many Quechua receive holy communion when it occurs in connection with the pilgrimages to certain shrines, such as that of the Lord of Huanca.

The Quechua culture has its own system of ethics, in which the great universal principles written in the human heart appear, redefined by the Andean ancestral heritage and in part also by the first catechism introduced by missionaries. In general, because the Quechua live in a society based on the principle of reciprocity and face-to-face relationships in an overall environment marked by poverty and struggle to assure survival, we can affirm that the ethical behaviour of the Quechua is very good, judging this goodness not only from the values of their own culture, but also from universal human values, and even from the gospel. They consider the worst sins to be incest, defined as a sexual relationship between relatives, not just those related by blood or kinship, but also those related spiritually, such as the *compadres*, and the three sins indicated in the classic Inca variation of the Ten Commandments of the Incas: Do not steal, do not lie, do not be lazy.

> These four sins mark four aspects in the lack of reciprocity in social relationships:
> - theft, is the lack of reciprocity in the interchange of assets;
> - lying, is the lack of reciprocity in the sharing of information;
> - laziness, is the lack of reciprocity in the interchange of the work force;
> - incest, is the lack of reciprocity in the interchange of sons and daughters in marriage.
>
> These four levels of reciprocity are fundamental for the Andean social organisation (Ansion 1986, 161).

Unfortunately there are still no good monographs about the values and sins of the Quechua world available, as there are about the rituals and their forms of religious organisation.

Catholic marriage or *casarakuy* is quite normative among the rural Quechua. However, almost all couples begin their marital life by a kind of pre-marriage of Andean origin called *servinakuy* (a Spanish word that has been accommodated into the Quechua language meaning "mutual services"). This arrangement begins at a very early age with a recognised ceremony called *warmipalabrakuy* ("to make a verbal agreement on a woman"), in which the parents of the girl make a formal commitment of their daughter to the suitor and his parents. However, in many cases the young man simply "abducts" the girl with whom he has not had a long engagement in the Western sense. *Servinakuy* should not be understood in the sense of a trial marriage, an expression often occurring in popular literature, but rather as the first step in marriage, which is thought of as a process in which the willingness for permanence and mutual obligations become increasingly more sacred. From the beginning of their marital life the couple has the desire to establish a permanent marriage, even though they know that the commitment taken on in the *servinakuy* is less sacred than that promised in the *casarakuy* and that the former may be broken for serious reason (misunderstanding between the couple, though not necessarily because they are unable to have children), while the *casarakuy* is considered to be indissoluble.

Christian and Andean Specialists

Since Quechua Christianity, as we have seen, has a double—though integrated—system of rituals, it must have two types of specialists: the Catholic priest and the Andean priest. The latter is generally known by the generic name of *pago* and a specific name for each of the roles that he plays. The Quechua continue to accept the Catholic priest for the role that he plays in the church, although since the beginning of the century there may not be a priest physically present in each village. This acceptance, however, is somewhat ambiguous: on one hand, he is respected for his role as a man of ritual in a very sacralized world and for his history of service in the field of education, community service, and even for defending the Quechua against the dominant white world to a certain extent; on the other hand, he is not trusted because they do not value or they do not believe that he remains celibate, because they do not believe in him because of his origin or his training in the dominant mestizo culture, and because many priests have come from the dominant part of the world and may be implicated in some forms of exploitation of the Quechua. Beginning with the ecclesiastical reform begun at Vatican II and in the episcopal conference in Medellìn, it is possible to talk of two classes of Catholic priests. The one is more traditional, the members almost totally Peruvian born, belong to the most ancient colonial or republican dioceses. The second is more modern, the majority foreigners who belong to the prelatures created out of dioceses and entrusted to religious communities. There one finds a great concern for pastoral and social work, but seldom do those persons remain in the region for a long time. The negative traits noted above appear to a lesser degree among these pastoral workers.

Although an Andean priesthood with a number of ritual functions exists, its members do not form a real Quechua religious organisation, and for this reason we cannot speak of a parallel Andean church. The most important among these Quechua specialists is the *altomisayoq*, the man whom they say has been struck by lightning and who possesses a mysterious stone, like the altar stone of the Catholic altars, by which he is able personally to carry on a conversation with the Apus and fulfil most of the ritual duties in the Andean religion, such as *waloq* (divination), *hampeq* (healer), and so forth. It seems that the practice of the *laika* (sorcerer) is excluded from these duties; they attribute malicious powers to the *laika*, who fulfils the social function of channelling revenge upon one's enemies.

3

The Historical Formation of Quechua Christianity

A history of the Christianisation of the Andean Trapezoid has not been produced yet. My book *La transformación religiosa peruana* (1983), which, because of the broad sweep of information collected and because of its emphasis on the cultural process in the formation of new belief systems, rites, kinds of organisation and ethical norms coming from Andean and Christian roots, continues to be the most ambitious work about Peruvian Christianity, refers to the entire country and not just the Andean Trapezoid. However, I believe that what is said about the whole country can be applied to the region under study, but one must bear in mind that this region, having been one of the strongholds of the Quechua culture (Quechua continues to be the mother tongue of the majority of the population) can be expected to offer greater resistance to evangelisation.

From the point of view of the results obtained in the study, a history of the evangelisation of Peru can be divided into four periods: formation, consolidation, resistance and renewal.

1) The formation period extends from the celebration of the first Council of Lima in 1551 to the end of the great campaigns to exterminate idolatry about 1660. It includes the first stage of intensive Christianisation, focused on the twenty-five years of the episcopate of St. Toribio de Mogrovejo (1581-1606) and in particular on the celebration of the Third Council of Lima (1582-1583), which was most significant with regard to the Peruvian religious model and ordered the trilingual edition of the catechism for teaching and confession; and a second stage of the uprooting of the persistent Andean religion (campaigns to "exterminate idolatry") as a result of the discoveries of the Cusco priest, Francisco de Avila, in his parish of Huarochiri. These campaigns served not only to eradicate many practices of Andean popular religion but also to gain a better knowledge of this popular religion (Arriaga 1621, Avila 1987, Avendaño 1649 and Villagomez 1649). Thus the church, now fully established and organised, could count on a good synthesis of Andean religion and on sermon texts that were more pastorally adapted to the culture than those previously published in 1584, giving rise to a more thorough evangelisation of the Indians.

2) The consolidation period began about 1660 and ended some two centuries later. During little more than 130 years the indigenous popula-

tion was dispossessed of the official Inca religion, which fell almost at the same time as Tawantinsuyu because of the close connection between the two, along with the destruction of Andean popular religion in the "campaign of extermination," and was subjected to a compulsory evangelisation centred around the acceptance of baptism. From 1660 onwards they could at last take their own religious inventory within the bosom of colonial society and adopt a worldview and a characteristic religious disposition which crystallized throughout the second half of the seventeenth century and remained substantially unaltered until the middle of the nineteenth century. Thus the Indians ended up accepting Catholicism but making a series of reinterpretations of it from an indigenous cultural matrix, even to the preservation of many aboriginal religious elements.

> Through the acceptance of a collection of beliefs, rites, forms of organisation and ethical norms, such a transformation came about in the population of Tawantinsuyu on a whole, though not in the same way in each and every one of the coastal and mountain peoples. Many Indians, especially those in the southern Andes, had ceased to maintain or even to integrate the elements of their old Andean religious system in order to form a system that was more or less syncretistic . . . but, at any rate, I judge the indigenous Christianity to be more than a simple mask, nor does the ancient Andean religion live on beneath the surface.
>
> Also I reckon that some "categories of Andean thinking," especially those which have had a new system of classification imposed upon them, have not continued intact because the classification systems are modified at the same time as profound cultural change takes place, such as that which was seen in the region of Tawantinsuyu (Marzal 1983, 439-440).

3) The period of resistance spans the second half of the nineteenth century and the first half of the twentieth. This period of resistance is due more to the gradual decrease in the numbers of the clergy than to the impact of modernity that arrived to a limited degree and then only reached certain sectors of the cities. From the three thousand priests who were in the country during the period of the struggle for independence—to attend to the pastoral needs of a population of some two million persons—the number of clergy present declined drastically, especially when viewed relative to the growth of the Peruvian population, to the point that around 1950 they had to seek help from foreign clergy. Even then it was impossible to cover all the parishes, especially those in the Andean region. Throughout this century, in many regions of the country and in

particular in the rural areas, certain Christian practices which had been established during the colonial period have disappeared, and the Catholic religion has been reduced more and more to the patronal festivals and the rites of passage (baptisms, weddings and funerals) performed by priests who make occasional visits to the outlying communities from the cities or larger towns where they reside.

4) The renewal period covers the years from 1950 up to the present. It is characterised by a series of innovations in catechesis and in the broad field of social improvement due to the arrival of a clergy with a new outlook and to the creation of prelatures or new ecclesiastical constituencies from the most neglected areas of the old dioceses. These efforts were immediately joined to the church renewal promoted by Vatican II and its Latin American application in the episcopal conferences in Medellín (1968) and in Puebla (1979). However, we must not forget that though there has been an indisputable pastoral renewal in method and approach with some very interesting aspects, such as the birth of one of the versions of the theology of liberation, the ordinary pastoral attention in Peruvian society today, which is much more involved in modernity, more pluralistic and much pursued by the proselytizing of the new churches and sects, continues to be quite deficient and has not been able to resolve the old problem of self-sufficiency with regard to native clergy. According to the last Ecclesiastical Directory in Peru (1987), for a population of almost twenty-one million Peruvians, the church depends on some twenty-three hundred priests, of whom more than half are foreigners.

Within this global historical panorama I think it is possible to analyze the formation of Quechua Christianity, starting from the Andean religion that existed in the southern Peruvian highlands. When two religions come into contact, in theory, three things can happen: they are blended into a new religion, producing a synthesis; they are superimposed and maintain their own identity, producing a simple juxtaposition; or they are integrated into a new religion where it is possible to point to the precedent for each component, producing a type of syncretism. In practice, the process seen most frequently is the third one, which can be defined as the formation, starting from the point at which two religions came into contact, of a new religion which is the result of dialectic interaction of the elements (beliefs, rites, forms of organisation and ethical norms) of the two original religions. Such interaction results in the persistence of some of these elements in the new religion, the complete disappearance of others, the synthesis of some elements that are similar in the two religions, and the reinterpretation of some followed by a change of meaning. It is evident that in the southern Andean evangelisation a true syncretism took place, one which does not prejudge the value of southern Andean

Quechua Christianity as a way "in spirit and in truth" (Jn 4:23) to come to the Father.

THE ELEMENTS OF CHRISTIAN ORIGIN

Among their beliefs, the southern Andean Quechua have fully accepted God, the saints and the devil. They accept the Christian God, not so much because his character is equal to the Andean creator God, whose existence is defended by several chroniclers (Acosta 1588 and Cobo 1653, for example), nor because this equality was preached as is seen in the widely circulated sermon text of Avendaño (1649), but more because the catechism and the Christian rituals, especially the more popularized prayers, the Mass and the sacraments were so focused in this belief that it could not help but be accepted. This is confirmed in modern ethnographical studies, including the Quechua communities that are quite marginalized (Flores 1984). This creator God, though, is not the object of a systematic cult, for if this were the case he could never be the supreme God of the popular religions.

The Christian intermediaries are also accepted, those who are represented by means of images or "saints," such as Jesus Christ, the Virgin Mary in her various invocations, and the saints of heaven. These are accepted for the following reasons: first, because of the importance held by the cult of the saints in a church that had just defended the legitimacy of the saints as symbols and as mediators against the Protestants in the Council of Trent; second, because the saints correspond to the Quechua religious class of the Wakas, who grant favours in exchange for cultural services and who have attributes and specialists for their own cult (when the missionaries introduced the cult of the saints and founded brotherhoods with lands and cattle, these gradually replaced most of the cult of the Wakas by their substitutionary functions); and third, because many Quechua came to the conclusion that their prayers were heard by the images, and some went so far as to give testimony to having seen apparitions or experienced miracles, which were attributed to the images in question.

This occurred not only with the appointed saints in the great shrines, centres of pilgrimages of a regional nature (the Lord of Huanca and the Virgin of Cocharcas are two typical cases), but also with the images venerated in virtually unknown villages. Such is the case of the Immaculate Conception of Anan Cusi in the village of Acoria, province of Angaraes (Huancavelica), which in 1687 on three occasions "miraculously moved" to various different places from the altar of the old church, which was almost demolished by an earthquake. This caused an enormous commotion among the Quechua and is related in a detailed account which is kept in the bishop's palace in Ayacucho. One of the witnesses, the sacristan Marcos Condor, tells of the first move, which happened one night in August, when a new tremor was felt, strong enough that several neighbours with their families took refuge in the lean-to which had served as a provisional chapel as a result of the first earthquake. His statement in Quechua, translated by the interpreters of the process, declares:

> Everybody began to pray (the "Te Deum") and plead to God for mercy; because they were without light, the night was dark and it was raining, they decided to pass the night there until dawn. When all were quiet they heard a noise as loud as an earthquake, with the sound of chimes and bells, which frightened and startled them all so that they could not speak for fear. When the noise stopped, they said to each other, "Perhaps God wants to punish us like he did to the Pallalla, burying then beneath these mountains," and, "So that God will have mercy upon us, let us perform acts of contrition and penitence."
>
> To this end they beat themselves . . . , asking God in a loud voice for mercy and pardon from their guilt. A while later, Mateo Quispe told this informant to go and bring a light; so he brought it . . . Carrying the light to put it at the foot of the cross, this witness and all the others who were there with him saw the image of the Conception of the Most Holy Mary, which was standing on the right side of the cross, with her garland of flowers in her hand and her cloak. Everyone asked this informant who had brought the Virgin, because they had left her the previous night in the church, fallen over in her niche, and this informant answered them that he did not know (Marzal 1983, 205-206).

It is not possible to analyze here the long process that reflects the prevalence of a Christian way of life. But it is undeniable that the saints are completely accepted among the Quechua, not only because they have been functional, but also because they are ethereal.

The missionaries explained evil by the presence of the devil in the world and gave him the name Supay, a word meaning "good or bad spirit" (according to the first dictionary of Quechua, compiled by Fr. Domingo de Santo Tomás in 1560). The Quechua completely accepted him as an evil spirit, without removing any other evil spirits from their pantheon.

As the beliefs of Christian origin have been passed on to the rites, without doubt the most widely accepted has been the patronal festival. The festival itself has become a catalyst for the Quechua colonial society. Although the missionaries established the festivals in order to create certain critical points in the ritual life of the Christians and to be able to celebrate the mysteries of the life of Jesus, along with the great saints of the Christian calendar, and because these festivals arrived in the moment when the Quechua colonial society was emerging, they became the crucible for its formation. Actually a strange convergence of interests appeared in connection with the festivals. There were the interests of the missionaries who wanted to evangelise the people; the interests of the colonial functionaries, who were trying to establish village settlements in order to control the population; and the interests of the Quechua themselves, who wanted to restore their religious world and to reestablish their social cohesiveness in view of the breakup of their *ayllus* (rural communities). Therefore the festivals immediately began to fulfil important social functions. This is one of the reasons that they have survived even though in many places the clergy have lost interest and have ceased to believe in the pastoral opportunities the festivals present.

Another fully accepted rite is baptism. It seems that by the beginning of the seventeenth century the majority of the population of Tawantinsuyu had been baptised (Armas 1953, 266). This owes not only to the narrow interpretation on the part of the missionaries of the old axiom "Extra Ecclesiam nulla salus" (Outside the church there is no salvation), but also to the fact that during the first years of the Conquest the ones placed in charge saw baptism as a form of legitimization, and the Indians viewed it as a social price which had to be borne. Little by little they were obliged to change things, undoubtedly due to the influence of the hierarchy, which, in the Council of Lima in 1567, stipulated that adults were not to be baptised before they had received instruction for an entire month and children were not to be baptised without the agreement of their parents (Constitutions 29 and 27 about the Indians). This acceptance of the first Catholic sacrament, which eventually became a type of requirement in the Andean culture, did not exclude certain reinterpretations by this culture, as we shall see later.

The other sacraments were accepted to a lesser degree by the Indians, though they were obliged to receive them with the same regularity as the Spanish settlers during the period I have referred to as the period of consolidation. Confession and Eucharist, once the Second Council of Lima got over initial distrust of giving communion to the Indians because the council doubted that they "qualified," were received regularly at Easter. Ordination to the priesthood was not administered to the Indians, except in exceptional cases. Matrimony was fully accepted, although the Andean *servinakuy* survived as a premarital practice.

If the sacraments faced certain difficulties in being accepted, the same was not the case with the sacramentals. The great diversity of the sacramentals allowed them to better respond to the religious needs of the

Indians, who lived in a sacralized world, full of insecurities; the Spanish, too, had much faith in the sacramentals, as can be deduced from the testimony of St. Teresa of Avila, who relates in her autobiography that the demons fled from the holy water "so that they would not be turned away . . . This must be the great virtue of holy water. For me it is special and a well known consolation which I feel in my soul when I take it" (Avila 1977, 188). The priests also believed in the efficacy of holy water and the rest of the sacramentals, even to viewing them as the most appropriate pastoral instrument for the "poor Indians," apart from the economic advantages that their administration provided for them. Taking all this into consideration, I believe that the sacramentals were accepted completely among the Quechua and took on relatively greater importance when the decline in the numbers of priests from the middle of the nineteenth century made it more difficult for the people to receive the sacraments.

Finally, since the rites from Christian origin evolve into forms of organisation, the Quechua have ended up by accepting the Catholic priesthood and the confraternities. The acceptance of priests by the Indians has been marked by their own exclusion from the priesthood. The Second Council of Lima decided that "the Indians should not be ordained into any order within the church, nor should they wear any ornament, even though it be just to chant the epistle" (Constitution 74 about the Indians). On the other hand, for the mestizos there is no prohibition of any sort, and initially they were ordained, as is evident from the example of the Jesuit Blas Valera. But in 1578 Philip II gave the command to the bishops that they were not to ordain any mestizos until further notice, which gave rise to the beautiful letter that a group of mestizos sent to the pope in 1583. In this letter they pondered the advantages that they had in exercising the office of the priesthood (knowledge of Quechua, permanent residence in the land, etc.) and they asked: "If the Spanish have their Spanish priests and the French, their French priests . . . why is it that the Indians cannot have mestizo priests?" (Marzal 1983, 322). Nevertheless, during the greater part of the colonial years the clergy were almost exclusively from the Creole class, because there was an abundance of ordained persons in the dominant group and because they continued to distrust the Indians, considering them to be "new Christians." In spite of all this, the Creole priests were accepted by the Quechua to administer some rites which they had incorporated into their religious world (baptism, festivals, sacramentals, etc.). These Creole priests, because of their continual presence, also exercised a supervisory social role in the indigenous world, in accordance with the Toledo ordinances. This necessity for a priest, despite his belonging to the dominant world and at times being involved in the colonial exploitation of the people, explains the "distant nearness" in the way the priest is perceived by the Quechua today.

Confraternities soon were imposed upon the people as an expression of transplanted Catholicism. Here too there was a convergence of interests. For many of the priests they were an excellent pastoral instrument for the promotion of veneration of images, the receiving of the sacraments, and mutual help and charity; for the Quechua they were a way of reforming the rotation of services and acts of solidarity, in essence, the "*ayllus* managed to be revitalized by functioning as *cofradías*" (Celestino and Meyers 1981, 127).

THE ELEMENTS OF QUECHUA ORIGIN

After analyzing the contributions made by Catholicism to the Quechua religion of today, it is necessary to analyze pre-Hispanic Quechua religion. Unfortunately, we only know of it through the writings of the chroniclers who, as men of their day, wrote from the perspective of their Spanish and theological categories. To read them today frequently requires a careful hermeneutic. If we were to compare the Andean religion of the chroniclers with the present religion among the Quechua, we would arrive at the conclusion that many Andean elements have survived and certain Christian elements have been reinterpreted within the Andean religious matrix.

Among the first, the cults of Pachamama and the Apus are prominent. These cults have survived not only because they respond to the current sacral vision in the Andean culture, but because the missionaries did not offer a real alternative to support the agricultural activity and the husbandry of the Quechua in a ritual manner, in spite of the abundant rites of blessing found in popular Spanish Catholicism. Furthermore, as these agricultural rites in honour of the Pachamama and the Apus were so tightly bound up with the day-to-day life of the rural people and only were celebrated in the family group, it was not difficult for the Quechua to hide them from the possible inspection of their priests.

Many aboriginal healing rituals still exist also because Spanish medicine is not always considered a better alternative to indigenous medicine (and in some cases it is definitely inferior) and because the Quechua did not know about the Spanish methods, which, in addition, were more costly. On this point the attitude of the hierarchy was more tolerant. While the Third Council of Lima in 1583 ordered that the "sorcerers, confessors, diviners . . . be shut away in a place separate from the rest" to examine them and instruct them (Constitution 37 about the Indians), they also ordered that "the empirical and experienced medical practitioners who usually administered cures among the Indians should not be impeded in using their skill, but fortunately, they were to be examined first by the diocesan ordinary to ascertain whether they healed with words and superstitious ceremonies or, missing this, they were able to heal with herbal medicines and roots . . . , giving them written permission" (Constitution 110 about the Indians).

Lastly, an oral tradition survives to a large extent, although it does not preserve its aboriginal originality but has suffered a series of transformations, as happens with all oral tradition. A couple of examples: In the oral tradition about Huarochiri which Francisco de Avila collected (1987), there are five myths which are quite similar. They speak of a divine being who was in attendance at a festival in the disguise of a poor man; when he was not received by the participants—with the exception of a woman—he punished the guilty ones with a flood (1987, 121-125). This myth continues to be told in many southern Andean villages to explain the origin of the lakes. Jose de Arriaga (1621), in the oral tradition collected during visits for the elimination of idolatry in the central highlands, records, "The souls of those who die go to a land called Ipamarca . . . ; they say that before they arrive there is a big river which they must cross" (1968, 220). This myth has been preserved up to the present.

However, just as some of the rituals and myths from the surviving Quechua religion have taken on Christian elements (as happens, for example, with the rite of Pachamama, when the priest holds a cross or certain Christian prayers are recited; in the myth of the river that the dead must cross, in some communities this is the Jordan River), the Christian rites also have received Andean elements that amount to a veritable reinterpretation of these Christian rites. We recognise that reinterpretation is a process whereby cultural borrowings are redefined, taking on different or additional meanings from the matrix of the receptor culture. The culture unleashes such a redefinition of the borrowed element, not only to preserve its own identity in a case of compulsory acculturation, but also to render the borrowed aspect understandable in the new cultural universe into which it is received.

I offer two examples. Christian baptism, fully accepted by the Quechua, is reinterpreted in its meaning as well as its organisation. When the Quechua take their children to be baptised, they want to make them Christians, but in addition they want to ensure that lightning will not take hold of them because if it does and they die, they will be changed into spirits. When they search for godparents for the ritual, they do not so much want new spiritual parents who will ensure that the newly baptised will receive a Christian education as much as they seek the social and economic support of the *compadre*. This role is so institutionalized in Quechua society because the Conquest broke down the old cohesive groups based on kinship and evangelisation offered this new relational tie of godparents.

Catholic marriage, *casarakuy*, has been accepted by the Quechua too, but they have changed it into a three-stage process in which mutual commitment and the will to make it permanent are even more sacred. Before *casarakuy* the couple live in *servinakuy*, which is not a trial marriage but the first stage toward a binding marriage. It is not clear how this came about. It seems that the *servinakuy* was the only type of marriage that existed in the Quechua world before Tawantinsuyu; it consisted in a monogamous and stable union preceded by a rite similar to the *warmipalabrakuy*, although there was a certain degree of premarital sexual liberty, and the bond could be broken and a new one formed in certain circumstances. With the Inca conquest the union became indissoluble by a ceremony at which some state official presided. After the Spanish conquest this ceremony was replaced by the Catholic sacrament, which is also dissoluble and by nature more religious in character. Beginning with independence from Spain civil marriage was established, which has been accepted by the Quechua to an increasing degree, although without becoming an alternative to either *servinakuy* or *casarakuy*.

4

The Transformation of Quechua Christianity in the City

As I have already indicated, the rural Quechua religion will become more understandable if we analyze how it changes in an urban environment. Many peasants from the Andean Trapezoid, compelled by chronic poverty in their agricultural lands because of periodic natural disasters (and in recent years, because of terrorism) must emigrate to the city, most often to Lima. In Lima, confronted with a concentration of the work force because of the persistent economic crisis, they usually find work as street vendors. In the city they must not only satisfy their need for the basic necessities of life but also reorganize their social and religious world. In spite of the presence of certain secularizing forces, this situation offers the immigrants many religious opportunities, primarily, the great shrines of popular Catholicism located in Lima (foremost is the Lord of Miracles). They meet young people from parishes with a pastoral approach different from the tradition in the rural regions, one centred on biblical reflection and social commitment. Last of all, they come into contact with the abundant religious market that produces an explosion of new churches. Faced with these religious opportunities, many immigrants limit themselves simply to living their popular Catholicism in the city, but others take one of three choices. Some recreate their Quechua religious world in the city, especially their most meaningful ritual, the patronal festival; others join Christian communities, where they try to live out a spirituality that is more biblical and more involved with social change; and still others end up in one of the new churches which take advantage of the peculiar psycho-social situation of the immigrants in order to attract them with their persistent proselytism.[6] Although I cannot analyze here each one of the three choices, I shall address two points that seem to be significant: the appearance of the spontaneous cults with the re-creation of the patronal festivals in the cities, and the Quechua heritage in the new churches. In both, a fundamental continuity with the patronal religion which was de-scribed in the first part can be found, though the social and even the religious context has changed.

SPONTANEOUS CULTS AND PATRONAL FESTIVALS

Although the urban invasion and later settlement of El Agustino, a Lima *pueblo joven* or young town, began in the mid 1940s when the wholesale food market, La Parada, was established, the parish was not founded until 1968. Because of this time lapse and the nontraditional pastoral approach taken by parish priests, this parish did not promote the spontaneous cults in honour of the crosses and the saints (the images of Jesus Christ, the Virgin Mary, the saints of the Catholic calendar); none-theless, these cults witnessed an explosive growth. In effect, the appearance of these cults has continued on a marked ascending curve: the four initial cults from the 1940s became sixteen in the 1950s; in the 1960s the number grew to twenty-nine, in the 1970s to forty-nine, and from 1980 to 1986 to sixty-four. This proves that the organisation of cults of the cross and reli-gious images is not just a remnant from the past but the most important cultural response of the immigrants in their new urban environment.

Of the sixty-four cults, nineteen are focused on a cross, six on an invo-cation of Christ, seventeen on a Virgin and the other twenty-two on some saint. The importance of the cross as a religious cult symbol among the immigrants is noteworthy. It is explained not only by the place of the cross in Catholic worship, but also because the cross is the symbol of an occupied territory both in the Hispanic tradition of the Conquest and in the ecclesiastical tradition of the Lima councils, which ordered that a cross be placed over the mountains and the pre-Hispanic centres of wor-ship. Therefore, when the immigrants started to occupy El Agustino, they felt the need to erect a cross to mark their conquest and assure themselves of God's blessing. The cross is the guarantee of divine blessing, because it exorcises, sanctifies and makes the new space habitable, converting

"chaos" into a "cosmos" (Eliade 1967). This action is especially significant when a new town is established on the sides of a mountain, in an
area which has never been inhabited before or perhaps inhabited in ancient times by the *Ñaupa runakuna*, whose bones appear when they dig
the trenches for the cement foundations of the houses and who fill the
nights of the immigrants with fear until they erect a cross.

Although the crosses that are venerated are more numerous than the
images of Christ (nineteen to six), because many crosses bear the face of
Christ in their centre and because for the majority of the devout the crosses
are clearly associated with the death of Christ, it is interesting to note that
the piety of the immigrants is quite Christocentric. The fact that the cult in
honour of the Lord of Miracles has the largest following in the parish affirms this. The four most popular religious images in the parish, judging
from the number of spontaneous cults and by the crowds of people who
congregate around them, are the Lord of Miracles, the Virgin of Carmen,
San Martin de Porras and Santa Rosa de Lima. None of these has a provincial origin, which shows that the general tendency to venerate crosses and
rural-based saints has more influence on the emergence of such cults than
their automatic transplantation; actually only fourteen of the sixty-four
(little more than a fifth) are cults which have been transplanted to Lima.

Why do cults spring up spontaneously among the immigrants? The
main reasons seem to be as follows: First, the blessing of God, understood as an application of the working of faith to the solution of the
problems faced at the outset of life. Second, a bond or a social identity—
the cross or the saint becomes a bond of identity for the young town, the
block, the street, the lane or the labour union—which is capable of mobilizing the people through the creation of a nucleus of symbols, attitudes
and shared feelings.

The presence of the miraculous is the third reason, because religions
need divine legitimization through miracles, the same thing that happens
in the spontaneous cults, although in these they call anything extraordinary a miracle. One cult is prestigious because the miracles it produces
not only contribute to a solution for limit situations in a world full of
need but also reveal the presence of a providential God concerned about
people. However, although there are miracles associated with the origin
of the informal cults, there are punishments too, which are another form in
which the presence of God or the saints is revealed. In such cases they cease
to be simply benefactors and become demanding and jealous beings.

The fourth reason is the presence of a revelatory dream. If a miracle
legitimizes the appearance of a cult, so can a revelatory dream. This is
what has happened with some cults in El Agustino, when a founder of a
cult had a dream, then told his neighbours about it and they found a
sufficiently legitimate reason in it to start a new cult.

The last reason for the origin of the cults is the weight of the tradition of the family or the person's own group, as occurred in the fourteen cults of provincial origin which have been organised in the parish. In these cults the religious sentiment of devotion to the saint is coloured by a feeling of social connection with one's own group, which frequently is very strong among the immigrants as a way of compensating for the break with the village itself.

As an example of the origin of the spontaneous cults, I relate that of the Lord of Huanca, established in 1970 by a family from Cusco. The head of the family, a merchant, supplies this information; in his narration the interweaving of the various reasons are seen:

In 1962 a friend of mine told me that he had a linen cloth belonging to the Lord of Huanca, and he gave it to me because I am from Cusco. My mother-in-law, who was a very devout follower of the Lord of Huanca, was living with us, and she usually went to the festival in the shrine each year. When my friend gave me the linen cloth, I put it in the living room of my house. A little while later I heard my wife and my mother-in-law start to weep and to embrace each other, speaking Quechua. At first I didn't pay much attention to them and thought that perhaps it was because they were drinking liquor, but, when I took more note of what was happening, I heard them singing in Quechua the traditional songs of the Lord of Huanca, and they asked me to sing with them. The thing that greatly impressed me was that they had the Lord, and from then on we began to pray to him regularly in the house.

Later my daughter wanted to offer a Mass to the Lord. The idea was her own. She saw that we had the image in the house, and also she was pregnant and desired that her baby be born healthy. Thus the first fiesta with a Mass was in 1970. The following year the celebration was organised by the family of my brother-in-law, and that year there were vespers and a procession with a band. Since then the festival has been celebrated every year, attended mainly by relatives and people from our rural area.

I attribute all my success in the merchant business to the Lord of Huanca. He performs miracles for those who ask in faith, but he also sends punishments. When I was remodelling my business I asked the Lord of Huanca to touch this property, because it is large and well situated, and he granted my request. When my niece, recently graduated from high school, was trying to gain entrance into the University of Cusco, I took her to the shrine of the Lord of Huanca, committed her to the Lord and with tears pleaded that he help her. She got in on her first try. A woman acquaintance from the market came to the house a little while ago to place candles before the Lord (because we had built a small chapel to the Lord on the flat roof of the house), to thank him that her stall had not been burned when there was a fire in the market; when the woman had seen the blaze, she had shouted, "Lord of Huanca, Lord of Huanca, help me." The fire did not reach her stall. It was a miracle.

But, the Lord of Huanca also punishes when he is not obeyed. One time, after the festival was over, my brother-in-law did not do the accounts correctly; in addition, his wife had paid more attention to the dancing than to celebrating the Lord. The day after the festival she woke up with terrible stomach pains and had to be admitted to the hospital. When she was released, she came to pray to the Lord, recognising that he had punished her.

This testimony shows that the family cult of the Lord of Huanca follows exactly the model of the patronal festival with vespers, a Mass, a procession with a band, a communal meal, and so on, on the eve of the festival. This is the most important cultic form of Quechua Christianity, as we have already seen.

As the Lord of Huanca receives great devotion in the Andean Trapezoid, I believe it is fitting to now give an account of the vision of Christ in Quechua Christianity. This will complete what has been previously said about the Quechua religious worldview, because this view is seen more clearly in the city. The majority of the Quechua believe that Jesus Christ is the Son of God in human form and that he came to earth to redeem humanity by his death on the cross. The way they perceive and relate to Christ, however, is different from the official church of the hierarchy, the priests, those in the religious orders and the better trained members of the laity. To analyze this difference it may be useful to compare, by means of two ideal types at opposite poles, the vision of Christ in the official church and in the Quechua church, using the scheme laid out in the following chart:

THE VISION OF CHRIST IN THE OFFICIAL AND QUECHUA CHURCHES

	The Official Church	The Quechua Church
1. How is Christ revealed?	the Bible	images
2. How does he function?	an intercessory model	intercessor, motivator
3. How is he celebrated?	in the Eucharist	the patronal festival
4. How do the people relate to him?	prayers, intentions	prayers, promises
5. How does he relate to the people?	mercy, trials	miracles, punishments

How Is Christ Revealed?

In the official church, Christ is found and revealed to believers mainly in the Bible. Although members of the official church offer worship to Christ represented by images, their spirituality is not focused on the image but on the Book.

In the Quechua church Christ is revealed principally in a particular image, such as the Lord of Huanca or the Lord of the Tremors (Cusco), for it is through these that the Quechua know Jesus. Although they accept the authority of the Bible and even listen to it when read in church or on the radio, their experience of Christ is not focused on the Book but on the image. All this is explained by Quechua religious socialization itself; they either read little or are illiterate, so the church does not foster Bible reading but rather devotion to some images who listen, comfort and perform miracles. Although this spirituality can change with the emigration of the Quechua to the city, the spontaneous cults still reflect the old spirituality.

How Does He Function?

In the official church Christ serves as a model, and the imitation of Christ is the nucleus of spirituality. Christ is also recognised as an intercessor, for the prayers in the official liturgy are made in his name; but it is an intercession directed towards receiving grace to imitate him more fully.

In the Quechua church each concrete expression of Christ (the Lord of Qoyllur Riti or the Lord of Achajrapi) functions as an intercessor, as one who grants favours on behalf of God, but not as a model to follow. Although the Quechua know the history of Christ in the gospel, they only know his principal characteristics (that he was born in Bethlehem of the Virgin Mary, preached, performed miracles and died on a cross for the sins of humankind), but they do not know the richness of his life and teaching, so he cannot be a model to imitate. However, although the Christs venerated by the Quechua are not models to imitate, they definitely are very important motivating forces, reminding the people to remain true and to renew their Christian faith.

How Is He Celebrated?

In the official church Christ is celebrated in the Eucharist, especially in the Sunday Eucharist, which the Christians celebrate "in remembrance of him" (Lk 22:19). It is the desire of the church to make this a grand Christian celebration, even though for many it is not "alive" like a real festival.

In the Quechua church Christ is celebrated mostly in the patronal festival. Although there is usually a Eucharist in the festival, the Quechua do not perceive it as the central element. There is a harmonious synthesis between the sacred and the profane elements in the celebration and in the euphoria that gives life to the celebration in contrast to the rest of the year, which is dedicated to work.

How Do the People Relate to Him?

In the official church Christians relate to Christ through prayers and intentions, by which they endeavour to imitate the Lord.

In the Quechua church the intention takes on the form of a promise, which is a serious commitment to perform some difficult task in honour of Christ. Ordinarily, though not necessarily, this task is linked to the condition that Christ first grant the favour that is sought, which is often of a material nature.

How Does He Relate to the People?

In the official church Christ relates to the people through his mercy and grace—which are bestowed in the form of illumination or strength of will in order to find the solution to the problems of each day. To this believers must apply every personal effort and all the technology that is available in order to perfect their imitation of Christ. When things go wrong and one does not attain the spiritual goals as planned, and when life is interrupted by moral distress or bodily sickness, it is seen as Christ testing the faithfulness of his people.

In the Quechua church Christ relates to the people through miracles, by which solutions are brought to limit situations, particularly in the material order. Thus when things go wrong and disgrace falls upon them, they see Christ as punishing them. Such punishment, however, expresses the zeal and the demands of God, and thus is so numinous and such an obvious sign of the divine presence that it is like a miracle.

Let us return now to the role of the festival in the city. Testimonies collected in the study of the informal cults confirmed that the festivals almost invariably are like those in the villages of origin. Some festivals, organised by village leaders or by those who possess the image, later have evolved into a system of shared responsibility, which is proof of the costly weight of the tradition. If the history of each one of the festivals were written, it would be seen that each year new elements are added to the celebration, as in the Quechua model. This occurs not only in the trans-planted festivals but also in those of coastal origin. Is it possible to talk of a re-creation of the festival by the immigrants? In a narrow sense it is impossible to answer this question, because I have not done a comparative ethnography of the Quechua festival and its Lima version, as Zoila Mendoza (1985) has of the patronal festivals in San Jeronimo de Tunan (Junin) and the "Association of the Sons of San Jeronimo," made up of provincial residents in the capital. However, in a broader sense, yes, there is a re-creation, for the Lima festival fulfils the same social and religious functions as the Quechua one does in the place of origin.

In the first place, it fulfils the social function of connecting the immigrants with their cultural past and fixing them in their new environment by means of a common symbolic strategy. It also fulfils the social function of granting status to those who bear the responsibility for the organisation of the festival within a scale of values that continues to be valid for the majority of the immigrants and which in any case gives them an identity, something that is especially important for people in transition who are seeking a new identity. Thus many leaders of the young towns in El Agustino have been interested in organising the patronal festival, so as to ritualize an emerging solidarity among them. In the past the festival was a means of resistance of the colonial Quechua to the disorganisation that followed the Conquest, as well as being the crucible of a new cultural identity (Marzal 1985, 110-111). Today the patronal festival, transplanted or accepted from other immigrants in the city, is for many a means of resistance against the disorganisation of emigration and a vehicle for redefining or preserving their identity.

Second, the festivals fulfil a religious function. By means of the celebration the people make their supplications to God and the saints, give thanks for the miracles they have received and fulfil their vows. Although from the point of view of Catholic theology the festival is a simple sacramental which bestows divine grace in a substitutionary way through the institution of the church (in contrast to the ways instituted by the Lord himself to grant full mercy through the sacraments), the festival has become a "popular sacrament" through which God is revealed, communicates with the people and is celebrated. Furthermore, through the festival the devout are put in touch with the institutionalised church (the presence of the priest at the festival and the celebration of certain sacraments) to maintain the religious dimension in their lives.

Although I have limited my analysis to the appearance of the cults and the re-creation of the patronal festival in the city, I want to add a brief reference to what has happened in the city to the other elements of the rural Quechua religion. On this subject there is useful information in other studies (Matos Mar 1986). It is recognised that because of the work load that is imposed on the immigrants, they leave certain rural religious practices behind without remorse, for example, the "sacrificial offering to the earth." This disappears in the city as a social event because it is tied to agricultural activity and is only a personal problem for those few recent immigrants who have experienced the offering as a religious feature in their lives and now must experience the disenchantment of their worldview through contact with modern technical culture. In general, those elements of the Quechua religion most closely bound to rural life or to the Quechua language are rapidly disappearing, because many immigrants no longer regularly speak Quechua at home in order to facilitate the change to Spanish for the second generation. Meanwhile the elements of a system independent of the urban lifestyle weaken (for example, beliefs such as those regarding unbaptized children who can be changed into spirits, because in Lima the lightning does not appear so they can detect them). Still, certain beliefs and practices related to health and beliefs in punishing damage or sorcery to explain trouble can live on for a long time. This transformation of Quechua religion in the city does not come about just because of the loss of certain characteristics that are tied to the rural life, but because of the acquisition of new traits that are connected with the city. For example, the move to the city brings the immigrant into contact with books and with Bible reading. Other effects occur among some immigrants who re-create their patronal festivals, but more often among those who commit themselves to the Christian communities or end up joining the new churches.

THE QUECHUA HERITAGE IN THE NEW CHURCHES

Just as Quechua religion reappears in the city in the spontaneous cults and patronal festivals, it also reappears in many of the new churches, even though this seems paradoxical. These churches are recognised for persistent proselytism among the inhabitants of the marginal areas, especially the immigrants. In the case of the parish under study, El Agustino, there are fourteen different religious denominations (four are mainline Protestant, six pentecostal and four fundamentalist), and 12 percent of the heads of the families declare themselves to be members of these churches, a percentage much higher from that of metropolitan Lima (which was only 3.5 percent in the 1981 census). When we analyze the reasons that move the immigrants to convert to the new churches, we can refer to a continuity/break between the new church and the cultural world of the convert, which, in this instance, is the Quechua heritage. Continuity is found in ritualism, emotionalism, a sense of procession, miraculous healings, imminent eschatology, and so on, which feel "the same"; a break is present in the suppression of the festivals, the Masses for the dead, the veneration of images, and others, which conveys a sense of being "converted."

It is not difficult to discover the Quechua heritage in the pentecostal denominations which are so focused on emotional religious experiences and on miraculous interventions. R. Poblete and C. Galilea (1984) connect popular religiosity and pentecostal religiosity when they analyze the growth of Pentecostalism in Chile, making an analysis that is valid for our purpose:

> Popular religiosity may indirectly be a decisive factor in the expansion of Pentacostalism. This religious feeling can be found in a way that fits this substratum in the pentecostal message, which offers health and salvation to those who choose to participate in the pentecostal doctrine.
>
> Folk Catholicism, which is benevolent, not too learned, traditionally devoted to the saints, ignorantly confident in their prayers, blessings and sacramentals to which they attribute infallible and magical powers, with great nostalgia believing in the dead and in the possibility of receiving some sign from them, of a magical worldview, easily persuaded about outside forces, influences and effects that are somewhat mysterious, is fertile ground to latch onto this novel message which places religious expectations within reach of these people.
>
> In effect, Pentecostalism brings emotion to bear more than reason, offers the assurance of salvation, announces the kingdom beyond this world, and proclaims a Holy Spirit who has extraordinary manifestations of the senses (gift of tongues, gift of prophesy, revelations, visions, dreams). They preach an omnipotent God who heals and forgives sins, who regenerates and sanctifies, who promises changes in life and who gives a guarantee against all evil. With this kind of message, Pentecostalism places the element of feeling in first place . . . , in harmony with the religious dispositions . . . of folk Catholicism (1984, 28-29).

Nor is it difficult to discover the Quechua heritage in the fundamentalist denominations such as the Seventh Day Adventists, the Mormons or the Jehovah's Witnesses, which are so focused on the imminence of the end time. We recognise that the Andean culture speaks of a cyclical history, in which each cycle is separated from the following by "turning the world upside down" (*pachacuti*). Cristobal de Molina of Cusco (1574) described the Taqui Ongoy movement of 1565, which was led by the

Indian Juan Chocne in Ayacucho and in a short time spread throughout the greater part of the Andean Trapezoid. He relates that the Indians "believed that all the Wakas in the kingdom . . . had risen from the dead . . . and walked about in the air, commanding that the battle be given to God . . . , that the world was turning upside down, and that God and the Spanish would be conquered this time . . . Later many preachers appeared among the Indians who preached this resurrection of the Wakas . . . , who were now present in the Indians and caused them to speak" (Molina 1943, 79-80). Molina was referring to the trances into which many of the participants of Taqui Ongoy fell and explains the name of the movement (*takiy* means "to sing while dancing" and *ongoy* means "sickness"). Such movements of indigenous resistance continued to appear among the Quechua, although the religious elements became increasingly less Andean and more Christian, as illustrated by a simple comparison between the ideology of Juan Chocne and that of Juan Santos Atahualpa or that of Tupac Amaru II, who is more of an indicator of the Christianisation of the Quechua. Thus, the preaching of the fundamentalist denominations concerning the imminent end time and the millennium of Christ finds fertile soil in the Andean background of many immigrants.

However, the Quechua heritage is discovered most easily in the Evangelical Association of the Israelite Mission of the New Universal Pact (AEMINPU), the official name of a new church founded in 1968 by Ezequiel Ataucusi Gamonal, a Quechua-speaking peasant from the Andean Trapezoid. In the present day AEMINPU numbers some twenty thousand followers ("Israelites") in the whole country, both in the rural areas and among the urban migrants of Andean origin. In this case we see once again the continuity/break with the Quechua culture and the new religion, which is expressed as much in the life of the founder as it is in the religious system of AEMINPU. Brother Ezequiel personally told me his life story in a long recorded interview, and we can mark three periods in his life: infancy and youth in his native village of Cotahuasi (1918-1941); work in the regions of Arequipa, Pasco and Junin until his conversion to Seventh Day Adventism (1941-1955); and "the great revelation" and activity as preacher and organiser of the new religion (1956-1988). The first two periods of his life were much the same as any Quechua peasant. He was only able to study through primary school in his community and then was forced to leave the community in search of work in various places. Then several events took place, which he now considers mysterious and which seemed to prepare him for the "great revelation," in which he was caught up into the third heaven. When he was six years old he said to his mother who was worshiping a Christ figure: "This saint is not God because he is dead and God is alive in heaven." At twelve, one night he saw a white light in the form of a morning star and this vision was repeated quite regularly. At fourteen, a mysterious old man revealed to him the origin of the saints in the images that the priests made in their houses and later hid in certain spots so that the Indians, when they discovered them, believed that it was a revelation and established a festival. Finally, at eighteen, when he was bathing with some friends in the river one day, he was on the point of drowning when a fish with a "long reach" appeared to him and saved him. Years later, when he had converted to Adventism, he had the great revelation, which he related to me in this way:

When I was caught up into heaven, in the first heaven there is no light; in the second heaven there is no light, everything is dry; in the third heaven, there is brightness, there it is day. I was walking along in a hurry as though someone had called me. When I went up to the third heaven, I approached a large door that was open and I went in. I stood amazed; I had never seen a place like this, so big . . . I looked to the far end, and there was a big blackboard and two libraries. I was going towards the far end when someone spoke to me from behind: "Brother Ezequiel, have you arrived? We have been waiting for you. Sit down." I turned around and saw a little table with one chair, and a big table where three persons were seated, the Father, the Son and the Holy Spirit. The Son was reporting to the Father, and the Holy Spirit was the one talking to me. It was there I received the order which I was to write on the card: "Sit down and write the ten commandments on the card, exactly as they are written on the blackboard, without adding to them or omitting anything." When I had finished writing, they approved it.

From this revelation we can see that Brother Ezequiel sees himself as a new Moses, one to whom God confided the Decalogue and sent out to preach repentance. Although Brother Ezequiel only appears with the titles of founder, biblical compiler and missionary general in the official publications of AEMINPU, the great mass of followers attribute to Ezequiel a kind of divine character, even though they do not speak about the subject easily. In a long interview one of the principal leaders told me: "Like the Son of God was incarnate in Jesus of Nazareth, the Holy Spirit has become incarnate in Ezequiel Ataucusi Gamonal." Ezequiel himself often applies the gospel texts about the Son of Man to himself. During the interview, after we had read some fragments from a sermon together, I asked him who this Son of Man was. He replied in a solemn tone: "The Son of Man walks about the city and when the people see him, they do not see him . . . Believe it or not, he comes from Peru. Now he is on his way, and very soon he will be known everywhere." In addition to the great revelation, Ezequiel had others which led him to discover the new way and he still continues to hear a voice within.

So a new religion was established with Peru the privileged country, because here God had made a new universal pact with humanity. Such a religion could be considered a truly cultural creation. It was considerably inspired by the Old Testament, had a strong eschatological flavour, and now, twenty years after its foundation, numbers some twenty thousand followers, some recruited from among the rural Indians of Bolivia and Ecuador.

A fundamental characteristic of the "Israelites" is that they follow an Old Testament liturgy. With the exception of baptism, which is administered according to the example in the gospels, though with a different meaning, all the other rites follow the Jewish model commanded by Moses. In addition to the Sabbath rest, which is celebrated in *cecabi* (centres for biblical training, equivalent to synagogues) where the "Israelites" meet for eight hours every Saturday to pray, sing and listen to brief Bible studies, their liturgy includes a celebration of the new moon each month and the three great annual festivals (Passover, Pentecost and the feast of the Tabernacles), which are celebrated in the main temple in Cieneguilla and in the temples in each area, in strict accordance with the rules laid down in the book of Numbers (chapters 28 and 29). In these festivals the "Israelites" pass long hours alternating between studies and singing praises. The first are brief catechetical expositions on biblical subjects and ethical orientation; the second part consists of singing psalms and songs from the hymnbook, most of them in Spanish, though some are in Quechua with *huayno* or *chicha* music (a mixture of indigenous South American music), and popular *cumbias* from Colombia with the help of tambourines and other musical instruments, while everybody claps hands and the women move their bodies and arms in rhythm. The most solemn ceremony in the new moons and the three great festivals, however, is the holocaust. Here is the testimony of one who was present in Cieneguilla:

> After we finished the study, all those present processed out of the temple towards the esplanade in front where the holocaust altar was set up. This was a platform of stone with three layers of wood where the priests had placed a young bull which had been sacrificed earlier by the Levites in the slaughterhouse, and then prepared with olive oil, salt, flour and incense. The assembly, some eight hundred persons, formed a large human circle around the altar, maintaining as always a strict separation between men and women. They began the unending song entitled "Praises of the Congregation of Israel,"

which is full of verses from different psalms and other books of the
Bible. The Andean "Israelites" sang with enthusiasm:

> Who is like Jehovah our God,
> who had raised up his dwelling place,
> who stoops to look upon heaven and earth?
> He lifts the poor and the beggar from the ground,
> he raises them from the dung heap,
> to cause them to sing with the princes,
> with the princes of his people.

There was a gathering together and many were deeply moved. They
continued singing. From where I was located I could distinguish
three men—an adolescent, a young man dressed in the traditional
long tunic of the AEMINPU and an adult—who showed signs of
ecstasy or of being possessed by the Spirit; they moved their heads
and their arms in a strange way as if they absent from the body. The
same thing happened with a number of women whom I could see
from my place (of the some four hundred women in attendance, a
third wore the long robe of the AEMINPU). Some seemed to have
the gift of tongues, and when the singing stopped, they continued to
pronounce strange sounds. [As Brother Ezequiel told me in the interview, "There are persons in the congregation who have the gift
of tongues, some speaking as many as eight, ten or even thirty
tongues, who are possessed by the Holy Spirit."]

When the singing of the first praise was finished, which had lasted
about half an hour, Brother Ezequiel knelt before the altar and with
his arms raised to the sky, offered the holocaust with a brief prayer.
One of the priests lighted the bonfire, a huge cloud of smoke rose
and the second "praise" commenced, which lasted another half hour,
with the same emotional and mystical aura.

It seems pertinent to ask why the "Israelites" celebrate a liturgy that
so imitates the Old Testament. Brother Ezequiel justifies it by saying that
"the Lord made me understand these things when I was a child" and
other "Israelites" repeat the saying that Jesus did not come to destroy but
to fulfil the ancient law (Mt 5:17). However, in order to understand the
historical and social reasons, I believe that we must search in the brief
encounter that Brother Ezequiel had with Adventism, where he stayed barely
a few months, and in certain traits of the Quechua culture, from which
Brother Ezequiel and the majority of his followers trace their origins.

In the first place, the same importance is attributed to the rite and
symbolic language. The "Israelites" participate in the ritualism and rich

symbolism that are distinctive of the archaic cultures. They meet in the *cecabis* for eight hours each Saturday and for two hours three days of the week. The majority gather in the temple at the time of the new moons and for the three great festivals (Passover, Pentecost and the feast of Tabernacles). In addition, they participate in a series of more individual and family rituals: circumcision (which refers to the heart and is a type of anointing), presentation of a child in the temple, baptism, purification of individual impurities in accordance with Leviticus 15: 1-28, commitment, marriage, etc. All of this ritual life helps "Israelites" to feel as though they are within a world that is blessed by God and which must be preserved ritually, as is the case with the Quechua culture as well. On the other hand, the "Israelites" impute much importance to symbolism. In the liturgical meetings many women and some men wear long robes, which are costly and not very functional. The women wear them in their secular life as well, while the men, who have taken the Nazarite vow (Nm 6:2-4) do not shave their beards or cut their hair, both signs that easily distinguish the "Israelites" on the streets of Lima.

Second, the "Israelites" make sacrifices of animals, sprinklings with blood, and in the festival of Passover they eat lamb with unleavened bread, all the while applying the gospel texts associated with the Eucharist. All of this is similar to the sacrifices of llamas, the ritual sprinklings of blood and the feasts of sacrificed meat which are still celebrated in some parts of the Andean Trapezoid (Nachtigall 1975).

Third, the "Israelites," like the Quechua, believe in a severe and jealous God, Jehovah of the Old Testament, who makes his presence known on earth by bringing punishments. Their preachers in the *cecabis* and in the popular plazas of Lima deliver apocalyptic sermons about the natural and social ignominy of the human race, and announce an end to it all because the sun is getting closer to earth. This is a reference to the rains in Piura caused by the Niño current, the droughts in Puno, the volcano that erupted in Colombia, the earthquake that devastated Mexico, terrorism, drug traffic, military tensions. Above all, this is a reference to the imminent end of this world, which has a cyclical history like that of the Andean world. In the interview Brother Ezequiel explained the text of Ezekiel 34:7 this way:

> As it states clearly here with respect to this: that I will visit the evil of the parents (time of Noah) upon their children (time of Lot), in the third (present day is the third) and in the fourth generations of those that hate me. Then, to clarify what is the fourth generation, after this third judgement another thousand years will pass. After a thousand years, all of the dead are going to rise again. Immediately

the fourth judgement will take place and this will bring about the purification of the earth.

The purification of the earth will take place during 1,335 days, according to Daniel 12: 12, and it will be accomplished in the same manner as a blacksmith heats the iron. And when the earth begins to get hot, the people will be jumping and leaping about; they will not be able to sit down, lest they be turned into ashes . . . It is necessary that the dragon be punished for having won over so many souls during all this time. Then, at the last, the city that is above will descend on top of the head of the dragon to crush him. Thus, the dragon, the old man, Satan, the devil, dies.

In other words, the first judgement is in the time of Noah, the second, in the time of Lot, and the third, in the time of the Son of Man. In the fourth judgement there will be no liberty. The redeemed from the third judgement are going to be moved to new planets until the fourth judgement is passed . . . The third judgement is near. This is written.

This belief in the imminence of the end time is given voice in the long chants of the liturgical hymnody. One of them, which is entitled "The End Is Drawing Near," repeats the title twice as a refrain between the stanzas, which have been written in a peculiar Andean Spanish. I quote the first five stanzas:

> All the earth will be renewed,
> listening, naturally, to this warning.
>
> The third judgement will come very soon,
> peace will be taken from the world.
>
> Michael, the Archangel, is already on earth,
> to begin the conflict among nations.
>
> Among the people there will be no respect now,
> silver will not be worth anything either.
>
> Among neighbours hatred will spring up,
> all the people will go about in a troubled state.

Note that in this "Israelite" eschatology, Brother Ezequiel is not only the Son of Man, whose arrival announces the third judgement, but also the Holy Spirit, who presides over the future world, according to the myth of the three eras of creation.

Fourth, the "Israelites" have not only restored certain symbols, attitudes and values of Quechua culture in the new religion but have also promoted a kind of Quechua nationalism that considers Peru to be a privileged country, an idea found in the titles of other hymns. Furthermore, they have adopted as a symbol of the new pact the colours of the rainbow, which many think was the banner of Tawantinsuyu. They recognise Manco Capac as the first Peruvian prophet and repeat the Incan *ama sua, ama quella and ama llulla* as a principle of morality, which is completed by the Decalogue which Brother Ezequiel came to restore. In the interview, he said:

> Peru is a privileged country. The scripture declares it so in Isaiah 66:18: "A time will come to bring all people and languages together, and they will come and see my glory." This means, then, that the generation of the four provinces of earth or the four *suyus*, as the Incans called them, will kneel before God. Even though we do not want to do so, my dear brother, that which God says must be fulfilled . . . Many are now acquainted with the things of the Lord, but from now on they will be much greater, more fearful, than that which has never ever been seen.
>
> For this reason I sometimes say: "Up until now the Israelites are looked down upon, but they are wrong, because God is manifesting himself among the Israelites in different ways as a testimony to all peoples. The generations of the four provinces of the earth will be reunited in Peru. It is written." In the temple in Cieneguilla we already have the flag of Bolivia, but very soon other flags will come. From now on not much time remains.

Thus I conclude this composite but provisional picture of the Quechua religious world with its past roots, Christian and colonial, and its future profile, which becomes more urbanized each day.

PART THREE

THE AYMARA RELIGIOUS EXPERIENCE

Xavier Albó

1

Introduction

The reader must take into account the provisional nature of this effort to transmit the religious experience of the Aymara people owing to two limiting factors: the author is not Aymara, and there is a wide variety of religious experience within the Aymara world.

An outsider never can manage to perceive, let alone transmit in all its varied richness, the personal religious experience of others. This is especially so when confronted with enormous cultural differences and when one is dealing with a culture, like the Aymara, in which the religious dimension is so strong and penetrates every sphere of life. The Aymara people themselves are the only ones who are qualified to express their personal experiences through their most representative exponents of that experience and in so doing, enrich us all with their own witness. In no way do these reflections seek to replace such a work. I shall consider them of use, however, if they serve as an incentive so that in the future we have more direct testimonies.[1]

The second limiting factor is more intrinsic. In reality, perhaps, it is impossible to speak of *the* Aymara religious experience but only of an infinite number of Aymara experiences. I refer not only to the uniqueness of each personal religious life, but also to the great multitude of variants, symbolic languages and microcosmic, local syntheses found across the length and breadth of the high plains and valleys that comprise the world of the Aymara.

THE GREAT TRADITION, LOCAL TRADITIONS AND COLONIZATION

Studies in religious phenomena tell us of the coexistence within the same cultural current of a "great tradition" and "little local traditions." The first covers the major areas and is endorsed and guarded mainly by the leading sectors of the society, who—if they are literate—even have it codified in their sacred texts. The little traditions, in contrast, are found deep within the memory and praxis of each specific group and show a greater variety and flexibility from one place and time to another. This dialectic between the great and the little tradition is found, for example, in the Hindu world and in countries with a Muslim tradition.[2]

Something similar occurred in the original Andean societies, within which the Aymara society plays a part, along with the Quechua society. Since 1532, however, the history of these societies has been cut short and shaken by an invasion and conquest from Europe and the subsequent establishment of a hybrid colonial society. Such a situation—only partially accepted by the Aymara people, who have felt "oppressed but not conquered"[3] ever since—allowed the preservation and relatively autonomous development of many little traditions, while making the perpetuation and growth of a great tradition—which binds people together and lends a sense of total belonging to the system—more difficult.

As a substitute for the Andean great tradition, the Christianity of the conquerors and colonizers was introduced. Independent of the good or bad character of the new evangelizers, it is natural that a system of exogenous beliefs, brought in from a place so distant and formed in social and cultural situations so different, would not be equally weighted against the old great tradition, which it battered and persecuted. The new Christian matrix represented not only a faith system but also a completely new symbolic and cultural system. It was, furthermore, in league with the dominant colonial society and accomplished at the most the creation of new syncretistic religious forms, differing greatly from one another as a consequence of the diversity already found among the little traditions and the kinds of impact that the colonial experience had and continues to have throughout the length and breadth of the Andean and Aymara world.

To the above we must add the impact of changes of the present century, multiple and equally diverse in nature, that come from primarily two sources: a) the penetration of modern society through the schools, pro-state and anti-indigenous legislation, access to national politics, syndicates, etc., and b) the proliferation of new religious options which come from the outside, both from Catholics of different origins and from a whole range of evangelical denominations that increases daily.

The result of this pluralistic experience, undoubtedly painful and not without trauma, is the multiplicity that faces us today. However, behind the differences we can also see the underlying continuity. Each variable is like a reproduction, more or less modified with some deficiencies and mutilations, of the same ancient and venerable image. It is as if in each place the same sculpture had been smashed to bits and restored, but in the process some of the original pieces were preserved better than others; then the holes were filled in in a different way in each place, according to the local creative talent, and in agreement with the new model presented by those who wished to destroy the original statue in the first place. In this process of continual reconstruction within each community, the roles are played by the Andean tradition—more than the actual linguistic differences between the Quechua and the Aymara—the local tradition, the Spanish-Creole cultural tradition, within that, and the Christian tradition.

The whole religious system, however, continues to be reinterpreted, particularly with regard to its function, from the specific viewpoint of the receptor, who in our case is obviously the Aymara people. The old Latin saying *Quidquid recipitur ad modum recipientis recipitur* (What is received is adapted to the worldview of the person who receives it), has ample application here. In the new colonial society, regardless of the situation, the Christianizer came from the dominant sector and the receptor, the Aymara, were the oppressed people. Therefore, everything received from outside and from above was added to their life, logic and millennial existence.

AYMARA RELIGION, CHRISTIAN RELIGION AND THE EXPERIENCE OF GOD

When we speak of the Aymara religious experience today, we are speaking of the personal religious experience of a people who have called themselves Christians for four centuries. These people have incorporated many symbolic and ethical elements of a Christian origin into their religious experience. The Conquest—colonisation—oppression and the evangelisation, with the bright side and shadow side of their histories, are parts which cannot be separated easily from the life and concrete memory of the Aymara people living today. Nevertheless, this religious experience is Aymara, preserved and consolidated throughout these centuries and those that preceded the invasion. Thus we can still speak of a genuine Aymara religion, given public expression in some parts and cultivated in others in a clandestine form.

Perhaps it is more artificial than real to ask whether we are dealing with an Aymara religion that has been covered over with Christian concepts and symbols, or the opposite, a Christian religion in which, more or less, Andean traditional elements live on. To decide which one is the veneer for which depends greatly on the narrowest and the broadest concept that each one has with reference to the two ends in question. To some, the two concepts will appear incompatible, and they will lean towards the side which satisfies them more. Others, however, who are more flexible, will see a possible Andean-Christian synthesis.

The specific form in which Christianity has been incorporated into the present Aymara experience opens immense questions and challenges for those who, calling themselves Christians, have tried to "convert" these people in the past or present. If we reflect more deeply on what St. Augustine called "the seeds of revelation" or on that which Karl Rahner calls the "existential supernatural," the Aymara experience without doubt includes an experience of God, always present in history and perceived through a thousand crystals of different reflections by all the people of the earth. Here we have much more than a mere theoretical consideration, for we are speaking of the experience lived by so many among the Aymara with whom we have had the privilege to share food and home during a number of years. We give witness to that which we have seen and heard.

In any case, what we are looking for here is precisely what is the religious experience—for us, an experience of God—of the present-day Aymara people, whose roots penetrate into the depth of the past and have been exposed to Christianity for half a millennium.

I cannot refer here to all the religious experiences that stand out so differently in today's Aymara mosaic. Such an effort would require several volumes. Neither would it be appropriate to limit ourselves to showing just one of these experiences in detail. We would run the risk of losing the global perspective. So I have adopted a middle road. Starting from the reconstruction of the experience that an individual in their culture gradually accumulates from birth until death, I have tried to call attention to some characteristics, in my opinion the most central, of the conception and experience of Aymara religion. There is still much which has not been said. For example, we barely begin to hint at some highly developed dimensions, such as the vast world of myths of origin, the symbolic richness of so many highly elaborate rituals, or the long list of religious specialists, each one with his own special charisma. Rather, I have concentrated on identifying some profile sketches that will help us to understand this varied and fragmented "statue," with yet so much in common, which is the Aymara religious experience today.

Despite what has been said above, in the bulk of the text I shall speak only of religious experience and belief without any desire to prejudge what is and what is not an experience of our idea of God. It seems to me to be less ethnocentric, more realistic and more respectful to try to present, at least in the first instance, the manner in which the Aymara develop their personal experience of the very real world which overwhelms them and with which they have a permanent relationship. Only in the final pages do I take up again the complementary theme of the experience of God, endeavouring to point to some more precise ways we might perceive the personal experience of the Aymara as effectively an experience of the One who is for us the living God.

2

The Aymara

It is impossible to understand the religion of a people without some general knowledge of their life and environment. Here, at least in broad strokes, are the traits which are most typical of the Aymara.

A PEOPLE DIVIDED BY THREE NATIONS

The Aymara, who number almost two million people, occupy the greater part of the high plateau, a wide mesa four thousand metres above sea level, which extends for almost a thousand kilometres from around the lakes of Titicaca and Poopo to the large salt lakes further south. Their territory also embraces mountains, inter-Andean valleys and the semi-tropical regions (Yungas) surrounding them, with heights that range from more than six thousand metres in the snow-covered peaks to less than one thousand metres in the areas settled most recently. This territory is distributed—actually cut into—by three nations: Bolivia, Peru and Chile, in decreasing order of numerical importance with respect to the Aymara population. The great-grandparents of the present-day Aymara occupied an area much larger, partially shared with the Quechua, the Urus and other ethnic minorities. The colonial Spanish government, with its policies of population concentration in order to levy taxes and promote missionary expansion, gradually diminished the Aymara territory to its present size. In spite of everything, other regions which are populated by the Quechua today still maintain some traces of their Aymara ancestors, for example in their religious world.

The majority of the Aymara population live to this day off agricultural activities in the rural areas, mainly on the freezing high plateau. There are, however, 500,000 urban Aymara in the city of La Paz, the capital city of Bolivia, and from 100,000 to 200,000 spread throughout the cities of Oruro, Arequipa, Tacna, Arica and other smaller towns and villages of the region, including some as far away as Lima, capital of Peru.

THE EARTH ONLY GIVES SO MUCH

The greater part of the rural high plateau, the area to which this work makes specific reference, combines subsistence agriculture, cattle raising and sometimes other seasonal work within or outside of the community, in proportions which vary according to the resources and opportunities of each place. The principal agricultural product is the potato, native to the region, of which there are hundreds of varieties. This crop is complemented by that of other indigenous products (like quinoa) and some that have been introduced (like barley). The llama and the alpaca are the main livestock native to the area, but since colonial days almost every family has its flock of sheep, at least a pair, or other small domestic animals.

In the valleys corn abounds, and in the subtropical areas, the famous coca leaf, both of which are indigenous plants. In these more temperate climates it has been possible to introduce other products from outside, such as fruit trees, coffee and rice; goats and cows also have been brought into this area, including some raised for export on a commercial scale when the roads are passable.

Especially on the high plateau the agricultural activity is full of natural risks from drought, frost (which can happen in any month of the year), hail or, for those close to the lake, floods. For this reason the traditional plan was for each community to have access to all the different climates or ecological zones. Since colonial times, however, the majority of the communities have been confined to only one microclimate; in addition, the better lands passed into the hands of the *patrons*, leaving some Aymara holdings reduced to marginal and scant properties, and other Aymara in the situation of being peons on the haciendas. The agrarian reforms in Bolivia (1953) and Peru (1969) returned the land to many who had become peons, but only in a haphazard way. Although in many of the original villages property was held in common, the use and economic unit of production is now basically in the hands of each family of small farmers.

Outside of the Yungas and some of the more privileged valleys which produce mainly for the market, the majority of the people cultivate their land primarily for their own consumption. However, almost everybody takes agricultural surplus to market (when there *is* a surplus)—a cow, some piece of handicraft—or work for hire. In this way the families purchase a range of manufactured goods they now consider indispensable for consumption in the festivals, for example, a few or many pieces of clothing, a radio, a bicycle.

FROM THE COMMUNITY TO THE AYMARA NATION

The ancient communities, known as *ayllu* or *jatha*, were brought together into larger units until they formed several nations, which in turn, towards the eve of the Spanish Conquest, established the Qollasuyu, one of the four constituent parts of the Inca Empire. After colonization these larger units were broken apart, but the smaller communal units have survived to the present with major or minor changes depending on their location, including the former haciendas which have been reconstituted as communities. In the rural areas there are hardly any Aymara who do not live as part of some *ayllu* or community.

Since the colonial period, groups of ten to forty farms, ranches or communities have been amalgamated to form a central town, more and more of a mestizo character, on which they are dependent and to which they owe service on certain occasions. With the agrarian reforms of this century, these traditional ties have been weakened. On the other hand, the majority of the communities, including the new ones formed from old haciendas, have gone on to form the so-called peasant unions. These bring together all the rural people of Peru and Bolivia in organisations with a national organisation, though they continue to have the community as the minimum unit with the traditional organisation only superficially changed.

The entire process was violent and has bred a constant resistance, sometimes accompanied by uprisings. Although these have occurred in every century, the most general uprising was in the years 1780-1783, involving all the Aymara territory plus the southern region of the Quechua world. Tupaq Katari, then the principal Aymara leader, is still recognised as the symbol of the struggle of the Aymara not to surrender. In the last decade several parties and Aymara political movements have emerged, most of them in Bolivia. These include among their principal objectives the official recognition of the language and culture—of which a central element is their religion—of this people increasingly called the Aymara Nation.

A BELIEVING PEOPLE

These Aymara, who for centuries have lived in one of the wildest and most impressive landscapes on the planet, among snowy peaks, interminable high plateaus and deep valleys, have developed a sacred relationship with this natural surrounding. They see it full of life, inhabited by powerful and extraordinary beings, as real as themselves, with whom they must learn to relate and to dwell amicably and whose presence they must acknowledge in all their activities. These spiritual beings protect their existence and grant them their favours—as long as they feel duly recognised and served. If they are ignored or not given the affection that they deserve, they can react, like any other living soul, and withdraw their favours and protection or even send calamities.

The ancestors help the Aymara to orient themselves within this sacred universe. The bearded men who in latter times have come from over the sea did not bring any alternatives so convincing that they abandoned completely their previous personal experiences. The invaders, despite their endeavours to explain, sometimes verbally, other times with the sword and burning at the stake, only managed to add new elements to the established universe. In some cases they imposed names and new symbols on ancient existent reality; in others they achieved genuine transformations or the inclusion of new interpretive keys and approaches to the unknown and the sacred. These new faces of God, however, did not eclipse the old ones; they complemented them. The Aymara still feel surrounded by an extraordinary universe, sacred and full of life, and present in all their activities.

In the following pages I shall attempt to show something of this religious experience, just as the Aymara demonstrate it in the present. In chapters 3 to 7 I present the development of this experience throughout the natural life cycle, with emphasis on that which occurs in the rural sectors of the high plateau and taking advantage of those experiences which are expressed more directly in their symbolic religious code. The majority of the data comes from the northern high plateau, both Peruvian and Bolivian, though some supplementary information from the southern, more traditional area (Oruro, Potosi and northern Chile) is included as well. In the final chapters I shall broaden the horizon to grasp some idea of other variants, such as the miner and the city dweller, returning to the basic question: What is the Aymara face of God?

3

Arrival in This World

Birth is a key moment to determine the relationship of the new person brought into this world (and those that give the child shelter) with all of the sacred universe into which the infant comes to find a place.

BORN AS CHILDREN OF ACHACHILA

Birth merits special care. The expectant mother receives special foods, definitely without salt, perhaps as an indication of her greater exposure to the forces of nature. The helpers pray and in addition prepare a special offering for this moment, called a high Mass, which is directed to all of the ancestral beings for the mother's health. When the child has been born, several precautions are taken which emphasize the sacred nature of the event, as well as the danger: nobody should look at the door of the place where the "sick" mother lies, neither persons nor animals; the umbilical cord is cut with a piece of ceramic or glass, not with metal objects, so that the baby will not become a murderer or be murdered; the placenta, called *jakana* ("like life") is washed, so that the infant will be comely; the placenta is inspected in detail for omens about the future of the infant, adorned with flowers, and sometimes prepared as though it were an exquisite dish. Some days later it is buried in the yard or burned, and the ashes are thrown on the roof of the house.[4]

The preceding description demonstrates the profound relationship of the newborn to the ancestral and sacred forces of nature. However, it is precisely here that a dilemma arises. The child belongs to this ancestral world: When he is born, he is born of Achachila, the "grandfather" or "ancestor spirit," which is also the name of the most important mountain in the vicinity. He belongs to Achachila, and so if he should die in such a condition, he must be returned, ritually carried to the top of a mountain or at least outside the boundaries of the community, so that if anything happens, it will not harm their land. Otherwise grandfather spirits will reclaim the child by sending a hail storm. Therefore, whenever there is a bad hail storm, the communal authorities begin to investigate who has transgressed this sacred obligation. If necessary, they search from house to house until they find a woman whose breasts give evidence that she has given birth, but who is not nursing a baby. The guilty one has to reveal where the infant (or perhaps the foetus) is buried. It will be exhumed and returned with rituals to the mountain of the Achachila, to whom it belongs, in order to restore equilibrium to the community.

As long as the child stays in this situation it is *muru wawa* (a Moorish baby). If it dies like this, it is *limbu* (in limbo). Both these terms are borrowed from the Spanish, but reinterpreted to mean beings belonging to the ancestral world. Soon, with baptism, the child will enter society and the Christian world.

BECOMING A CHRISTIAN AND RECEIVING A NAME

When they have managed to get the acceptance of suitable godparents, people who can act as models for the child through the years, these godparents take the child to the church and to the priest (which may lie at a distance of many miles), in order to anoint the child with salt, oil and water, and in particular, to give the child a Christian name. The latter is likely to be that indicated by the almanac on the day of his birth. In accordance with their functions, the godparents are called *ichu tata, mama* (the father and mother who carry in their arms) and *suti tata, mama* (the father and mother who name). The tie with the child and its family becomes something sacred, the fount of many reciprocal relationships in the future.

In this way, baptism introduces the infant into the social world, and at the same time stops the all-prevailing power of the Achachila and other ancestral forces, at least balancing them with the power of God. With this the community is also protected. Thus baptism has become an essential rite of passage into the world and into society. When it is necessary, they even baptise dead foetuses in order to rescue them from Achachila. Father Monast tells of cases where godparents have traveled more than one hundred kilometres in search of baptism.[5] In emergency cases the families rouse themselves to fulfill minimum requirements; for example, they give the newborn a little bit of salt, a symbol of the social world as opposed to the natural world, and say, "Now this child is a Christian." However, the other elements, particularly the oil, which frequently accompanies the naming ceremony at baptism, are usually administered by an official minister of the church.

4

Living with the Spirit World Below and Above

The same passage into life is marked by the presence of those from both worlds: the ancestral, which is closer and more dangerous, sometimes called *manqha pacha*, the world below and within; and the other, with closer ties to the established order, under the control of what has gone before, which is usually called *alax pacha*, the world above. Those of us who live in this world (the earth) (*aka pacha*) are perpetually exposed to the forces from above and below and we must learn to live in a respectful manner with them both.[6]

The present-day rituals of entrance into life show that the colonial missionaries had a measure of success in guaranteeing baptism and in relegating the ancestral forces to the world of evil beings. Baptism, however, is only the beginning of a life full of a complex and evolving set of religious experiences, involving those below and within as much as those above, in a way that is more complementary than contradictory.

STAGES IN RESPONSIBLE PARENTHOOD

The social growth stage that follows, between three and five years of age, is the first haircut. Hair, like fingernails and perspiration, is an important and dangerous element and symbol. As a part detached from the organism itself, hair can be used as an object for harmful ends. Sorceries performed on hair affect the person. For this reason, children's hair requires special treatment. During the early years the hair is left loose, without cutting or parting it; it forms knots like that found in wool.

When the child reaches the right age, a special ceremony is prepared. Godparents, preferably people of good social standing, who may or may not be the same ones who were present for the baptism, are selected. On the appointed day, the parents invite the godparents and all their friends, offering them good food and drink. The child is placed on a table or some other prominent place and surrounded by symbols of abundance. The ritual begins by asking permission of the various protecting spirits: Achachila, Mother Earth, the spirits of the hearth, our Father God, and so on. Immediately following, all are invited to take a drink. Then the godparents and after them the others cut off a lock of hair. They place it carefully on a plate, together with a gift of money or a gift in kind. At the conclusion, the honored child is dressed in new clothes, which are a gift from the godparents, and the mother keeps the hair in a special place. All the gifts constitute the initial capital investment for the real life of the child. Thus the child leaves infancy, which is free of obligations, and enters into life as one more person to help with the routine tasks in the home, and later, in the community. In this ceremony, which marks a new step in the socialization of the child, no conflict is noticed between the Christian and the ancestral symbolic worlds.

THOSE WHO PROTECT THE HOME

As children develop the ability to reason, they discover a complex world around them, both in the home and in the fields and pasturelands. One of the first truths that children learn, under the guidance by their parents, is that their own house with the space that surrounds it is much like the sacred space of a church; it shelters the spirits that protect it. These are given the generic name of *uywiri* (caretakers) and become the guardian angels of the family.

The child learns to invoke and respect a masculine protector spirit, called Kuntur Mamani (Condor Falcon) or, among the shepherds of Puno, Mallku (Chief), and a feminine protector, sometimes called Qhiri Awicha (Grandmother of the Hearth). The former is associated more with the home.[7] The patio and the corrals are also objects of many religious practices, directed to these and other protectors. In the centre of the yard there is usually a *misa qala* (a stone altar for sacrificial offerings). Possibly there will also be a cross on the wall or on a table and a picture or an image of a saint who also protects the house. When the saint's day arrives, the picture or image is taken to the church for Mass, and later is the object of a family festival.

If shame falls upon the family, it may be because the family has not reverenced all these protector spirits adequately; therefore, they have forgotten to protect the family.

THE WHOLE LANDSCAPE IS ALIVE

One of the children's first productive tasks probably will be to accompany those who lead the flocks of sheep to pasture. On these walks throughout the communal territory they will rapidly learn the names of many spirit beings and sacred places. They will know which are the most sacred peaks, the well-known ones like Achachilas (the grandfather spirits). Furthermore, they will discover that the Awichas (the grandmother spirits) are found mostly in the steep, narrow valleys.

Children will hear talk of Mother Earth—Pacha Mama or Wirjina (Virgin). Libations are poured on the ground to her on any occasion when drink is shared and in all the rites of the agricultural cycle; she is feared, too, when they travel about in solitary pairs.

Crossing between two peaks, as they move from one landscape to another, adults will speak to the children about Apachita, who is venerated by hikers, truck drivers and by all travelers. In the mountain pass, everybody greets and makes supplication to the spirit of the place for a good journey. They rub the body with a stone to transfer their weariness to the stone and gain strength; they leave the stone on a pile of stones and throw the coca leaf that they were chewing on it. Thus, they leave one world behind to enter the new one that lies ahead; before they continue the journey, everybody exchanges greetings as though they had just met for the first time.

Places that could pass unnoticed, perhaps in the middle of a field or at the far end of a cultivated patch, are sacred for other reasons. Perhaps there is a special stone there, which is also Achachila Protector or Wak'a. Maybe lightning, the "breath" of Mother Earth, struck there, making it a privileged place in the contacts between the world above and the world below. Many types of duplicated beings may have emerged there, twins— mountains, agricultural products, animals, people—even *yatiris* (those who know, the shamans or priests of the Aymara religion), precisely because they had been touched by the lightning and had been returned to life by it.

However, the young people, who are discovering the life and sacredness of the whole landscape that surrounds them, are even more impressed when they hear that there are certain places that are very dangerous, sometimes right beside the house. Those are *phiruni* (wild and fierce spirits), because in such places there are devils of all kinds—*saxra, ñanqha, supaya, anchanchu*—or because there are remains of a very ancient people, from the time of the *chullpas* (Aymara circular tombs), who lived before the existence of the sun, or a place of the *jintila* (the gentiles), who did not become Christians. Even the wind that blows in these places can be harmful. Other spirits are dangerous for other reasons, for example, the souls of the dead who committed serious crimes and cannot rest in peace, or the *kharisiri*, a priest or another person associated with him who took the fat from his victims in order to use it later as oil in the baptismal rite.

In reality, the spirits and places described are all somewhat ambiguous.[8] They are dangerous and must be treated with due respect, receiving offerings from human beings. However, none of these spirits is completely bad. They all have great "hunger" and must be well cared for so that they do not just take what they need, inducing illnesses, deaths and natural disasters. When they are well cared for, however, they offer protection with their extraordinary gifts and grant necessary provisions. The Achachilas and Earth Mothers are the special protectors of the community. In one way or another, all can contribute to the well-being of the group. We saw this in the case of when lightning strikes. Even those who are identified as devils and evil ones have control of certain blessings, such as riches, minerals and music. In reality, the dividing line between the devil and progenitor, between menace and protector becomes increasingly more blurred the further we go into this world. The double role of each of these spirits is its most characteristic trait and gives vitality.

THE PROTECTORS AND THE SPIRITS OF PRODUCTION

The main occupation of the Aymara is small-scale cattle raising and farming, concentrating on cultivated crops or shepherding, depending on ecological conditions. The essential activities of subsistence farming are full of risks, particularly on the high plateau. A frost can defeat the efforts of many months in one night, a heavy snowfall can kill the yearlings and a prolonged drought is the cause of great concern, obligating many families to emigrate temporarily.

For these reasons, Aymara agriculture is dependent upon the smallest signs of nature in order to anticipate the future and organize farming activities: a clear or clouded sky; the changing colours of certain constellations and even the dark spots in the night sky; the behaviour of certain plants and animals, such as the time of flowering or the height of the nests around the lake; the signs and messages of the coca leaves when they fall on the *inhuña* and *awayo* (ritual cloths); the metal when it melts in the fire on the night of St. John, the coldest of the year ushering in the winter solstice. All of these are indicators of what will happen during the following agricultural cycle.

Naturally, in this mixture of worry and trust, both the ancestral and the modern methods must complement each other in the perpetual dialogue with the supernatural beings who govern the climate and the forces of nature. The Achachilas are masters of the clouds, the water, the snow and hail. Our Father who in is heaven regulates the seasons and the sun, which gives the warmth that is necessary for life. Life springs from the earth and therefore, once again, the great intermediary for production is Mother Earth. Pacha Mama is both one and many. She is present everywhere, even in the wild and dangerous areas, and she is distinguished in a very personal and particular way in each parcel of ground as *uywiri* (caretaker) of the family that cultivates it. She can also be personified in an image of the Virgin in the local chapel.

Together with Pacha Mama are all the generative spirits attached to the various animals and crops. They are the ones who, when they are called upon and tended with affection at the high points of the annual agricultural cycle, ensure abundant fertility of both animals and plants, and also in money and among people. These spirits, whom the Peruvian writer Jose Maria Arguedas defined as "germinating archetypes" of each species, receive many different names according to the produce and the location.

One of the names most frequently used is Illa or Mama Illa, referring to the multiplying spirit of the cattle and livestock. Her name possibly is related to *illapa*, meaning lightning, which has the power to duplicate spirits, and to the names of some of the most majestic snowcaps of the high plateau, like Illimani and Illampu, sources of lightning and rain. Illa are not spirits of the cattle exclusively; they are also for other benefits which make life in the home possible, such as clothes, money and agricultural produce.

One of the names that appears frequently when referring to the spirit of agricultural production is Mama Ispalla. This applies especially in connection with the potato, and by extension, to that which is produced on the same ground in the following years of the crop rotation cycle.

In reality, the Aymara see in every agricultural product and in every animal a living and venerable being, with whom they carry on conversations, whom they adorn, to whom they offer coca leaves and drink for their use and whom they reverently kiss. On ritual occasions, connected with the spirit of production, each species of animal and plant has its own name: The potato is Mama Jatha, "Mother Seed, the germinator," or Imill T'alla, "girl, wife of the communal chief." The barley is Phisqa Qunqur Tutu, "the grain with five knees" or Waranq Ispilan Mallku, "the chief with a thousand ears (as in ears of corn)." The sheep is Niña Luisa or Kumpitisa (sweets). The llama is Tata or Mama Sulla, "Mr. and Mrs. Morning Dew."

As with the Pacha Mama becoming the image of the Virgin, Ispallas, Illas and other spirits take on concrete form in certain objects, such as a potato of exceptional size and shape, brightly coloured stones, even elaborate amulets carved into the shape of animals, a hand that weaves, a couple making love, a house full of all kinds of possessions, and so on.[9] All these help the Aymara to remember the perpetual presence and action of these spirits of agricultural production, just as the images remind them of the saints.

THE AGRICULTURAL AND THE CEREMONIAL YEAR[10]

Production has to deal not only with places, spirits and seeds full of life, but also it is a process in time. Thus, there is a close tie between the agricultural cycles and the annual ceremonial cycle. Each day and each period has its message and demands certain religious ritual practices.

The Aymara new year does not begin in January but in August, when the preceding agricultural year has reached its climax and the most pressing preparations for the coming year are under way. They say that at the beginning of August the ground opens and the devils hand over their treasures. It is a windy month during which the spirits walk free, a month when the new *yatiris* (shamanlike priests) are initiated in the communities. The first days of the month offer signs of what will happen throughout the new agricultural cycle. In this month they make special offerings upon the most sacred mountains "in order to leave all the evil of the community there and ask for pardon so as to receive the good."[11]

Another high point is in the month of November when the first rains begin and with them the great annual plantings. With All Saints' Day—the day of the dead, the festival of life[12]—the most dangerous and, at the same time, the most laborious and productive period of the year commences. During this time they maintain much more contact with the powerful generative beings of the earth. They observe fasts, present offerings and perform other celebrations related to fertility. There is music appropriate to this season. This stage comes to a climax at Carnaval, sometimes called the middle of the year before Lent, or in other places, immediately before Easter.

Then the other part of the year begins, much happier and more festive, characterized by its own music. During this time important celebrations take place, such as the harvest festival at Pentecost, various festivals for the animals (such as the feast of St. John at the end of the lambing season), and above all, the patronal festivals in each community. These are concentrated largely in the dry season, when they rejoice over the fruits of the harvest. A good celebration of the festival to the patron saint of each village brings the strong support of this protector spirit, providing good production in the immediate future.

Other saints in the Christian calendar are introduced into this same frame of reference. Tata San Andres (St. Andrew), for example, is commemorated at the end of November and sometimes is identified with the devil; he has power over the rains, which are so necessary at this time of year. Mama Candelaria, the second of February, is connected with the growth of the plants. The days in the almanac that are dedicated to a saint who was a pope are good days for working with the produce by the same name (*pope* and *potato* are the same word in Spanish). On the other hand, the days of martyred saints are not good days to work in the fields. The festival of Corpus Christi—the Most Holy or Nostramo—is related to Father Sun in a season close to the winter solstice. There are many other examples as well.

GOD, CHRIST AND THE SAINTS

In the celebrations dedicated to saints, as well as in many others that are for the most part dedicated to the indigenous pantheon, the Aymara make reference and address their prayers to someone who is less visualized when they invoke Tatitu or Tatala, meaning Lord (with diminutives that convey affection and supplication), Suma Awki, good Father, and Tiyusa, God (that is, the God of the Spanish). There are many more references to the supreme God of the Christians incorporated in the Andean world. They associate the supreme God not with this near and earthly world, but with *alax pacha*, the world above, to which the sun, the moon, the stars, and some of the saints also belong. Father God is providential and in some way is superior to all the other protecting spirits. There is, in addition, a myth with precolonial roots that is very commonly accepted, according to which God attended a festival dressed as a beggar. The people did not recognize or pay any attention to the Beggar God, thus bringing about the destruction of the place. Many ruins of abandoned villages are explained this way.

Around the regions of Oruro and Potosi, the people often identify this good God with the sun, whose mate is Holy Mother Moon. The llama shepherds from K'uta (Oruro) tell the following myth of origin, which sets the world above, the conqueror, against the world below:

It is said that Tatala and the evil spirits residing in and around *chullpas* are enemies. The evil spirits managed to capture Tatal, an old man who was a stranger, and at last killed him, because they were very much at odds. They buried him and placed thorns on top of the grave. They watched for a while, then finally went away. Later they discovered that he had escaped. They grabbed him again and buried him a second time. This time they placed a huge stone on top. They watched and watched. But when at last they went away, Tatala escaped once again. They went back to hunting him down. On the road the evil spirits asked other people if they had seen an old man running away. These people showed them the ashes of a bonfire which seemed older than it really was. So the evil spirits thought that their enemy had already gone a great distance and they were frightened. They thought that if he could escape in this way, he could conquer them. So they rapidly began to build good, solid houses with doors facing east to protect themselves from the heat and light of the fire of Tatala, who has been changed into the sun, which comes up over the firmament from the east and murdered the evil spirits in their own homes, scorched by the heat. Today we can still see the ruins of the *chullpas* and the sun, Tata Awatiri (Lord Shepherd of the flocks), who continues to travel in the heavens. Some evil spirits managed to escape by getting into the centre of Lake Poopo, and they live there yet today. They are the urus, the chipayas and the muratos.[13]

Similar myths about the end of the era of the *chullpas* with the arrival of the sun are still told in the Aymara world. In many areas, however, especially the north near Lake Titicaca, there are only a few indirect traces of this God-sun relationship; for example, the care that is taken when addressing this deity in certain prayers and supplications as Suma Awki, identifying him as God.

The explicit references to the person of Jesus Christ, though present, are much scarcer. Christian prayers, such as the Our Father and the creed usually form part of the Aymara prayers, even in many rites that are directed to the ancestral spirits. The same thing happens with the sign of the cross, always present in the rituals, in the homes, chapels and the shrines in the mountains. Even when one piles up the coca leaf for the first time, he makes the sign of the cross first. Few people, however, are aware of the historical person of Jesus Christ, except for those who have recently been exposed to some study of the Bible through their relationship with priests or pastors. The commemoration of Jesus' birth at Christmas, which is so central in the religious life of the cities to which the rural Aymara constantly travel, passes almost unnoticed in the countryside. Holy Week is the time of year for the major celebrations that are explicitly related to the mystery of death and resurrection. Even then it is more frequently a generic reference to the death of God, in a way that can be reinterpreted cosmically, like the preceding myth.

When the name of Christ is invoked along with other saints and the ancestral gods, or when Jesus is represented or celebrated in the churches in some of his many attributes in a manner similar to devotions directed to the rest of the saints, he is often perceived as just one more or several more within this vast pantheon by which the Aymara approach their deepest roots that impart meaning to life. As Jorda (1981, 333ff.) summarizes, the idea of a cosmic Christ is prevalent, much as in other times and places in the primitive church.[14]

Many who as a result of biblical catechesis have a good understanding of God the Father and of Jesus Christ still often revert, with reverence, to other tutelary spirits. For example, not long ago a devout Aymara woman, a prominent member of a Methodist church, told us:

> I believe that God is one, that it was Jesus Christ who died and rose again for us, because he had defended the poor. I believe in this one and only God, and I also venerate my Mother Earth, asking her for her blessing. The truth is that God exists and that in this world the Achachilas, our protectors, exist too.[15]

5

The Mature Person

Community Is Sacred

The growth of the person also means increasing involvement in the surrounding world. This begins with the family and later moves to the community, society and, as we have already emphasized here, communion with that great cosmic collectivity that lives below and above. This process of incorporation, both sacral and social, commences with birth and baptism, when the person acquires a name and some new "naming parents," and reaches its fullness with marriage, by which he or she passes from the state of the young to that of personhood (*jaqi*), reaching fullness in becoming a married couple, and takes on communal obligations.

Such an important change implies a long ritual process, often observed several years.[16] The climax is not marriage, per se, but the permanent establishment of a new home. This happens when the person completes the construction of his own dwelling place—the roofing done ceremonially and by the parents of the new couple in competition—and with the birth and ritual incorporation of the first child, who often has the same godparents as those who fulfilled this same role for the marriage.

When a new couple through the process of marriage become *jaqi* (persons), it is as though they are reborn. For this reason they need new parents—the godparents, called "great father" and "great mother"—who must accompany and help their adopted children in everything during the celebration. They take them to church, as though they were to be baptised again; they offer them a special drink, which they call *puqi* or colostrum or first milk; they teach them to dance; they even have to accompany them when their adopted children need to leave the celebration to answer the call of nature.

The community, in turn, accepts the new couple, ensuring that they have access to the parcels of land—the virgin mother, holy earth—that they need.[17] In a reciprocal relationship, the new couple enter into their long *thakhi* (road) of growing obligations to the community, which they will perform as a sacred duty. This has to do with social responsibilities which range from small things, such as supporting the school or the socioritual control of the planted fields,[18] to bigger ones, such as taking their turn as the principal community authority who "tends as a shepherd" the community or being the sponsor for the most important patronal festival.

The characteristic seal of each responsibility ought to be generosity and service towards the rest of the people in the community during the year of commitment. More than a source of power, a responsibility is for the Aymara an economic responsibility in money and time. In some places they go so far as to call the one who is responsible *juchani*, the one who bears the sin, perhaps because with his dedication and temporary impoverishment in order to fulfil his duties in communal celebrations, he assumes the role of scapegoat and, in so doing, ensures blessings for the whole community. In order to fulfil the responsibility the diverse community leaders must develop a myriad of reciprocal ties with his family members, *compadres* and friends, among whom help is given and returned for a previous favour. In this way the reciprocal net and communal solidarity continually grow stronger.

The final result is that the community, and in particular the family of the leader, receive a blessing both when they have fulfilled their important annual responsibility and especially at the end of the long "road." This blessing is symbolized in many areas by covering those retiring from office with breads and fruits; they dance on and on covered with abundance. When they have finished the last stage, they enter into the group of the former leaders. These are the most respected people in the community, because they have given of their time and their savings to bring blessings on everyone, so that everyone can celebrate—eating and drinking well in the festive occasions when communal life is shared most. It is in this same spirit that those who follow them in taking on the responsibilities always invite the elders first as a sign of respect. Further, when important decisions are to be made, the communal assembly, presided over by its authorities who are exercising the year of responsibility, does not make a decision without taking into account the opinion of the most prominent elders.

We shall underline two religious experiences which are part of this whole process of maturation in the life of the community: the sacred character of the service authority and the festival.

To fulfil a term of service as an authority is not just a reciprocal response to the generosity that the community has demonstrated towards the couple. It implies a special relationship with all of the spirits that protect or threaten communal life. Especially in the southern region of the plateau, one of the main symbols of communal authority is the *vara*, a rod of office inlaid with silver.[19] This rod is full of religious significance. Depending on the area, it is called "three kings," "holy father Rome," or "Nostramo," Spanish Christian names that simultaneously indicate authority and close ties with the ordered world above. The last title is used in connection with God, the Blessed Sacrament, or the sun. There are masculine and feminine rods. They can come to represent a whole lineage, are objects of ritual and special libations, are taken to Mass and at times are kept in a privileged place in the home like the image of a saint. In short, to become an authority is not an ambitious undertaking, but rather an obligation, difficult but sacred, which the people take in turns and from which one retires with blessing, both for the retiree and for the community.

Nor is the festival simply a diversion, but an occasion when religious experience, which has an important festive dimension, becomes a major communal effort. Besides the importance of the festivals, so that each "person-couple" continues to advance on the "road," there are many collective experiences during the festivities: the back-and-forth invitations between the officials and the people of the community, always sprinkled with libations to the tutelary spirits; the enduring ties of reciprocity that it all implies; the musical ensembles and dances that accompany each festival sponsor, which, with the mix of orchestras and dance routines plus the abundant food and drink, create an atmosphere of massive euphoria. Everything contributes to this personal and collective experience, which is predominantly religious in nature.

Unlimited amounts of drink and alcoholic consumption even have a religious dimension. In contrast to the countries in the First World, there are no alcoholics among the Aymara. The people drink basically in the context of important social and ritual events. Furthermore, they drink only when invited to do so. Therefore, to arrive at a state of inebriation is what is expected, for it is an indication of the generosity of the host and the appreciation of the guest; according to some, the loss of control is in itself a measure of the degree to which one hands over control of the body to the supernatural beings that are involved in every aspect of the festival (Abercrombie 1986). The one in charge, the sponsor, "ought to give with all his heart" food and drink so that the others will be satisfied but he himself must remain sober in spite of his participation in the invitations, because this time he is the host.

Limiting ourselves to the patronal festivals, the religious heart of the celebration is usually the saint who presides in the local church. Normally this saint is associated with the world above, even more so if the celebrations are graced with the presence of the priest[20] to celebrate Mass with the host and the wine, to walk in a procession with the saint and to perform baptisms, weddings, and all kind of blessings.

The connection of the patron saint with the world above is not always so clear. We have already indicated the association of many female saints or Mamitas with the Pacha Mama. Neither is it unusual for the image of the saint to be simply a stone; sometimes it is not even painted. Perhaps they attribute to the saint some miracle or power connected to either of the two worlds. The good or bad celebration of the patronal festival is reflected in a good or bad climate for the following agricultural cycle. It is often the case that the same church that gives shelter to the saints from above has other kinds of symbolism; the tower is male and is associated with the mountains, ancestral grandparents; the patio, on the other hand, is female and is associated with Mother Earth. In several areas, from one extreme to the other of the territorial landscape, they perform a rite in which seeds or other products are thrown from this male tower as though to make the patio-earth fertile.[21]

Occasionally the collective religious experience of the festivals goes beyond community boundaries. In the recent past, the communities that were part of the same mestizo town often met one another ritually in the town for an "Indian" religious festival (Indians, in contrast to that of the dominant town). However, exploitation by the townspeople has led to a decline of such celebrations since the agrarian reforms of 1950-1970. In other regions, such as the northern area of Potosí, where an important annual interchange between the high plateau and the valleys persists, the collective pilgrimages to certain shrines, such as those referred to as "twelve miracles," are regular events. In several of these intercommunal celebrations they carry out the *tinku*, a ritual battle between two communities or regions that are symbolically in opposition; this gives the gathering a dialectical idea of a paired set, conveying the idea of unity through the conflict.

6

Overcoming Crises

Throughout life unforeseen crises do occur, large and small, such as sickness, a terrible crime in the community, a flood, a landslide or a war. In these situations, when faced with the great difficulty of finding ordinary solutions, the need to seek help from all the available means within the supernatural world grows. Help is sought from those who are better acquainted with this area and exercise more influence in it, including the distant *yatiris* with special powers, such as the *ch'amakani*, master of darkness, who is able to communicate with the spirits of the dead and the mountain ancestors. Likewise they ask for the priest's blessing, for his special influence with the world above so that by his rituals and his holy water he can counterbalance the power that the devils have unleashed.

THE RESTORATION OF COMMUNAL EQUILIBRIUM

All means are considered to find the most efficient manner to restore the equilibrium which has been lost. The cause of the problem must be investigated; possibly there was a serious crime or perhaps the people have not adequately fulfilled their obligations to the superior beings. More than anything, they must find the manner in which they can compensate for the damage that has been done.

For them, a key concept is *kuti* (a return to the point of departure). It is used, for example, to call upon the spirit that has abandoned someone; when dealing with sickness, it can consist in stirring up the evil and transferring it to some animal. This concept is present in some form on many occasions: in many rites in which something is done "in reverse" (weave threads with the left hand, put one's clothes on back to front, etc.); when it is necessary to return a favour or an insult by means of the principle of reciprocity, which rules daily life as well as the relations with the supernatural world in extreme cases.

With or without the need to restore the balance which has been lost, one of the most significant offerings for serious situations is the sacrifice of animals, called *wilancha* (*wila* means "blood"). This is not something exclusively reserved for a crisis; it can occur in the normal course of events in the annual cycle, particularly in the pastoral regions where many pairs of male llamas are sacrificed in a single ceremony, both to the divinities above and to those below.[22] In other areas also, *wilancha* is the ideal offering in moments of serious crisis and other extraordinary occasions, such as the construction of a building or road that could disturb Mother Earth and the beings who live in the place in question.

The animal or animals that are chosen for the sacrifice are treated with much affection. The people adorn them with grooming preparations and streamers; they give them cocaine and alcohol until they are drunk; they speak to them, begging for pardon and making supplications relative to the occasion. Simultaneously they pour out libations and offer prayers to all the gods. Then comes the time to slit the animal's throat. All the blood is collected immediately by the participants in special containers, and with it they *ch'allan* (sprinkle) everything they want to bless: the cattle, the planted fields, the walls and foundations of a new building, even, at times, those in attendance. The bones and some selected organs, particularly the heart, preferably while it is still beating, are reserved as offerings to the spirits addressed in the invocations. The bones are burned in a ceremonial fire and the rest are buried. The conclusion of the ceremony is marked by a communal feast, in which everybody shares the roasted meat from the sacrificed animals, carrying any leftovers to their homes.

Extremely grave situations can occur when the sacrifice demanded is more than an animal victim. Two different situations can precipitate such action: an extremely serious crime or an occasion when the danger from the spirits below is extraordinarily threatening. In either of these cases, the demand for the restoration of equilibrium can go so far as to require a human sacrifice.

Examples of crimes that can bring the community to such an extreme solution can be the systematic theft of cattle, which causes the community to lose the security of its economic base; or sacrilegious theft or incestuous relationships between *compadres*, which put at risk the moral and social base of the community, and, in addition, can bring disastrous climactic conditions. When crimes such as these become an insufferable threat, they demand, as the sole solution for restoring the balance, the expulsion of the guilty ones from the community. However, there is an alternative solution, sometimes preferred by the transgressors: they may remain in their community, but only as a sort of participant like those in the mysterious world of the dead, who, in a way, continue to participate in the life of the community.[23]

A second reason for reestablishing equilibrium arises when the spirits from the inner world within demand more than the usual compensation. Although I have never had direct evidence of human sacrifices, references to them as a last resort to obtain a desired result are frequent. Whether these occur or not in the real world, the important thing is that in the universe of religious experiences this possibility is not excluded. The most cited cases are to bring an end to accidents that have already cost many lives—the Achachila's appetite is too great—for example, in especially difficult constructions (bridges over rivers with constant landslides, large churches or skyscrapers) or in the dangerous tunnels of the mines. The chosen victim is to be an asocial person, such as some habitually drunk person without family or someone insane. Like all sacrificial victims, the person must be treated with special affection, given abundant food and drink, until the moment when—already unconscious and before just a few witnesses—he is buried to commit him to the inner world. Then, surely, the balance will be restored and the spirits below will stop threatening and once again return to being those who do good.

In a more implicit way the possibility of offering human blood is always present in the ritual fights, *tinku*, or other kinds of conflicts against another group which may precipitate a violent death. It is understood that should someone happen to die in a *tinku*, there will be a good harvest in the coming year. If the victims are enemies in another form of combat, it may be that they are objects of special rites. For example, in one revolt against an abusive landowner in 1927, he was not simply executed but sacrificed on the top of a sacred mountain, which was at that time the border between the *ayllus* that reclaimed his lands.[24]

THE STRUGGLE FOR THE FREEDOM OF THE PEOPLE

The Aymara idea of freedom is both broader and narrower than that of a social and political struggle against the oppressors of this people. For a simple villager, who lives on his plot of land, the big problems that he must overcome each day are threats to his health and his survival in a precaroius environment that is none too easy. In this sense the activities and ritual celebrations, such as those discussed thus far, effectively fulfil a liberating role in that they encourage communal spirit, solidarity and help the Aymara peasant to accommodate himself better in the natural and social surroundings in which he carries on his daily existence.

This does not mean that the Aymara are not aware that they suffer social and political oppression. As we indicated at the beginning of this work, since the colonial period they have felt "oppressed but not conquered." In a society which clearly marginalizes and exploits them, they search for a thousand ways in which they can continue being themselves, sometimes combining dependence and resistance, or being cunningly silent. In their stories, their songs and dances, many of which are associated with religious contexts, they find subtle ways to laugh at the oppressor: the rabbit and the weak partridge always trick the fox who wants to eat them; the dance, *awki awki*, or the modernized version of *doctocitos* ridicule the Spanish and the white authorities; and many other examples.

The Aymara are constantly expressing their awareness of feeling exploited as a class and as a nation through the concept of *q'ara* in their references to the dominant group. *Q'ara* is the opposite of *jaqi*, a person who has reached maturity and acts in a responsible way within the community. In contrast, *q'ara* (literally, "the bald one") means one who does not even fulfil the minimum requirements of social convention (reciprocal work), which are so important if one wants to behave as a human being. They are called "bald ones," because they do not have anything except the fruit of their own labour. The term is applied principally to whites who exploit the Indians and mestizos in the towns and cities; however, an Aymara who has abandoned the community and assumed the same type of activity also is seen as *q'ara*. For the *q'ara* there were no reciprocal relationships. In contradistinction to what occurs in relation to the Pacha Mama, with whom the *q'ara* are not in a reciprocal relationship, at best, the Aymara just put up with these who have strayed and hope for better times (Albó 1985b).

From time to time, however, moments arrive when they cannot endure any longer and nothing remains except to confront the oppressors. Historically, one of the most frequent causes is the defense of the communal land, whose sacred character we now understand better. There are many other motives: excessive taxes, high prices, opposition from those in power to a rural school, etc. Traditionally, these struggles have had strong religious references, with similar arrangements to those mentioned in connection with serious crises. On such occasions offerings are presented to the ancestral beings to guarantee that they will support those who belong to the community, the *jaqi* as opposed to the *q'ara*.

A short while ago a leader, a *yatiri* from the northern area of Potosi, gave us the following explanation with regard to the sacrifices that are performed on behalf of the struggles of the *ayllus* to defend their territory and their school against the *q'aras*:

> We sacrifice a llama on the mountain peak so that the Urqu or Achachila are fed on the offering that has been prepared for them, meat, bones, wine, incense and copal. In the sacrifice the blood is very important. It is necessary to scatter the llama's blood around; it serves as a kind of shield. So that they will enter into the fight

with their whole heart, they put the heart of the llama into the offering. With this, then, Pacha Mama and the Urqu take action and impart the strength for the battle. We, who live in the northern area of Potosi, always offer llamas when we make a sacrifice. Therefore, we continue to be strong and we are still the masters of the land.

They took me prisoner because I wanted to erect a school. They threatened me with a gun saying, "We must kill this communist chief. Such an act is not sin." I said to them, "All right, kill me. Cut me up piece by piece. This accursed body will be dying, but the spirit will not die because Pacha Mama and Urqu will save me."

For the same cause they arrested and killed Apolinar Qalani. The *q'ara* drank his blood in order to ruin the community. When the blood of a brother killed in the struggle spills on to the earth, it is of great benefit for the whole community. But if the *q'ara* drink it, it is disgrace. When they drink our blood, we feel robbed of strength and fearful; the courage for the fight is ruined. However, this blood can be recovered; if we sacrifice a llama it can make *kuti*. The blood of the llama is poured on the place saying to Pacha Mama and Urqu, "I am not going to remain in the grave. Give me back my strength. Give me back my spirit. You know me." The body is not resurrected but the community is. It will rise with incredible strength. And something will happen to the person who drank the blood, no matter where he is. Pacha Mama, who is incomparable in this world, will drink his blood.[25]

This story reflects a kind of experience that, according to several sources,[26] has been very much part of the Aymara struggles and rebellions almost continually since the colonial period.

In recent decades a certain change has been operative. Especially since the agrarian reforms (1953, 1969) and the proliferation of the so-called rural unions, which are related to the government and political parties who are not always aware of the mobilizing force that is found in the religious arena, there has been more of a secularization in the way the rural struggles are articulated. In huge blockades, land take-overs, congresses and other actions taken in search of justice, the discussion now is more secular in nature.

We ought not, however, to interpret these actions only from their public appearance. When they are analyzed more carefully and from a local perspective, a certain continuity with the past surfaces. Before one of the land take-overs, for example, it was widely known that the authorities had previously visited a *yatiri* so that he could confirm whether the decision was wise and to guarantee them the support of the tutelary spirits to ensure a positive outcome and also to prevent unnecessary deaths. As one Aymara told us, "This is not printed in the papers." The following testimony from a young leader, born near La Paz, points in the same direction:

> When I was ten years old, my grandfather, who was an authority and a *yatiri*, interpreted the coca leaves and told me, "You will be a shepherd of the flock[27]; you will be a guide to the community, to the people. You will suffer much and be persecuted. Therefore, you must invoke the Achachilas, your deceased grandfather spirits, and Pacha Mama." At first I did not believe him. During my education, I came under the influence of priests and pastors who preached that God would save us and heal us. But my grandfather's words of advice kept coming back to me. Later I committed myself to the union and have become a young leader in the Rural Confederation. As Aymaras, we leaders visit the *yatiris* to make offerings to the Achachilas, asking for their blessing on our mission of leadership and for their protection in the difficult moments of the struggle. Then the *yatiris* assure us that the grandfather Achachilas will protect us from all ill. The prophesy about the persecutions was true, and I am aware of their protection because I have been saved from death on many occasions.[28]

The religious experience in the struggle on behalf of the people is not always linked to the ancestral world. We know of several other cases of Catholic catechists and Protestant pastors, perhaps separate from the Andean symbolic universe because of the kind of evangelisation to which they have been exposed, but who nonetheless have managed to develop a strong sense of solidarity with their people. At times they have been among the most stalwart defenders and organizers in the community when facing the aggression of the powerful factors within their governments. During the reign of General Garcia-Meza's dictatorship in Bolivia (1980-1982), we have seen instances when catechists and deacons were tortured and even killed without denouncing anyone among their people.

7

The Supreme Experience of Death[29]

We have thus arrived at the final stage of the journey in the Aymara religious experience: death. Like birth, it is a liminal moment. As such it is particularly exposed to the action of supernatural forces who have so much influence on humans, but, because it is the end of human life, the religious intensity of this moment is much greater than in the case of one's arrival to life.

A primary verification of this is that, unlike the usual attitudes in the dominant society, the Aymara do not feel any fear when confronting the idea of death. They accept it, not in a fatalistic way, but as a natural course of events, as one more stage on the road of life. Death is not the end, but the beginning of a new stage. Perhaps behind this calm exterior is found security in the thought that there are ways by which, with the help of the community, their situation in the world of the dead can be peaceful for them and even beneficial for those who continue to live on after they have gone.

However, this change from a living being to a soul, to death, is much more serious and complex than the previous changes, such as the change from being a *moro* (pagan) to Christian or from child to *jaqi*, a married person and a full member of the community. If this latter step implies a long matrimonial process, how much greater will be the ritual process required for the *jaqi* to pass into being a soul, and subsequently with the passage of years even an Achachila, without creating continual danger for the living.[30]

In addition to the grief and the sympathy shown when someone close dies, particularly if the person was loved and respected, this event inevitably confronts those present with life beyond the grave, the existence of which is not in doubt. How can we face this reality? It is necessary, first, to have a clear line of demarcation between the newly dead and those still living; second, to dedicate carefully all the necessary rituals to the dead to guarantee his or her gratitude and future well-being, thus showing that the person has become a potential danger to the living; third, to look for the indications and signs about who will be the next to die. The first two are more important to our central theme.

The need to mark the difference between the dead and the living is seen in a number of details. For most of the care that the dead need after death until burial, they look to those who are not relatives, because those closest to the deceased run the most risk of danger. When they return from the cemetery, if there is one,[31] the people take an alternate route from that taken on the way out. In some places they put thorns on the road to prevent the soul from coming back, and they shake out the clothing so that no part of the spirit of the dead person can remain there. In the north of Potosi the cemeteries are in distant spots, preferably on the mountains, and the funeral procession goes as fast as possible, as though the people want to rid themselves of the dangerous corpse as fast as possible. During the days that follow, several other rites of purification are performed to guarantee that there are no remaining parts of the spirit of the dead in the house. They erase the footsteps and clean out all the holes, which some call tombs, in the house where the person died. They wash the person's clothing, so that no part of the living spirit remains through perspiration in the clothes, burning those items which were worn the most. In northern Chile they even strangle a dog that belonged to the person. If the deceased's clothing is still of use, they fabricate a story so that some traveling merchants will buy it.

The motives behind all this behaviour is that the dead person is very dangerous, because he or she is one of theirs who now belongs to the lower world. Perhaps it is not just chance that they mark the grave with rosemary; both belong to the world of the Achachila.

At the same time this danger explains the second concern, to dedicate to the newly deceased all the ritual care necessary to satisfy the person. If they do not succeed, he or she will wander around as a soul bothering the living until they do. For that reason they make every effort to do all that needs to be done. These rites include a Mass said on the eighth day (if a priest is available) and attention given to the soul during the three years following death on the first days of each November, when they prepare food to serve to the dead. The important role given to the world of souls is also significant, that is, along with all of their predecessors, particularly from those who belong to the same community, in making present life possible. In several places, during the time of the dead the community selects two skulls as symbols of the deceased, places them in a prominent location and then venerates them in a special way.

What will happen to the dead in the future? There is no clear-cut answer to this question. They talk of heaven and hell, but they also say that the dead go towards the west, to the side where the sun disappears, where with the help of a dog they cross a lake to reach their world. The belief that eventually the dead who are attended properly become protecting beings for the living is equally deeply rooted.

Some of the older ones who are more respected become Achachilas in the course of time. Several prominent mountains of the high plateau bear the names of ancient persons whose stories are still told today. One of the most famous is that of Tata Sabaya, in the high plateau of Oruro in northern Chile. Present-day tradition even marks the place of his old dwelling. They tell of his adventures as an authority, his conflicts with the priest, how and when he died, the way the various parts of his body gave rise to the main towns and *ayllus* in the region, and how, later, he was changed into a volcano and had fights with the other mountains.

The return of the dead is only partially limited to the first two days of November. In some way the dead are continually present during the entire rainy season until Carnaval (or sometimes, even until Easter). In several areas they formally speak of the Achachila's Carnaval and visit the cemetery again as they do on All Saints' Day. After all, the dead have everything to do with the growing season.

Furthermore, the dead are the seeds of the future for the whole oppressed Andean society. The mythical Tata Sabaya is not the only one who planted new towns and *ayllus* when he died. Another widely known myth tells of the Inca king (Inkari)—who now has become a great symbol for the entire Andean population—putting his body back together from the pieces scattered about several places below the earth.

Tupaq Katari, the great anticolonial leader in 1780, who is today a main symbol of the constant resistance of the Aymara people, was also executed and his body quartered. By order of the Spanish, the principal parts of his mutilated body were sent to separate places in order to perpetuate the ignominy and lesson of his punishment. However, to this day the popularity of his memory and the hope it inspires provide another interpretation to his martyrdom. In all areas, in the revindicating actions of the Aymara people, his last words are repeated—whether historically accurate or not, "I shall return as a million more of my people." This hope is rooted in the conviction that death is not just the end of an individual life, but also that the world of the dead and the Achachilas contains the seeds of the future. When this era comes to an end, a change will occur for which the driving force will come from the world of the dead.

Scholars of precolonial Andean religion reveal that many beings now considered to be evil devils were identified with the dead before the advent of Christian preaching.[32] This identification has not been completely erased. The idea, however, that the devils are not so bad is still alive. The best expression of this is found, perhaps, in Oruro at Carnaval, when the whole town is filled with thousands of devils dancing, lively and happy. It represents a kind of symbolic freedom from the Conquest (see chapter

8) and a hope that this present world, which is chaotic and unbalanced, will some day turn right side up and a new *kuti* or *pacha kuti*—that which is presently below (oppressed) and within (hidden)—will return to the top in an obvious way, "made into millions" (whereby the present millions of Andean peoples will enjoy the fruits of their past glory).

This seems to be the symbolic sense of the design of a weaving[33] secretly called *jiwiri* (the one who dies). He descends to the world below in order to be changed into new life in the future, so that between this life and the life to come there is a continual parallelism and counterpoint.

8

Other Trends and Experiences

It is impossible to speak of uniformity with regard to the Aymara religious experience today. In the preceding pages we have emphasized the possibility of an internally coherent Aymara theology as seen from the experiences of the traditional community. However, even to achieve this goal we have had to put elements of it together that today, after so many centuries of being stepped on, are sometimes scattered about in several places. At the same time we have oversimplified what in each place is a much richer and more complex interior universe. This chapter gives an overview of the variety that exists, particularly emphasizing diverse effects on present society, in different areas of the Aymara world.

Without leaving the rural areas, we can find a great variety of interpretations. In some cases we are only dealing with different ways of organising the traditional universe. Other differences are more basic, owing to the growing social diversification within the area and to the new ideological influences, religious and secular, coming from the dominant society. We shall say something about each one of these sources of diversity.

ALTERNATIVE EXEGESES

The idea that has guided the preceding pages has been a balanced inquiry into the upper world, which is more ordered and distant, and into the lower world and within this lower world, which is more dangerous, nearer and more creative. This present world (*aka pacha*) is primarily one of living beings, who have to learn to live with both worlds. This is the conclusion that has been reached by a number of scholars who have worked in the more remote regions respectful of the Aymara religious universe.[34] However, in other areas that have come under the influence of Catholic catechists for a long time, the Aymara have gradually made more of a correlation between these worlds and heaven as the realm of the good, the evil place and the visible world. For example, in reference to the Puno region where there was intense indoctrination carried out by the Jesuits and others, Victor Ochoa says:

The Aymara person . . . sees three worlds, which have their own order and are related to, or involved with the person in the real world. These three worlds are: *alax pacha* (heaven), *aka pacha* (earth or this world), and *manqha pacha* (hell). Each one of these three has celestial supernatural beings or evil spirits. In heaven are God the Father, who rules the whole universe, the angels, the saints, the sinless and the saved souls, and the rest of the celestial beings. In this world (earth) are the Achachilas (grandparents), Wirjina (Mother Earth as a protector goddess), the *uywiri* (those who protect the home or homes) and other spirits. In hell are *supaya* (demons or devils), *antawalla* (evil spirits who walk with fire), *sajjra* (an evil spirit who walks with the winds), and other spirits.

Ochoa adds:

All these worlds are very involved with human beings. When the people realise this reality, they have to offer certain rites and sacrifices to appease God and the gods, without specifying which, to demonstrate their true affection.[35]

The *yatiris* themselves do not seem to agree on this issue. Ochoa bases his observations on a *yatiri* from Zepita, who is a relative of his. However, in the same region around Lake Titicaca, another *yatiri* from Chucuito told me that the devils are of *this* world. A third from Tiwanaku laid emphasis for us on the greatest prominence of Our Father the Sun and Mother Moon in the world above; for him evil was in the world below—theft, lying, adultery, anything that makes the people cry—but immediately he clarified that it is not such a bad world; it is just a question of how to deal with it.[36]

These examples show that there can be many variations not only from one region to another, but also in personal interpretation. Indirectly this indicates that the general systematization is not as important as the experience of life. Activities are influenced by many beings and to all of them we owe attention and respect.

NEW SOCIAL POSITION, NEW RELIGIOUS EXPERIENCES

In recent decades the growing impact of a hegemonic society over the Aymara has resulted in the emergence of a greater social differentiation in the rural sector. Particularly in the towns, but sometimes even within the same community, there are groups that are richer, involved in transportation and commerce; in addition, there are residents from the community who are now in the city and considered more civilized. Many of the latter group have become mestizos (*q'aras*), from the point of view of the poor majority in the communities, but have nonetheless not abandoned the symbolic Aymara universe.

In the past, this differentiation within the religious matrix was confined to a polarisation of town and rural community. There are towns in which this contrast led to visible expression in the existence of two churches with two plazas, one for the neighbouring mestizos and the other for the Indians. In some of these they even celebrate at different festivals catering to the two social groups, and in each one symbolic elements are present to stress the subordination of the Indian (*jaqi*) to the mestizo (*q'ara*).[37]

Since the agrarian reforms, the emergence of the rural peoples and the strengthening of their negotiating organisations have weakened the traditional power structure of many towns and have brought about the downfall of this type of ritual reenforcement of the structure. However, at the same time something similar has started to spring up within the heart of the community, such as in the distinct behaviour of the leaders, who now are not simple farmers but businessmen or community members who live in the city. These people have a tendency to impose spending levels and certain lifestyles to which other community members cannot aspire. In this way, in their own place of origin, they underline their newly acquired status, which the still-hostile city does not want to acknowledge.

Community members who climb the social ladder maintain, from their perspective, some ties with their place of origin. They accept the honour of being godparents for other community dwellers, who will later grant them favours or perhaps, in exchange, their godchildren will farm their semi-abandoned fields or offer them produce at reduced prices. The patronal festival in the community continues to be seen as a pilgrimage that generates a great deal of activity for months preceding the festival date. It can also be the occasion on which, out of "devotion," they present gifts or even works to the community. The relationship with the rest of the community, however, gradually becomes more one-sided, as in the old towns. The more powerful residents gain recognition of their new status, but at the cost of disrupting the traditional balance of community reciprocity.[38]

Other members of the community emigrate to the tropical regions where colonisation is encouraged. Although there is neither drought nor fear of freezing conditions, the problems there include excess vegetation, continual threats to physical health and new difficulties that emerge from their greater incorporation into the market economy. In the tropical areas spirits like the *kharisiri*, who can bring harm to one's health, are always present. In contrast, they speak of Mother Earth much less and, in general, less about the sacred relationship with nature. Thus with the passage of time the sense of community is weakened.

THE WAR ON BEHALF OF THE GODS

The factor that has brought more diversification to the religious universe in the very heart of the communities on the high plateau than any other, however, is the veritable avalanche of ideas coming in from the outside. Many have to do with the modernising influence of schools, emigration and commerce; many development institutions are trying to sell their ideas to the rural Aymara. The package which is offered usually includes abandoning their "primitive" customs in order to become civilized.

The proponents of different religious traditions exercise more direct influence on the Aymara religious experience, each one presenting itself as the proponent of the "true" faith. Each brings its own message, its own style and cultural baggage, perhaps even foreign, along with its own collaborators, including its own organisation in the heart of the community.

It is impossible to take the space to review the full range of possible ideas and counter proposals here. In some cases they attain a greater degree of orthodoxy, including a greater orthopraxis, within the Christian ideal. However, nobody is surprised that the most prevalent result among the Aymara is confusion and division. In recent workshops on this theme, the Aymara participants have expressed this feeling in words like the following:

It was as if they were throwing mud in our face, leaving us blind and confused. Our Aymara people had a bedrock religious foundation. We knew where we were treading. It was the earth. But now it is like walking on sand. How can we unite this people that has been torn to bits? (A Catholic woman promoter)

They talk of love, but there is hate. They bring division to us. We had a walking stick, but they took it away and gave us a prosthesis. We suffer for having two religious faces. What internal strife we suffer! A war within ourselves, within each Aymara! (An Adventist peasant leader)

We are not the ones who have brought division to the church. They are the ones who have brought division under the names of Catholic, Methodist, Adventist, and so on. We speak of love, of unity. What unity? (A Catholic priest)

It is a sin that they come in without knowledge of or being acquainted with our reality, without at least the ability to speak our language. And then they want to teach us so many things! It is a continual invasion that we Aymara suffer. (A Lutheran pastor)

The new attitude that the fathers of the institutions have portrayed is good for us. They have begun works to help social, agricultural and husbandry promotion. But they do not even speak of God; they have lost all religious feeling. It seems that their new religion is the market economy. Some elders believe that the fathers practise two religions, Catholic and Protestant. (A Catholic catechist)[39]

Limiting ourselves to the effect of the avalanche of religions, it is not rare that proselytism on behalf of one creed is accompanied by an iconoclastic intolerance of all the other propositions, especially the traditional religious expressions. Although it is not exactly appropriate to generalize, the lack of respect for the Aymara religion is so common among many missionaries and their converts that frequently they even begin to distinguish linguistically between "religion" (the new idea that has come from outside through all these missionaries) and "custom" (the Aymara religion in its multiple syncretistic forms).

But with all their efforts, not even the most aggressive can manage to erase completely the old gods. They push them further into hell, as devils, but they never lose their influence over the living. Here are two testimonies:

We know that there are two powers in this world who manipulate us, the power of God and the power of the devil . . . The devil wants us to be embroiled in wars, fights and killings. But God says that we should not be concerned about this earth because it will come to an end. (An Adventist from the northern high plateau)

I am a Christian; I am a child of God the Father, not Pacha Mama, nor Virgin Tayka, nor *uywiri*, nor Mallku, t'alla. I do not love them any more. They are all screwed up[40] . . . They are all the work of Satan. ThMallku of Sabaya is a devil. There is no need to worship him. (A Pentecostal from the southern high plateau)[41]

The Aymara world, however, is not confined to the rural areas. We shall look at some things that occur among the hundreds of thousands who are now established in urban and industrial centres.

THE DEVILS OF THE MINE[42]

Mining activity has been present in the Aymara territory at least since the Inca period. Later, during the colonial years, the fulfilment of conscript labour or a term of work in the mines of Potosi became an obligatory routine in all of the original communities. Since then, with the ups and downs of life and with various technical and social innovations, mining has continued to be one of the more realistic work options for Aymara and Quechua who are in need of outside income. In the depths of the mining tunnels their identities are forged and transformed into something new, though with strong Andean roots.

This long history explains the important role that the Aymara religious experience (and the Andean) plays within the life of a miner. In contrast to the rest of humanity, the miner earns his living by taking riches from the bowels of the earth, working in dark tunnels full of risks. As the Aymara engaged in agricultural pursuits develops an intimate relationship with the spirits who provide good climate and fertility, in the mine something similar happens with divinities who are knowledgeable about minerals. What is new here is that their close tie, even physically, with the evil location of the world below and within is much more obvious; the miner belongs to the realm of the devils.

In effect, the axis around which the religion of the miners in the tunnel turns is the devil. They call him Tiu; his identity and location is both generalised and varied in each mine location. The tunnels are populated by images of Tiu, characterised by his big horns, a prominent male organ, and his arms in an attitude of embracing or grasping. His sole clothing consists of a multitude of paper streamers and confetti, reflecting the ever-present *ch'allas* (offerings or blessings) with alcohol, coca leaves and cigars which the miners offer him at Carnaval, during the month of August, and every Tuesday and Friday, which are the devil's days. To reciprocate, Tiu protects them against accidents and grants them the coveted vein of ore.

However, Tiu is not alone. The big pieces of high quality metal are Mamas or Awichas, with similar characteristics to the Illa or the engendering spirits of animals and plants. Christianity is not absent from the mines either. From the early days of colonization, within and outside of the mine, Tiu has as counterpart the Virgin Mary—of Candelaria, of Socavon (literally, the Tunnel)—and around Potosi, also Tata Q'aqcha, a dying Christ with a miner's mask, to whom they dedicate annual patronal festivals with all of the luxury of their annual sponsors, who by taking on the responsibility for the festival gain social prestige in the towns and cities.

In this whole picture perhaps the newest aspect is the unmasking of the lower world. The tunnel teaches the miner to live with the devil on a daily basis. He discovers, then, that in spite of the fact that the devil is dangerous and very avaricious, deep down he is not so bad as he is made out to be. He is, therefore, reinterpreted to appear as an elderly relative, an uncle (*tio*) who grumbles but in the end helps one to survive. Furthermore, the Virgin does not seem to oppose the devil but rather to complement him, at times even as his consort under a new name of Pacha Mama, while Tiu becomes Pacha Tata.[43]

The loss of a clandestine religious identity finds its greatest expression at Carnaval, particularly in the mining city of Oruro. There the streets are filled with thousands of devils decked out in flashy suits of brilliant colours, covered by extremely elaborate masks with figures of serpents, toads and dragons with bulging eyes, curved horns and sharp fangs. The principal devils bear the names of capital sins, and in a sacramental minicar that represents the feet of the Virgin of Socavon, these devils are brought down by an angel who is transformed into the leading figure of each devil dance troop. All the dancers have previously made their promises and lighted their candles in the shrine of the Virgin of Socavon, who is clearly identified with the Christian Virgin Mary. However, there is no doubt that the whole popular perception of this event is that the city is taken over by a host of fascinating devils who are near at hand. Their relationship with the Virgin is not seen in their downfall, but rather in a form of alliance with her.[44]

On a deeper level, everybody understands that behind each devil mask there is the face of a miner and that their large numbers reflect a multitude who, on fulfilling their promises, also express their real situation and their desires, though perhaps at a subconscious rather than a conscious level. In these festivals of the devils as well as in the routine *ch'allas* to Tiu—in the tunnels themselves, where they hold their union meetings in a time of crisis and persecution—there is logical correspondence between the proletarian reality of the miner and the symbolic expressions in his rituals. As one leader in the biggest mining company in Bolivia said:

There is no communication that is more intimate, more sincere or more beautiful than the moment of the *ch'alla*, the moment when all the workers chew the coca leaves together and present their offerings to Tiu . . . There we talk about our problems with the job, and there is born a generation that is so revolutionary that the workers begin to think about structural changes. This is our university. The experience that we have in the *ch'alla* is our best moment.[45]

THE CITY: GODS OF MONEY AND PRESTIGE

The majority of the Aymara who emigrate from their community end up settling in some city, especially La Paz, which continues to be Chukiyaw Marka, the capital of the Aymara world. There, for the most part, they become part of the poorer urban sectors, although there is already talk about the beginnings of an Aymara bourgeoisie made up of merchants. The urban Aymara continually discover new ways to find opportunities in the city, in many cases by hiding and gradually losing their old identity so as to suffer less discrimination. Some become part of the urban branches of the larger popular social movement and others accent their role as clients to their social superiors so that the latter will help them up the social ladder. However, in the city, where at least half of the people speak Aymara and many of these maintain ties to the rural areas, a total break with the past is not possible. Rather, they have gradually formed an urban variety of the Aymara culture.[46]

The religious experience of the urban Aymara also reflects these changes. Naturally, they have a closer experience of many other forms of popular religion than are present in other Latin American cities, as much from a traditional Catholic angle as from other more recent influences, Christian and non-Christian alike. For example, the person of Jesus Christ has now become a more central figure, especially at Christmas and during Holy Week. However, here we shall concentrate rather on the changes that their old Aymara religion suffers. Two prime considerations are money and prestige.

The urban Aymara are no longer dependent on the multiplication of seeds or cattle, or on finding rich veins of ore. Now money moves to occupy this place, perhaps because it is so elusive and capricious, like the harvest and the mineral ores. Through old and new rituals and prayers they constantly plead for blessings, which are mainly shown in obtaining money, an abundance of material goods and health. Particularly on Tuesdays and Fridays, the days of the devil, and other special dates, such as the eve of Pentecost, many Aymara homes and businesses in the city burn incense to their ancestors to this end. They make their prayers in a manner little different from the invocations to Pacha Mama or Tiu or Mama Illa, but now they turn her protecting and fertilizing power to act for monetary gain—ritually called Phaxsi Mama (Lady Moon)—which they desire to see multiply. At Carnaval the central rite for all the social classes becomes the *ch'alla*, libations of beer in the home, business, vehicles and on all the instruments of work to guarantee economic security and blessing for the coming year.

The most prominent ritual expression of this new religious concern for the merchant and monetary world is the annual festival of *alasitas* (literally, "buy me"), which is celebrated in La Paz as well as in the patronal festivals in the mestizo towns, and recently in some of the more market-conscious rural communities. The main rite of the *alasitas*, in which many non-Aymara peoples also participate, consists precisely in buying and selling miniature objects symbolizing what they hope to obtain in real life with the help of blessing—sacks of articles of basic necessities, along with houses, vehicles, university diplomas, airline tickets, and so on. For the occasion they print imitation money in miniature; dollars of high denominations have predominated during the recent years of financial crisis. They ask for blessing from the patron saint, but the festival has its own god too, Ekeko (Iqiqu).

Significantly, this god, whose roots are found in pre-colonial beliefs, had ceased to be an object of worship in the communities, but he reappears in the urban world, represented by a chubby little man of mestizo appearance carrying all sorts of goods.

The other big concern of the urban Aymara, especially the most successful, is prestige. We saw this when we spoke about the pilgrimages that they make each year to their place of origin. This is also expressed in many festivals in the city. The socio-economic dimensions and characteristics in the city do not permit a community atmosphere, where everybody knows everybody else and they lend mutual help to one another, and where people gradually advance in like rhythm along the "road of responsibilities," which at the same time yields a social recognition to which all have access. The most similarity is seen in family celebrations, attended by those closest to the family, and in some ways, the patronal festivals in the neighbourhoods and unions. On these occasions, on top of certain connections of restricted reciprocity, the most successful people look for ways to make ostentatious displays of their greater success and in some instances actually monopolize the festival. This is the dynamic that has led to the establishment of new festivals on a much greater scale and with great ostentation of costly fraternities in each one of the Aymara cities: Candelaria in Puno, Carnaval in Oruro (where this dimension combines with that of the devils) and especially the festival of the Lord of Great Power in La Paz. In these, reciprocity is limited to a small group within the confraternity, while the rest are reduced to the role played by "extras," observers or admirers. In the festival of the Lord of Great Power, even the colonial Christ, who originally was the reason for the festival, receives less and less attention, while the protagonist's role is being passed to this small group of people with a great amount of power and prestige.[47]

9

Religious Experience and Experience of God

Here we conclude our journey through the religious experiences of the Aymara throughout their life in the traditional communities of the high plateau, in the mines and in the city. To close the circle, we must return to the question we left hanging at the beginning of the study: Is this really an experience of the living God? We have given the theological reasons and personal testimonies, and we leave no doubt in responding in the affirmative. Here we want to emphasize certain traits that show this Aymara face of God.

SIGNS AND SPECIAL MOMENTS

We have confirmed those events we can call the special signs, places and times through which God shows himself to the Aymara people. Much that corresponds to what our brothers and sisters from the southern Peruvian Andes call the "core of the experience of God"[48] has been revealed through our own journey.

- The *home* itself, full of protectors, and through it, the *family* with all that makes its establishment and survival possible.

- *Agricultural work and animal husbandry* and, through them, the intimate and personal relationship with the earth, surrounding landscape, animals, plants, and their seeds. Because of this relationship, this work is one of the most ritualized activities throughout the year.

- All the occasions that have to do with fruitfulness and the *multiplication of life*, plant and animal as well as human, and including other assets, such as the veins of mineral ore and money, equally perceived to be full of life. In the entire society and in the cosmos, that which is not paired and does not reproduce is not within this creative dynamic process of the living God. Here, too, the family becomes a special place for the experience of God.

- *Health* and the care of it fosters much help between families and members of the community, and furthermore, is an occasion to appeal to God, to the protecting spirits and to the plants themselves to seek help and give thanks.

- The *community* in all its dimensions: its territory, marked and protected by the ancestral grandparents, who have become part of the landscape; its organisation, authorities and responsibilities of service; its deliberative assembly; its collective works; its fights, its festive celebrations around the church and the patron saint. The behaviour of each member of the community has repercussions on the well-being of the whole community.

- *The poor and needy.* One of the favourite images of the Aymara God is that of a beggar who tests the human solidarity of his children. Those who help those who are in need are showered with blessings; those who ignore them can be punished. Therefore, as poor as they all are, in the community there are no beggars, nor are they lacking in ceremonial occasions. When someone loses family or land, that person will be granted recognition in some way by another family or by the community.

- The *festival* at all levels: in the family and among families, around production, in the community, in the place of pilgrimages. In the festival the experience of God is expressed in all its sensory richness: with music, song and dance, flashy dress and showy costumes, smoke and the smell of the incense, the taste of the food and drink, the coca leaves and the alcohol . . . all this shared within the context of interchanges among the participants. In the festival, as in all the rites, the sharing of food and drink in abundance among all the participants, often in conjunction with offerings made to the protecting spirits, constitutes a special sign.

- *Crisis*—sickness, death, natural disasters, social conflicts—demand a review of the conduct of the people in relation to each other, to the beings that fill the cosmos and to God.
- The *struggle for rights* often combines several of the occasions already mentioned: the defense of land and life; community and inter-community solidarity; crisis.

The actual name of God, present in these signs and moments, can vary depending on the relative importance of the ancestral, European-colonial or modern traditions. Some speak more of Father Sun, Mother Earth, the multitude of spirits and saints; in contrast, others speak of God and Jesus Christ; a third group combines both systems in order to formulate its beliefs. However, in every case their contact with this superior world—which for us, under whatever conceptualisation, is a contact with that which we call God—takes place in a special manner around these central ideas, signs and moments.

PRINCIPAL VALUES

The great sign of the presence of the living God is not so much accuracy of a definite idea, but rather the values and attitudes it spawns. Orthopraxis is a more radical criterion than the orthodoxy of a definite theoretical foundation.

Through these occasions mentioned above, and undoubtedly there are others, a value system is developed which reflects not only the Aymara cultural matrix but also certain preferential traits in this people's experience of God. When we analyze these values, new reverberations that are forged in other cultural contexts are added to the Christian virtues such as justice, love, communication and pardon. Without any pretence of covering the subject completely, I shall underline the following:

- *Unity in diversity*. The family and the community are sacred and the obligations in connection with them must not be shunned. The Aymara culture and its language have a highly developed system of social behaviour with a thousand different shades of respect and etiquette. However, the kind of unanimity existing among the Aymara has two other important characteristics. First, within the growing circles of solidarity, the individual and the smaller units never are eliminated by the upper echelon. Even the model of the person is depicted as a couple, though even in that union, the wife does not lose her surname or her possessions. It is a dialectic kind of communion and unanimity in which each part is respected and, as such, maintains its own identity and specific contribution to the whole. Second, this solidarity is fundamentally operative among those who behave as persons (*jaqi*) and not with those who abuse it, developing domineering attitudes and persisting in them (*q'ara*).

- *Reciprocity.* This is the basis for social human relationships. In order to put this value into practice, the Aymara people have developed numerous cultural mechanisms. For the same reason, the model human being is not the individual, or the absolute master, or the collective group alone, but, once again, the couple. Each member of a pair has his or her contribution to make, and at the same time, exercises control over the possible excesses of his or her mate. We could also add that this reciprocity is not static, cyclical or sterile, but moves towards that which the church calls the dialectic of mutually enriching gifts.[49] If one party takes the initiative, the other responds with an even greater gift, and so on in succession. Thus an expansive dynamic is generated, not for the accumulation of wealth for oneself, but for the creative and shared abundance for all. The fullness of justice (or reciprocity) is a gift, and generosity an even greater one. The ideal of unanimity and of community emerges precisely in the midst of this kind of relationship.

- *Reconciliation.* Reciprocity has two faces: the positive is to return something more than was given; the negative is to reestablish the broken balance. Every misdemeanour demands a reparation. For this reason all the rituals, many times with the precise aim to restore the balance which has been lost, finish with a ceremony of pardon and an embrace of peace shared among the participants. In a similar way, in conflicts and fights the key is never to destroy, but to equalize or to level, that is to say, to restore the balance which has been lost through the abusive behaviour of one of the parties while still respecting the identity of the guilty party and recognising the possibility of his or her redemption.[50]

- *Communion with the whole universe.* Solidarity, reciprocity and reconciliation do not operate only among humans, but also with the whole cosmos and with each one of the beings that comprise them. Nothing is classified as disposable. Everything is treated as a living being, to which one must speak with respect and affection— even the stone and the worm. One must walk almost without stepping, must not loiter, must cultivate a conversation with the earth and kiss the seed, without provoking fear or bringing any

harm. This is because, in some form or other, everything participates in the comprehensive life that exists in the whole universe.
Francis of Assisi would feel quite at ease among his Aymara brothers and sisters.

• *Respect and trust in God and in the supernatural beings.* As a fundamental part of this communion with the whole universe, one must
maintain a respectful relationship with Our Good Father, Tatitu,
Suma Awki and the rest of the supernatural beings, including the
dead and the ancestors. In addition, with God and all the others
one must take the initiative in presenting gifts and generous offerings with the assurance that their response will be even more
generous.

THE LIBERATING AYMARA GOD

The experience of God among the Aymara people is the experience of
poor people who are believers, who seek to fulfil themselves in an especially difficult rural environment and who for centuries have suffered
greatly through the process of colonialization and marginalization. Under these conditions, how does the face of a liberating God appear to
them?[51]

In many aspects God appears in a way similar to the liberating God of
other poor and oppressed peoples. References to the poor who should be
freed from the abuses of the rich are present in the Aymara discourse and
also in their ideal of society. We have seen this expressed, for example, in
the opposition that the Aymara envisage between the person and *q'ara*,
or when they tell us about how God appears as a beggar, or the Tupaq
Katari, the Aymara Moses, "will return in the image of millions of other
Aymara."

Nevertheless, the experience of this people, who have been "oppressed
but never conquered," reminds us of the other dimensions of liberation.
Liberation, the same as any other task, is always perceived to be a task
which humans perform to the best of their ability and strength; God,
along with all the other protecting spirits, adds corresponding support.
Let us focus on three aspects of this liberation: the strengthening of life,
the community and the Aymara nation.

The first dimension, central to the Aymara experience, stresses that
the development of all forms of life to their full potential is liberating. We
have already seen that everything is filled with life and is in the process of
multiplying. Even death is really just a change of status, and the dead are,
in turn, those who engender new life. However, at the same time, life in

this world, and in the actual situation in the high plateau, is fragile and full of risks. Therefore, all that contributes to the maintenance and growth of this life is seen as liberating. This happens, for example, when, with the proper effort, with ancestral or modern wisdom, and with the fulfilment of sacred obligations, the harvest is assured or the sick are healed. A large part of the routine activities and the rituals of daily life has, therefore, a liberating dimension. In addition, the actions of God and all of the protecting spirits as support to these efforts are part of the Aymara face of the liberating God.

A second dimension is liberation seen as strengthening the community solidarity among and Aymara. Previously we showed how the Aymara saw their people as "broken apart," often with the aid of the churches who, calling themselves Christians, bring division into the very heart of the community. We have also seen how the community and its internal cohesion is something so sacred that it even guarantees divine support for the harvests and every kind of blessing. Therefore, every action that leads to the maintenance and the consolidation of this unity and sense of community is also liberating. Add to this the fulfilment of work and other communal activities, the active participation and service within the network of interchanges, invitations and celebrations, the special time of service on behalf of the others when it is time to take one's turn at shouldering the communal responsibilities, and more. For all of these reasons, the community also provides a special glimpse of the Aymara face of the liberating God.

The third dimension has to do with the liberation of the Aymara nation. The way in which the Aymara most clearly perceive their social oppression is through the fact that they are scorned and discriminated against by the others for being "Indians," the generic name which includes the specific Aymara identity. A certain class consciousness which is felt by poor, rural people who are exploited is also undoubtedly present, although now that they no longer work for large landowners, this exploitation is perceived in a less direct way. On the other hand, the experience of not being respected or treated as persons because of the fact that they are Indians is something that occurs in almost every contact they have with those who are not Aymara. Even the term *peasant* in practice is not seen so much as an economic classification but as a euphemism for Indian. On the positive side, social liberation is perceived as much more than simply economic and social improvement. In addition to all these factors, which are undoubtedly present, much importance is placed on the need to be respected as persons and as a people. The latter is the point that we wish to emphasize here.

Some who have been influenced by the dominant culture think that their freedom consists in ceasing to appear as Indians. For this reason they want to leave their community. They make every effort to speak Spanish, to adapt themselves completely to the urban culture, to join the "true" religion, even to change their surname, and to seek every possible means to whiten their faces. The majority only reach the halfway point through these efforts and then their frustration leads them into a kind of social illness which is a blend of servility, resentment, aggression and distrust. There are so many more psycho-social consequences of this collective sin called discrimination. It is a false road to liberation.

However, there is a growing awareness, particularly among the Aymara leaders and intellectuals, that their freedom ought to give them equal recognition and the strengthening of everything that identifies them as Aymara: history, language, culture, religion, social organisation within the community structure, people and nation. In some cases this awareness is so strong that it overrides all other dimensions. Still others see their freedom with "two eyes": as being part of an exploited class that breaks its chains, and as an oppressed people that recovers its identity. Their ideal is eventually to form a multinational society in which all persons have equal opportunities, all are respected and, at the same time, each cultural group can develop to the height of its own potential. Their social and political liberation ought to embrace their cultural freedom as well, and ultimately, their national freedom.

Aymara religious leaders, both traditionalists and members and ministers of the various Christian churches, are among those who think in this way about their liberation.[52] After having meditated on this theme for two days, a group of these religious leaders saw the intervention of the liberating God in their own lives in the following terms:

We affirm that both religions, Aymara and Christian, teach love and respect for life with its institutions. They are not religions of hate. However, by its actions the Christian religion is a sign of contradiction that divides the community and the Aymara nation. Nor does it put confidence in native leadership. We are its right arms, but we are not the head. In fact we cannot develop our own theology; a theological colonialism reigns. The churches among us must free us from all of this so that we can act like believers. Therefore, we demand a deepening practical knowledge of the Aymara culture. We, the Aymara, who have received the ideology that rejects our own things, must relearn its rudiments. Others who come here must acquaint themselves thoroughly with our ways not to dominate us, but to liberate us.

As yet we cannot count on an existing Aymara ideology of liberation. History shows us paths to follow, but it is not enough. The Aymara who have been modernised by schools and universities, we are the ones who must follow the example of Moses: raised in the palace of the Pharaoh, he learned the ways and thoughts of the oppressors in order to free his people. We, too, the new Aymara, must learn and later liberate our people.

We ought to formulate a liberation using all of the various points of view. We cannot just emphasize the religious aspect. The promotion, the training and the leadership must all be part of an integrated whole. Thus, by means of this "ecumenical" ideology, we can work out our freedom and take on strength, recognising our Aymara identity and seeking our Aymara unity. We are divided by political, historical and other reasons, but both the Christian religion as well as fraternal religion of Pacha Mama calls us to this unity.[53]

This, too, is the Aymara face of the liberating God.

RELIGION, CULTURE AND CONVERSION

Our journey through the Aymara religious experience has shown us developments which from our perspective are less Christian: for example, the manipulation of reciprocity by the rich godparents to ensure cheap manual labour, or using the festival to make an ostentatious show of one's wealth. That is, while maintaining the same appearance on the surface, without noticing we have moved from the dialectic of gifts to the logic of gain, the single-mindedness of egomania.

Actually, perhaps we can generalise that this type of change could occur in any area regardless of the Aymara religious experience. From an attitude of cosmic communion it is possible to cross over to the other attitude of fear and punishment. The reverence for all of creation and for the multiplication of life could hide idolatrous ideas towards the accumulation of money. The contrast between person (*jaqi*) and abuser (*q'ara*) can lead to a closed ethnocentrism that is racist in nature. Solidarity that starts with a respect for the dual nature of all relationships can degenerate into chronic factionalism between sides. And so on . . .

It is from within that any religion can develop and encourage opposite attitudes. It would be overly simplistic to think that a religion, with all of its structure and symbolic language, is *the good one*, while everything else is *the bad*. With any kind of structure and symbolism, any religion, including Christianity, can be used in favour of the status quo or to support liberation. Perhaps it is inevitable that all religion operates within certain limits of ambiguity. Religions are like languages, in which the same words and the same grammar can be used for opposite purposes.

Naturally, here too, there are certain socioeconomic conditionings. Each social class develops its own interests. Within the society called Christian we have already become aware of the fact that there is a chasm between the Christ of the rich exploiters and the Christ of the poor. Likewise, it is easier for the Aymara religion to provide an experience of the liberating God among the poor in the communities, and, in contrast, for it to express ideological attitudes towards power and money among the emerging Aymara bourgeoisie.[54]

It is certain that the "seeds of the Word" nourish all of creation and are expressed in any religion, but this does not lessen the impact of personal and social sin, which invades the whole of life. If God, the liberator, with the good news of incarnation, has an Aymara face, then conversion speaks Aymara also.

PART FOUR

THE GUARANI RELIGIOUS EXPERIENCE

Bartomeu Melià

I have longed for paradise all my life
I have sought for it like a Guarani
but now I know that it is not in the past
(a scientific error in the Bible that Christ has corrected,
    but in the future).
                    —Ernesto Cardenal, *Tocar el cielo*

The Guarani today take pride in who they are. With a very clear sense of their individuality, they speak of *ñande reko* as the most complete expression of their identity and the quality of their difference. This term has many meanings: our way of being, our present manner, our law, our culture, our norms, our behaviour, our habits, our human condition, our customs. These are the meanings that are given in the oldest dictionary, *Tesoro de la lengua guaraní* (1639), compiled by Father Antonio Ruiz de Montoya.

The Guarani character has two essential forms: *ñandé rekó katú* and *ñandé rekó marangatú* (our true and authentic way of being, and our good, honourable and virtuous way of being, with respect to the religious side of the person). How this religious side of the character is developed and lives in the present is the same as asking about the Guarani religious experience.

1

The Guarani People

A PEOPLE WHO TRAVEL

The Tupi-Guarani, identified by their language and culture, are from one of the oldest branches of the Tupi people. They began to take on their own distinct characteristics probably around the beginning of the first millennium before Christ, some three thousand to twenty-five hundred years ago. Migration movements, originating from the Amazon basin, were intensified, perhaps motivated, by a marked population increase during a period which coincided with the beginning of this era, approximately two thousand years ago. These groups we have come to know as Guarani moved to occupy the subtropical jungles of the desolate highlands, straddling the borders of present-day Paraguay and Uruguay. The Indians who were seeking new lands were not nomads who depended mainly on hunting and gathering, but farmers who knew how to use the jungle soil effectively, who felled and burned trees to plant corn, manioc, legumes and many other crops. They are skillful potters whose artefacts are needed in the preparation and serving of food. As energetic colonists, the Guarani continued their migratory expansion until the time of the European invasion in the Rio de la Plata area (c. 1520) and even up to the present. Migration, as history and as a plan, is a typical characteristic of the Guarani, although many of their groups have remained in the same territory for centuries and have never actually participated in a migration. As we shall see, the search for the "land without evil" and new land markedly influences their thoughts and their experiences. The "land without evil" is the historical and practical synthesis of an economy which is experienced prophetically and of a realistic prophecy, with their feet on the ground so to speak. From their point of view, the Guarani are an exodus people, though not uprooted, for the land that they seek is that which will serve as an ecological base tomorrow as it has in times past. Down through the last fifteen hundred years, the period of time in which the Guarani consider themselves to have been established as a distinct group with their own characteristics, the Guarani have shown themselves faithful to their ecological tradition, not because of inertia, but by active work built on the recreation and search for the environmental conditions most favourable for the development of their way of life. In this instance, tradition is prophecy that lives. The search for "land without evil" as a framework for the Guarani way of thinking informs the dynamic of the economy and the religious experience which is theirs alone.

In the sixteenth and seventeenth centuries, to the extent that the Spanish advanced in their voyages of exploration and their expeditions of conquest and the missionaries in their "spiritual conquests," they met the Guarani who were forming rather extensive areas of territorial control which they called provinces, recognised by their own names: Cario, Tobatin, Guarambare, Itatin, Mbaracayu, people of Guaira, Parana, Uruguay, Tape, and so on. These provinces embraced a vast territory which stretched from the Atlantic coast south of São Vincente in Brazil, to the right bank of the river of Paraguay, and from south of the river Parana-Panama and Gran Pantanal, or the lake of the Jarayes, to the islands of the delta, near Buenos Aires.

Soon the generic name of Guarani prevailed among the various groups, given the obvious linguistic uniformity among the dialects of these peoples and the great similarities in their socio-political organisation and their cultural expressions. Guarani was the common language of peoples who covered a wide geographic area.[1] They eventually formed a nation, though not in the modern sense of a nation-state. It is important to bear in mind, however, that within this area other "nations" were located; generally their presence in the area preceded the Guarani, with whom they were usually in conflict, and their occupied territories were very disparate in size.

THE COLONIAL INVASION

In the period when they first came into contact with Europeans, the Guarani population boasted considerable numbers. It is estimated that there were between 1,500,000 and 2,000,000 Guarani, although these numbers seem a bit exaggerated. They are given some serious treatment in the historical documentation, and they gain credibility in that they knew about the good productivity that could be achieved by neolithic societies based on a reciprocal economy, a fact that we shall return to because it is intimately connected to their religious life. During the colonial process, their demographic decline alarmed even their own governing authorities. Entire provinces were destroyed, especially those that fell under the domination of the assigned colonial administrators and those that suffered periodic attacks from ruling bandits in search of slaves. The province of Guaira, for example, which had a population of more than 200,000 Indians (perhaps as many as 800,000), was reduced to practically no inhabitants. According to Barzana, the greater part of the people died of disease, war, and maltreatment.[2]

A few thousand Guarani Indians were absorbed into the biological and social strata of the mestizos, while others were reduced to towns under the Franciscan missions (from 1580) and later under the Jesuits (from 1609). When these towns were disintegrating as communities throughout the nineteenth century, their inhabitants became members of the new state of Paraguay, which assimilated them and once again imposed upon them another process of settlement into reductions leading to the condition of poor rural peasantry.

The colonial oppression, especially the establishment of the Indian divisions under the assigned administrators (1556), provoked the uprising of numerous rebellions against the Christians. Between 1537 and 1616 no fewer than twenty-five revolts were recorded, and, remarkably, the majority of them revealed a prophetic structure. The rebellion stemmed from the religious tradition that the Indians sensed was under threat and was manifest through their actions as well as their religious language. One of the most significant prophetic responses against the colonial oppression took place at Obera around 1579. The Guarani who went to Obera sang and danced unceasingly for three days. They "unbaptised" those who had been baptised, and they gave them new names in accord with the indigenous tradition. This and other uprisings were liberation movements against colonial servitude, while at the same time reaffirming the traditional way of life, which finds its most authentic expression in religion.

If, during the time previous to the period of colonial rule, the Guarani were able to sense the times when the land in which they lived was full of evil—natural disasters, floods and droughts, diseases, internal dissensions, attacks from enemy tribes—there is no doubt that colonial domination, a system which took their freedom from them, amounts to the sum of all these and even more terrible evils. Even the Jesuit reductions with their declared intention to free them from the obligation to the administration and required personal service were nothing more than spaces where freedom existed only when the traditional religious way of life was seen to be discredited, ridiculed and even physically persecuted. The entrance of the Jesuits into the Guarani world was accompanied by a real "messianic war," to use the expression of a modern anthropologist. Though the Jesuits entered into a provisional dialogue when they were dealing with the linguistic communication and certain ideas about their economic and political life, the antagonism in the religious area, as much with respect to their beliefs as their ritual expressions, was total.

Old Paraguay inhabited by the Guarani Indians was the chosen land of indigenous messiahs and prophets for two centuries. No other region can lay claim to so many movements of mystical liberation . . . Its increase at the time when the conquistadors and the Jesuits established their rule and enforced it by destroying the old civilisation, could be explained by the despair that took hold of the Tupinamba and the Guarani. This despair encouraged them to listen to the prophets which were springing up among them and who offered them the solution of fleeing towards the "land without evil" or the next arrival of the golden age.[3]

Both in the area of colonial domination, properly speaking, and in the area of the mission reductions, the substitution of the Christian religion for the indigenous religion was progressing gradually and firmly, more of a superficial implanting than a shared inculturation. We are not negating, however, the authenticity of the conversions or the truth of the new ritual expressions. Neither do we doubt the depth of the Christian experience, even in mystical forms, among the Guarani Indians or the intimate quality of Paraguayan religiosity. These are the offshoots that set the religious experience of the tribal Guarani apart from all others and which must be treated as phenomena of popular Christian religion.

FREE MEN IN THE JUNGLE

During the entire colonial period, throughout the nineteenth century and up to the present, groups of Guarani have managed to survive free of the colonial system. Jungles which are relatively cut off from the colonial population centres, seldom or never crossed by "civilized" people, kept them sufficiently isolated so that they could preserve their traditional way of being from oblivion. As survivors of a world that is now outdated, they have been generically categorized as "Kaygua" and "savages." The outside world is barely acquainted with them; they were visited only rarely by some traveler or other during the nineteenth century and were able to live in peace until the twentieth century without any particular outside interference. Greater contact with some of these groups—there was a mission run by the Divine Word Missionaries between 1910 and 1925—reestablished the existence of three culturally well-differentiated subgroups: the Pai-Tavytera, the Ava-Katu-ete and the Mbya. These groups are more or less acculturated in their external behaviour within the rural Paraguayan population owing to the growing interchange of wooden artefacts and the processing of the mate leaves. In no way, however, have they ceased to be faithful to the fundamental structures of their tribal economy, social organisation or religion.

It is true that today they do not control an area of connected territories that serves as their homeland and that their numbers have declined; they occupy sections that range from a few hectares to colonies of more than ten thousand hectares, generally in the border regions of Paraguay, Brazil, Argentina and Bolivia. Faithful to their traditional ecology, they seek to preserve the land wherever possible, though often they face threats and actions to expel them from their lands, invasion by new settlers, intrusion on their cultivated fields by cattle ranches and, in a manner that seems to be irreversible, the destruction of their ecological environment. As never before, the earth is covered with evil, a concern and anxiety that penetrates their whole way of being.

The numbers of the Guarani tribes today present a relatively high demographic density, particularly when compared to the reduced population figures of other Amazonian tribes. The Pai-Tavytera (or Kayova) number some seventeen thousand (between Paraguay and Brazil), the Ava-Katuete (or Chiripa) some eight thousand (also divided between Paraguay and Brazil), and the Mbya, not less than twelve thousand (distributed in small nuclei scattered throughout what remains of the jungle in Paraguay, Argentina and Brazil).[4] The Chiriguanos of Bolivia and the border regions of Argentina and Paraguay reach numbers in excess of sixty thousand. As is evident, these figures are more estimates than proper census counts. Understandably, the Guarani do not trust the statistical controls that have always been aimed at integration projects which would alienate them from their culture and their lands.

2

Methods of Approach

A valid principle of ethnology assumes that researchers take into consideration their own experience in relation to that which they are describing and about which they are commenting, a principle which is rarely explicit in the theological task, although there are kinds of theologians whose main source is precisely the religious experience of others: prophets, mystics, saints, communities of Christian life.

The experience and the type of relationship that an author has had with the Guarani society constitutes the best hermeneutical key to be able to understand his treatise and put it into context.

If you were to ask me to give an account of my own experience with the Guarani, I should tell you that I have been in contact with them intermittently—the three subgroups on the Paraguayan side in particular—from 1969 to 1976. Since 1976 I have been acquainted with the Kayova communities of Mato Grosso in Brazil, and Ñandeva (or Chiripa) villages in the same area, as well as some pockets of Mbya in the southern jungle regions of Brazil. When on these visits and studies, I have always eaten and slept in the indigenous homes. They have permitted me to participate in their life, without any specific role, in their ritual songs and dances. I have heard their myths told in their own Guarani language, and have transcribed some of them word for word. Nevertheless, I believe that in their eyes I have never been seen as an anthropologist who is just on a fact-finding mission, nor have I ever exercised the role of pastor among them.

During this time I have set out to read the literature relative to the Guarani, both ancient and modern, from an ethno-historical perspective; that is, trying to read between the lines in the historical documents to catch a glimpse of the traditional memory of some Guarani whose happy and distressing lives are contemporaneous with my own, and whose struggles are not strange to me.

I have wanted to bring into the open my experience with the Guarani out of respect for the Guarani themselves and their religious experience, and in order to show how tentative and limited are the descriptions and interpretations I offer here. In the Guarani religious experience, their internal worldview is so imprisoned that the heart and the head cannot do theology. I hope these reflections are useful as a timid confession from someone for whom the acquaintance with the Guarani and their way of life has become an ideal of life that is just barely coming into light, but continually sought after.

THE COLONIAL AND MISSIONARY APPROACH

In 1913 Father Pablo Hernandez, in his attempt to give an account of pre-colonial Guarani religion, wrote that "very few facts, or none at all, are provided in the early documents with regard to the religion of the Guarani."[5] In fact, it has been said already of the ancient Guarani that they were "pure atheists, who did not worship any deity, rather ignored them altogether."[6]

However, a more careful reading of the letters, reports and chronicles from early colonial times gives glimpses of the religious character itself and the basic structures that have persisted up to the present among the Guarani. Prophecy, as a liberation movement against the colonial oppression, the song and dance in the so-called drunken orgies, the dreams and certain veneration of the bones of deceased practitioners of witchcraft, are all constant manifestations of the content and form of authentic Guarani religion.

In 1594 Father Alonso Barzana had already grasped some of the fundamental aspects of the Guarani religion. His text, when stripped of some of its preconceived notions, manages to relate the most important and essential elements of this religion. It is worth reproducing it at length, seeing that it is the first synthesis of Guarani religion written by a missionary:

This whole nation is very inclined towards religion, be it true or false, and if the Christians had provided them with a good example and they had not been deceived by sorcerers, not only would they be Christians, but even devout ones. They are acquainted fully with the immortality of the soul, and greatly fear the *anguera*, which are disembodied souls, and they say that they go about frightening people and doing evil. They show immense love and obedience to their parents, if they see them as good examples, and the same and even more so to the sorcerers who have deceived them with false religion, so much so that, if they command them to do so, not only do they give them their entire estate, sons and daughters, and they prostrate themselves before them, but they are not shaken in their resolve. This propensity of theirs to obey religious authority has brought about the situation that not only many unfaithful Indians among them have pretended to be children of God and teachers, but Indians who have been reared among the Spanish have fled among those at war, some calling themselves popes and others calling themselves Jesus Christ, and have stupidly set up monasteries of nuns whom they have used wrongly; and up to today, those who serve and those who do not serve (the Spanish) have planted a thousand omens and superstitions and rituals following these teachers, whose principal doctrine is to teach them to dance day and night, which leads them to die of hunger, in that they forget to tend their fields . . . They have so many dances that are so disruptive, as a integral part of their religion, that some die participating in them.[7]

Another historical account of Guarani religion is offered by Father Antonio Ruiz de Montoya, who has captured better than anyone else the structure of the Guarani language. He had decidedly committed himself to the defense of the Indian against the colonial administrators and the slave owners, though always looking to preventing and rejecting as diabolical the activities of the "sorcerers," whose prophetic depth he has perhaps brought to light—he himself being a mystic—though he could not accept it, owing to the theological and psycho-social conditioning of his time and his personality.

> They knew there was a God, and even in some way they were acquainted with his unity, which is inferred by the number that they gave him, which is *tupan*, the first word *tu* meaning admiration; the second, *pan* is an interrogative word, and as such corresponds to the Hebrew word *manhun* (*quid est hoc*) in the singular. They have never had idols, although they refer to the demon who imposed on them the veneration of the bones of some Indians who were famous magicians when they were alive . . . They have never made sacrifices to the true God, nor have they had more than just a mere acquaintance of him, and it seems to me that this is the only part of the preaching of the apostle St. Thomas, who, as we know, preached the divine mysteries to them, that has remained with them.[8]

Somewhat deformed or reduced, other elements of Guarani religion appear in the pages of Montoya's writings: belief in the mythical jaguar of the Gemini cycles, couvade and funeral rites that express their concept of the soul, the flood tradition and, in particular, the practice of divination and magic, generally understood to be evil sorcery related to diabolical powers.

Today these writings call attention to the fact that the very missionaries who ought to have been specialists in sacred things were so reluctant to appreciate the indigenous religious experience that they barely recorded a few isolated aspects and, even then, judged them negatively. Through the years these prejudices only increased, until they reached conclusions that are clearly both unjust and wrong.

> They did not know anything, nor could they find out anything, with any degree of certainty, about their ancient traditions, which they repeated with a great deal of obfuscation. They spoke much of some universal flood, but the term that they used to express the idea meant little more than the effect of a river overflowing its banks.[9]

However, despite these very negative ideas, they had to admit that it was the peculiar religious experience of the Guarani tribe that permitted and even favoured the noted religious experience of the Guarani in the reductions, when the formal religious structure was the recipient of new content, all the while preserving some of the forms of the basic Guarani experience, in which the inspired and audible word means everything. In effect, in the recently established missions not only did dreams and visions not disappear, but they gave evidence to the great power of symbolic language in the service of the task of converting the people. Among many of the Guarani there was a "rewording" of the message, which remained Guarani, in spite of the total impact of expressions and concepts aimed at steering them toward new meaning, which always was striving to bring about a substitution of religion rather than their conversion, per se.

If there had not been Guarani tribes who remained on the margin of the colonial culture dominated by Creoles and missionaries, it would be difficult indeed for us today to reconstruct the primitive religious experience with any probability of attaining a reasonable facsimile of it. Opaque and apparently discordant fragments, gleaned from the documents of missionaries and travelers, are highlighted and harmonised. When we can once again put them into context, even the modern Guarani, in turn, cannot tarnish their scintillating and even resplendent character.

Repeatedly, missionaries have demonstrated their relative inability to enter into dialogue with the "spirit" of indigenous societies which are so emphatically mystical, like the Guarani. This represents a rather critical theological problem, which seriously questions what kind of religious experience the missionary has had. The data from the documents show that the Guarani had more of spiritual openness to incorporate the religious forms of the missionaries into their system than the other way around. This openness and tolerance was not due to the weakness or inconsistency of the primitive people in regard to maintaining and knowing how to defend their religious principles, as missionaries have frequently thought, but rather the very way they conceive of the "word," which equips the Guarani for a sincere and true dialogue in the Spirit. It is this care that gave rise to the warning from the Guarani ethnographer Curt Nimuendaju, in a memorable page: "Though naturally a Guarani, in his intimate self, he is so convinced about the truth of his religion that the more he becomes a Christian the more fervent he remains, the more he is never intolerant again."[10]

THE ANTHROPOLOGICAL APPROACH

The beauty and depth of the Guarani experience was belatedly revealed to us, thanks to the participation of a few non-Guarani people who approached it with respect and have been able to describe and translate it correctly. Without renouncing the scientific objectivity to which they definitely laid claim, these people did not impede the spiritual insights, which they had shared, from shining through their writings. On the other hand, in the absence of an evangelising or civilizing project, they were not taken to a field for mere observation and for our benefit; rather, they put their own lives at risk to gain insight.

Given that in these pages I shall cite and make reference to the texts that were compiled almost in their entirety by three persons who entered into the Guarani experience in a notable way, I will briefly trace their human and scientific development in order to better place their literary presentation.

Curt Unkel Nimuendaju, a German, born in Jena in 1883, was in contact with the Guarani, who are called Apapokuva, starting in 1905. He was formally adopted by the tribe, who "baptised" him according to their own rites and gave him the name Nimuendaju ("He who knew how to clear his own road in this world and win his place")—definitely a fitting distinction and definition for someone who became one of them and took his place among them, who made him part of their world.

In being a new Guarani, Nimuendaju learned from experience the three essential elements of the Guarani religion: the importance of the word in all Guarani religious experience, the myth of the creation and destruction of the world as a foundation for the beliefs, and the dance-prayer that is the great ritual sacrament expressed with special intensity. The realisation of each one of these aspects takes specific forms in religious experience. It is this that enabled him to write his work entitled *The myths of the creation and destruction of the world as basic tenets of the religion of the Apapokuva-Guarani*, which was published in German in 1914. This work sheds more light on the authentic Guarani religion than everything that has been written since.

León Cadogan (1899-1973) defended the Guarani from the unjust and disreputable situation in which they found themselves in Paraguay. He was taken in among the Mbya, whose "first beautiful words" were entrusted and revealed to him; he managed to collect, translate and interpret them with the greatest degree of respect and reliability, aware of the fact that he was the recipient of a hidden wisdom, which is the strength of the people. The resulting compilation, which bears the title *Ayvu rapyta* ("Fundamental words or the basis of human language"), today is regarded as a classic of American indigenous literature. It is essentially a collection of theological hymns from these jungle prophets, from words inspired in dreams, from deep mysticism and from a broad spiritual vision. Through this writing and others by Cadogan, the Guarani appear as a veritable storehouse of spirituality comparable to other great religious traditions in the world.

The work of Egon Schaden (1954), which portrays the basic fundamentals of Guarani culture and, more specifically, their religious nature, also obtained by a sincere participation in Guarani life, is more systematic and more academic.

These are not the only ones who in recent decades have revealed the Guarani religious universe, but their contributions are certainly the most authentic, because they transcribed directly the indigenous words. Perhaps the most important thing about these scholars is that to the extent that they were able, and even with overwhelming limitations, they have captured the Guarani spirit. They have not put questions to the Guarani from other philosophical or theological systems, looking for similarities or differences, but have made themselves disciples of the word through the act of listening.

This anthropological approach is not only an excellent method to learn, but provides the condition without which understanding is not possible: experience. In fact, listening is not enough no matter how it is done. It is necessary to reconstruct the underlying principle that characterises the relationships and assimilate them in their entirety in the form of one's own personal experience. This approach, which was applied to a high degree in the case of Nimuendaju and Cadogan,[11] confers on the texts which they present to us this fascinating depth. The theologians who take up the task of reflection on the indigenous religious experiences, undoubtedly find much in these models to inspire them.

3

Ayvu Rapyta

THE WORD IS EVERYTHING

For the Guarani, the word is everything, and everything is word. These affirmations, which our ethnocentrism immediately attributes to some kind of "Western" influence from surreptitious Platonic origins, are, nevertheless, the most persistent expressions of what the Guarani are telling us through their myths, songs and rites. The characteristic which defines

Guarani psychology, sociology and theology is the peculiar religious experience of the word.

It is not easy to systematize all that the word is for the Guarani, given the various subcultures, each one with its own traditions, through which the Guarani way of being presents itself. The difficulties are similar to those one finds when attempting to formulate a theology of the Spirit or the Logos in Christian tradition. We shall have to turn to particular texts, examine their semantic value in a broader context, and verify their authenticity in the experiences of life.

A lengthy text of the Mbya, which is especially expressive, though not unique, will help us better understand and visualise the basis of the word:

> The true Father Ñamandu, the first,
> of a part of his celestial being
> from the wisdom contained in being celestial
> with his knowledge which is opening up,
> made the llamas and the clouds reproduce.
> Having begun and stood erect as a man,
> from the wisdom contained in his celestial being,
> with his expansive and communicative knowledge
> he knew the basic future word for himself.
> From the wisdom contained in his celestial being,
> in virtue of his knowledge that blossoms into flower,
> Our Father caused the basic word to be opened
> and it became as he is, divinely celestial.
>
> When the earth did not exist,
> in the midst of the ancient darkness,
> when nothing was known,
> he caused the basic word to be opened,
> which became divinely celestial with him;
> this is what Ñamandu, the true father, the first, did.
>
> Already knowing for himself the basic word that was
>   to be,
> from the wisdom contained in his celestial being,
> in virtue of his knowledge that blossoms into flower,
> he knew for himself the basis of love for another.
> . . . .
>
> Having already caused the basis of the word that was
>   to be to blossom into flower

having already caused a single love to blossom into
    flower,
from the wisdom contained in his heavenliness,
in virtue of his knowledge that blossoms into flower,
he caused a mighty song to be spread abroad.
When the earth did not exist,
in the midst of the ancient darkness,
when nothing was known,
he caused that a powerful song be spread abroad for
    himself.
. . . .

Having already caused the basis of the future word to
    blossom into flower for himself,
having already caused a part of love to blossom into
    flower for himself,
having already caused a powerful song to blossom into
    flower for himself,
he carefully considered
who would be made to participate in the basis of the
    word,
who would participate in this singular love,
who would participate in the series of words that
    would make up the song.
. . . .

Having already considered deeply,
he caused those who were to be companions of his
    celestial divine being to stand forth,
. . . .

he caused the Ñamandu of great heart to stand forth.
He caused them to stand forth with the reflection of
    his wisdom,
when the earth did not exist,
in the midst of the ancient darkness.
. . . .

After all of this,
from the wisdom contained in his celestial being,
in virtue of his wisdom that blossoms into flower,
to the true father of the future Karai,
to the true father of the future Jakaira,

to the true father of the future Tupa,
he caused them to be known as divinely celestial.
The true fathers of his own many children,
the true fathers of the words of his own many children,
he caused them to be known as divinely celestial.
After all of this,
the true father Ñamandu,
to she who was before his very heart,
to the true future mother of the Ñamandu,
he caused her to be known as (divinely) celestial.
(Karai, Jakaira and Tupa in the same way placed
      before their hearts the future mothers of their
      children.)
Because they had already assimilated the celestial
      wisdom of
their own First Father,
because they had already assimilated the basis of the
      word,
because they had already assimilated the basis of love,
because they had already assimilated the series of
      words of the powerful song,
because they had already assimilated the wisdom that
 blossoms in flower,
for this same reason, we call them:
sublime true fathers of words,
sublime true mothers of words.[12]

This text, heard and recorded by Cadogan, who also offers a version in the Mbya dialect, is not a fixed hymn which forms part of a ceremonially repeated tradition or any other form. It is simply a unique prophetic word, certainly uttered within the traditional formal guidelines, but without any dogmatic value. It is one of these songs, often in the form of a prayer, that the Mbya-Guarani chant, by which they make an effort to obtain strength from on high and to which a small group meeting in a house of prayer reverently listen with approving exclamations.

With Cadogan, we can affirm that these verses, transcribed almost in their entirety, constitute one of the most important expressions of the Guarani religion. When asked about the sense of the key concept of *ayvu rapyta* (basis of the word or basic word), two Mbya leaders offered this exegesis: "In the basis of the word he made it to open and to take his (divinely) celestial being Our First Father, so that it would be the centre of the marrow of the soul-word;" and, "The basis of the word is the original word, that of Our First Fathers, when they sent their numerous children to the earthly dwelling in order that there they might stand proud, distributed to them."

The gift of the word given by the "divine" Fathers, and the participation in the word on the part of the mortals, distinguishes who is a Guarani and what that person can become. It is certain that the life of a Guarani at every critical stage—conception, birth, receiving a name, initiation, parenthood, sickness, the shaman vocation, death and after-death—is defined within itself through the function of a unique and singular word which does as it says, and in some way is inseparable from the person. All this, which could seem like an arbitrary transposition of Western Platonic thought into the Guarani universe, has recorded documentary proof in several ethnographic sources; in other words, we are dealing with an actual indigenous experience.

"A being who will be the joy of the beloved ones is about to take his seat."[13] This metaphor expresses the Guarani idea of the conception of a new human being. Man (or woman), when born, will be a word that stands erect and grows until reaching full human stature.

> When he is about to take his seat
> he will bring joy to those who are adorned with
>   feathers,
> to the adorned ones,
> for he sends to our earth, a good word
> which will stand there,
> says Our First Father to the true Fathers of the words
>   of his own children.[14]

From their respective heavens, the Fathers of the soul-words generally communicate with the man who is to be a father through a dream. Then the dreamed word is communicated to the woman, takes its place in her and begins the conception of a new human being. The need for sexual relations to bring about conception is acknowledged. However, this act is only necessary because it is the will of the First Fathers. The baby is sent by Those Above. "The father receives the baby in a dream, tells the dream to the mother and then she becomes pregnant."[15] The word "takes its place" in the womb of the mother (oñembo-apayka), just as the word descends on a shaman when he himself is seated at a ritual banquet in the guise of a tiger. Conception of a human being and the conception of the shaman's song are identical. To the Guarani it is not an exaggeration to say that procreation is first and foremost a poetic, religious act, more than an erotic sexual act. Furthermore, eroticism among the Guarani has its own meaningful expressions during the ritual festivals, when they sing, pray, dance, participate in drinking *chicha* and in eating the corn cakes.

> The idea of the human soul, as the Guarani understand it in their primitive psychology, undoubtedly is the indispensable key for understanding their whole religious system . . . For that matter, the idea of the soul is more easily comprehended starting from the beliefs relative to conception.[16]

The doctrine of conception of the human being differs depending on the Guarani group, and even within the same group, at times, depending on the interpreter, just as their psychological theory differs. Two, three and even more souls can be present and active in a Guarani.[17]

However, for all of the Guarani the "sublime" and the initial nucleus of the person is the "word" (*ayvu o ne'é*), and as such a divine partaking through participation; it is the soul-word that, owing to its very origin, is destined to return to the fathers from whom it proceeds; it is both good and indestructible. Other souls are "shadows"—"passion," which embodies something of the animal character, and "the imperfect way of being," with its manifestations of bad character, aggressiveness, or simply an earthly and bodily condition.

However, the most important aspect of all of this theological psychology is found in the conviction that the soul, when given, is not fully formed, but is in the process of developing. The way a person develops is through making decisions: the history of the Guarani soul is the history of his word, the series of words that form the hymn of his life. "Our word is the manifestation of our soul that does not die; . . . *anq* is the shadow, the trail, the echo."[18]

Closely connected to the means of conception are the cautions marked by numerous tabus laid upon the father and the mother of the newborn. To ensure the development of the soul-word of the child is the main concern of the parents. In a relatively short time—two or three days among the Ava-Katu, up until the child begins to talk for the Mbya and the Pai—a ceremony is performed to determine the name of the person, which is the equivalent to determining "what is the soul-word that has arrived among us" and from which "heaven" it has come.

> The *payé* or shaman must submit himself to a superhuman effort in order to put himself in contact with the celestial beings, something that only happens in a state of ecstasy. To achieve this, when the sun has barely gone down he takes his place, sings and begins to

shake a rattle . . . The song continues in this way for hours. Through this procedure, the shaman receives supernatural faculties from the powers to whom the song is addressed that are transmitted to the child.

Among the modern Guarani there are some parts that show quite a similarity to the Christian ritual of baptism. However, what is unique and important is that the name which is discovered by means of the shaman's ceremony has a very special meaning for the Guarani.

Man is in a certain sense, in their eyes, a piece of the soul of the one who carries it or is almost identical with the soul, inseparable from the person. The Guarani is not "called" in this or that manner, he "is" thus and so. For example, when someone misuses a name, it can influence the one who bears that name.[19]

The Guarani think it is ridiculous that the Catholic priest has to ask the parents of a child what the child's name is.

Among the Mbya the process of receiving a name basically adheres to the same rules. When the child is yet without a name, it is the subject of anger, the root and source of all evil. "Only when they are called by the names that we, the Fathers of the word, give them, do they cease to get angry." He who gives a name to the child (*mita renoi a*) prepares himself to receive the revelation. He lights the pipe, breathes out puffs of smoke on the crown of the child's head and finally communicates to the mother the name of the one that he discovered. This name is an integral part of the person and is designated by the expression "that which keeps the flow of speech standing" (*'ery mo'ã a*).[20]

When the person has received a name, he begins to stand as his word is lifted up, that which imparts greatness to his heart and strengthens him, the two great virtues that are the aspiration of a good Guarani.

Guarani education is an education of the word, but they are not educated to learn texts, let alone to memorize them, but to listen to the words that have been received from above, usually in dreams, and to be able to tell what they have received. The Guarani seek for perfection in character through the perfection of speech; their worth and prestige among the members of the community and even among the neighbouring communities come from the degree of perfection, and even the quantity, of the songs and the different ways in which they are able to speak. As wisdom precedes the development of their word, which comes, in turn, from the property and intensity of their inspiration, it is easy to see how essential the appropriate religious experience is for the Guarani, which not everyone realizes to the same degree, but to which they all aspire in some way or other.

This phenomenon was noted by the Jesuit missionaries during the seventeenth century, and Father Antonio Ruiz de Montoya gives us an interpretation, though somewhat limited in scope: "Many ennoble themselves with the eloquence of their speech (they esteem their language so, and with reason, for it is worthy of praise and celebration among the famous), with it they gather people and servants to them, by it they and their descendants are ennobled."[21]

Potentially every Guarani is a prophet and/or a poet depending on the degree the person attains in religious experience.

When someone in a Guarani groups achieves his first *payé* song (shaman song), it is always an event of general interest. Only in the old stories about amazing things have I heard of children receiving such inspiration. Among older people inspiration is more and more frequent and among those who have passed their fortieth birthdays, it is exceptional if one does not possess a *payé* song. Some sing on the most meaningless occasion; for example, when crossing a bridge in order to keep balanced and not fall in the water, while in similar opportunities others are more reserved; on extraordinary occasions, especially when in trouble, some persons can be heard singing who did not even know that they had their own songs. In the majority of instances the individual receives his song while he is sleeping, with the apparition of some deceased relative who appears to him in a dream.[22]

The experiences through which the Guarani Indian receives the gift of mystical song are moving,[23] and their texts are of great poetic beauty and religious depth. Here is one that will serve for them all, in that a limitless number have never been recorded:

> Around the houses where they say beautiful prayers
> I go walking, dispersing the clouds
> (the smoke of ritual tobacco smoke).
> To preserve it so, I shall learn numerous words
> to strengthen my inner being.
> So that the true Fathers of my word will see it;
> that in a not too distant future they will cause me to
>   say
> many, many words . . .
> Although we love one another sincerely,

if we allow our heart to be divided,
we will never reach a greatness of heart nor be
strengthened.[24]

Very appropriately it has been said that "the whole mental life of a Guarani focuses on the Beyond . . . Their cultural ideal is a mystical experience of divinity which is not dependent on the ethical qualities of the individual, but on the spiritual openness to hear the voice of revelation. This attitude and this ideal are what determine the personality of the individual."[25]

Placing oneself in the proper state to hear the beautiful good words by fasting, sexual abstinence, and observing an austere way of living, eating and sleeping, is a practice that is still in vogue among the contemporary Guarani, especially the Mbya. There are modes of behaviour, attitudes and postures that favour the "talking to oneself" (ñembo'é); that is, prayer.

We said that the word is not humanly taught or learned. For many Guarani it is foolish and even provocative to try to teach children in a school; from this springs their suspicion and, at times, outright rejection of teaching in schools by Western terms. The word is a gift which is received from on high, not a bit of knowledge learned from another mortal being.

Even so, there are moments and situations of special inspirational intensity among the Guarani. These are connected with existential crises, through which all men and women pass while in this earthly dwelling. Some of the circumstances are fixed, such as menstruation in women, in a sense the initiation of a boy, and death; others are casual, even ordinary, such as roads and their dangers, the hunt and agriculture, invitations and festivals, sicknesses and paranormal psychological states.

Each one of these steps is accompanied by song-prayers, directed by the person, or someone designated by the person. Though the word is received individually and personally, it is almost never for individual use; it is preferred that it be used in public, at least for the edification of the others in the house, who through accompaniment, participate in the word and make it their own.

The initiation of boys, in force mainly among the Pai-Tavytera (or Koyova), with its intense exercises and ritual practices that last for weeks, can be compared to a formal kind of instruction, but it has nothing to do with schooling. It is true that the boys are taken to listen to mythological traditions which constitute the most important beliefs, but principally they rehearse songs and dances that can stimulate a serious and a profound religious experience. The initiation concludes with the piercing of the lower lip and the insertion of the "lip stone" (tembeta) or large button in the shape of a nail, which confers dignity and authenticity to the young man and is the mark of his identity.

The initiation among the Mbya and the Chiripa (or Ava-Katu) is less relevant, but it is a fact that the participation in the dances and the accompaniment to the songs from a very early age prepare Guarani boys for a religious experience that will make them the possessors of their own prayer identity and their own song identity some day.

"The resource which is always at hand, that the Guarani use to stimulate and at the same time, give vent to their religious experiences is a special song (*porahéi*) or prayer . . . The most valuable possessions that an individual has are his *porahéi*, to which he makes reference with pride and even a degree of reverence . . . "[26] These prayers and songs belonging to individuals, because they are the gift of the spirits to specific persons, are also a force in the community, for when the people hear the prayers and dance them, they identify with what is expressed and feel consoled. It is thanks to the prayers and chants that the Guarani feel that the world can delay its future and inevitable destruction, an aspect that we shall return to in relation to the "land without evil."

THE PROPHETIC WORD

It is always through the use of the inspired word that the Guarani grows in personality, prestige and even power, whether political power, magical power or both, which is usually the most common.

The classification of leaders, generally men but without entirely excluding women, is structured according to the degree of excellence in the "speaking of one's word," in the word. There are several types of sorcerers and magicians that are reported in the missionary chronicles of the colonial centuries, who are shamans, in anthropological jargon, or "jungle prophets," to use the modern term.

Nobody can become a shaman (*payé*) through learning, not even under the direction of the great ones, but only by inspiration. They do not belong to a closed caste, nor is the gift hereditary. According to the shaman song, the Apapokuva (Guarani) are divided into four classes: those who have not yet received any inspiration at all; those who have received one or more songs; the ritual leaders, called "our father" and "our mother" (*ñande ru* and *ñande sy*); and the shaman chiefs or community officials.

Generally those of the third class are the ones who officiate at typical religious functions. Among the Ava-Katu they are also called singers (*oporaiva*). Their song is available as a service to the community, to find the name of a newborn, to cure diseases, to lead a ritual ceremony, to speak prophetically concerning the way things are and the way they ought to be, and to remember traditional mythical stories. However, we repeat, this is not a profession or responsibility; that which makes a person a shaman is not an exclusive calling, in that to a greater or lesser degree every Guarani is a "chanter" and a prophet. There is no priestly class.

It is true that there are certain charisms that are held to be more important, such as that of a seer (*tesapyso*); being in the right conditions to find and give a name to a child; the ability to carry the "great ritual song" through to a good ending.

Several roles revolve around the two poles: a remarkable exercise of the word, and a providential patrimony.

If the fourth class, that of the shaman, is the most important, it is because, along with a remarkable ability with the word and the virtues belonging to a magician, they attribute to him the authority of a father who knows how to give counsel, how to organise a feast, how to provide resources and how to take decisive measures for the life of the community, even in the rural areas where the colonial societies are considered to hold the civil and material authority. The Guarani prophet and shaman is in reality by title more of a father figure than a chief; he brings all his powers to bear upon the perfection of his speech, of the word that fulfills, magically or persuasively, what he says. In principle, any Guarani can aspire to this category because as a potential prayer leader, singer or prophet, a person can also be a religious leader. Charisma, authority and leadership are aspects of fatherhood. In ancient times, probably, the Guarani had no other authority besides that of the head of an extended family, who, in his time, possessed the charisma of prophecy, the interpretation for healing and was the guardian of religious traditions. This is the figure who has remained as a prototype and reference point of true authority among the Guarani: "our father" who is also "our leader." The modern community officials and chiefs are somewhere in between the traditional concept from which they derive their authority and status as charismatic religious leaders, and the function that is imposed on them by the colonial and the neo-colonial societies of the "civilised ones," who want to see them simply as those who carry out the orders of others. The Guarani, even those who have adjusted to this modern kind of chief, remain loyal to their religious leaders, whose good and true words they respect.

And the sorcerers? It is true that there are "doctors" who heal by their prayers and their songs; there are also sages (*mba'ekuaá*) who use their knowledge to do evil. The Guarani fear them, and most of the time prefer not to face them, but when they discover who they are, they treat them as murderers and execute them. There are "masters of poison" (*moajary*), "ones who know" (*mba'ekuaá*), bad shaman (*payé vía*), "those who perform harmful works" (*poroavykya*) mentioned by the various Guarani groups. Many of these use elements of black magic, of which it is not appropriate to give details here, but to obtain the desired harmful effects they are accompanied by "prayers to do evil" as well.[27]

The remedy against sorcery is found in some therapeutic and magical practices, but mostly they rely on "good prayers." "Those who pray well, extract the noxious weeds . . . When a tree of the 'disobedient word' harms someone, those who possess the good science exorcise the curse, and draw out the evil."[28]

The word, name, prayer, chant, medicinal invocation, prophecy, political and religious exhortation, all these forms of "speaking one's word" are the special preserve of the Guarani religion. Guarani are religious because they create a word, and in making a word they participate with the First Fathers, Fathers of the soul-words. The Guarani religion is a religion of the inspired word. It is this way and practice of being religious that profoundly typifies their religion when compared to other kinds of religion, including Christianity—at least the Christianity that was presented to them during colonial times as a religion more of doctrine rather than inspiration, more of priests rather than prophets. The fact is that a synthesis never emerged when numerous Guarani simply converted to the religion of the Catholic missionaries; rather, a substitution process took place with deep rifts in the psychological, ritual, social and, naturally, the poetic aspects of their lives. We shall leave this aspect now, taking note of this fact in order to take it up again later at the level of historical analysis.

4

The Ritualized Word

The Guarani word is spoken and it has the power to be act; the way to the word, its "sacraments," is found in chant and dance. As religious people, the Guarani speak in signs and rites.

The chant, which is generally sung with very simple intonation and almost always accompanied by some instrument, is the most common ritual form in the Guarani religious expression. Although the chant is usually received in a dream while sleeping, its enunciation and expression is very conscious and clear, even though it comes with such intensity and metaphorical fantasy typical of poetic language. Of course, there are some chants which consist of repeated unintelligible words, but these are the exception.

Each ethnic subgroup of Guarani has its own special forms of chants and rituals that ought to be described separately. However, we shall make an attempt to summarize their basic and generic characteristics here, endeavouring not to lose the real picture.

INVOCATIONS AND PRAYERS OF PETITION

The Guarani are not acquainted with songs and dances that are specifically secular. Chant, dance and prayer are synonymous; a prayer is a chant that is danced, just as a dance is a prayer that is sung. There are three kinds of chant-dance: *purahei, kotyu* and *guahu*.[29] The last two can seem to be more secular or profane because frequently they have a lyrical, erotic theme, but even then they never lose their connection with the religious festival which is the preferred setting for their performance.

The Pai's prayers of invocation speak of the relationship with ecology and the economy in which the traditional Guarani life unfolded. The prayful Guarani are first of all farmers, though they have never given up hunting or gathering from the tropical jungle, which poses its share of dangers. In these chanted prayers the Guarani usually ask for protection from the spirit who is deemed master of that activity, or they ask for help against some danger, preventing the influence of an evil spirit. When burning off a plot in the forest, they will pray, alone or with the family, against rats, birds, dogs and wild pigs that can ruin the crops. They also pray when they want rain. In addition, there are prayers for blessing: blessing honey, fruit and meat. When they go out into the forest, they make invocation to attract the game; they talk to the traps so that they will catch a lot of prey, but they ask for forgiveness from the animal that is hunted, telling him that they only kill him in order to feed their family. Another type of prayer is made concerning travel on the road and its dangers. The Guarani are not nomads, but they are great travelers who like to roam the jungle and visit other communities. So when walking on the path, they pray that the jaguar, the vipers, the snakes and the evil spirit will be "shamed" by the travelers and will go away and leave them in peace.

When the Chiriguano-Isoceño of Bolivia go into the jungle they demonstrate with various songs and invocations familiarity and closeness of the sacred. A recent publication, *Textos sagrados de los Guaraníes en Bolivia*,[30] offers a good collection of these conversational prayers, full of respect and affection for the "masters of the jungle," who are treated with humility, though equally with familiarity and more than a little humour.

Just before daybreak or in the twilight of an evening, it is not unusual in a Mbya hut to hear a prayer. It is chanted by a man to music from a kind of rustic guitar, accompanied by the rhythmic beats of the pounding stick, which the woman holds vertically and beats on the ground. They are inspired songs, generally received in dreams from Those Above; their purpose is to obtain courage and reach greatness of heart.[31]

> Oh, Our First Father!
> it was you who first knew the rules of our way of
>   being.
> It was you who first knew within yourself that which
>   was
> to be the basic word,
> before opening and showing the earthly dwelling . . .
> Towards greatness of heart, some among us, from
>   among the
> few that remain, we are trying hard . . .
> To those of us who remain erect in this earth,
> grant that we may live, standing straight,
> with greatness of heart.

When analyzed in their context, these and other prayers, which sometimes seem to be intimate or introverted in character, are always a reflection about the human condition, between the society of the upper world and the actual historical society in this "earthly dwelling."

For these and other expressions that are included particularly in the work of Cadogan (*Ayvu rapyta*), the Mbya-Guarani have been called the "jungle prophets."[32] A prophetic and poetic inspiration is found in various forms and degrees in all of the ethnic Guarani groups, whether Mbya, Ava-Katu-ete, or Pai-Tavytera.

RITUAL SONG AND DANCE IN THE GESTURE OF INVITATION AND THE FESTIVAL

The festival is the real authentic time, the time for the use of the real names of the Guarani. What is prepared and carried out during this time is the "sacrament" of the Guarani society as a whole. It will suffice to analyse in detail, in its numerous unfoldings, what the festival represents among the Guarani to give us an understanding of their ideal for society and their Utopian vision. Today as yesterday, the situation, vitality and the expected crises take on meaning immediately in the light of the frequency and quality of their festivals.

The Guarani festival is not just a ceremony; it is the concrete metaphor of an economy based on the principle of reciprocity that is religiously observed. In this work we cannot adequately discuss what an economy of reciprocity is, its various forms and the social and religious practices which are part of it. The interchange of goods, whether for eating or for use, is guided by a principle of equal distribution, according to which the duty to give assumes the duty to receive as well, and receiving in turn brings one to the obligation to give. Thus, the interchange is a social dialogue, often religious, by which the thing that circulates the most is the prestige of the one who knows how to give and the joy of the one who knows how to receive, in accordance with the model set by the First Fathers and First Mothers, who in the beginning lived together, sharing life.

We shall look at a festival among the Pai-Tavytera as an example of the ritual and practice of a reciprocal economy. It is the festival of the green corn, of *chicha* or *kawi*, which is mentioned in the most ancient ethno-historical sources. Usually each community has its festival of corn, once a year, but these festivals happen in many neighbouring communities, one after another, and in one house after another, to the extent that the atmosphere of feasting and conviviality often lasts for weeks and even months.

It is important to understand that the festival is not an isolated or separate act of social and religious life but the metaphor inscribed in a network of relationships. It can be said that the festival has its origin in the obligation which was taken on at the close of the previous festival; the end and the beginning are intertwined.

To start at a specific point in the festival, which is first of all cyclical time, we can say that it begins basically when the invitation is sent out to the homes and neighbouring communities. This invitation establishes in the same spirit of generosity an obligation to receive. Not to attend a festival to which one has been invited is equivalent to an act of aggression, while the acceptance of an invitation is usually the most dignified way to put to rest any quarrels or misunderstandings, when there are any such problems.

Meanwhile, in the home the *chicha* is prepared several days in advance. The corn is ground in the mortar, mixed with water, boiled in huge pots—the ancient pottery bears testimony to the magnitude and importance of this preparation—cooled, chewed and mixed with saliva by the women of the house, and put into a tray or a "canoe" made from cedar wood, where it is left to ferment. Today the prosperity and well-being of a community can be measured by the number of trays that are available in the homes and by the homes that make the trays available.

On the appointed day, the guests arrive, usually in groups, and perform the ritual greeting. When evening comes they start the *mborahei puku* (the great, long chant), which lasts all night. It is sung by one of the rare men who is able to carry it through—on his feet without sitting down the whole night—without any interruptions or faltering. With his right hand he shakes the rattle; with the left he grasps the baton. The gentle rhythm and the somewhat monotonous dance suggests walking, although the dancers "walk" without moving from one place. Inside the big house the men who accompany the singer in the song and the rhythmic beat are lined up one beside the other in parallel rows. They stay in front of the *mba'é marangatu* (holy object), a kind of extremely bare altar, which consists of a few sticks stuck into the ground, without objects of veneration, sometimes barely adorned with some feathers. This "holy object" is not really a cult object, but rather just a point of reference.

In the morning after sunrise the *chicha* is served by the lady of the house, her daughters and other women. The following night they usually continue the festival with other kinds of chants: *kotyu* and *guahu*. These are sung and danced, most often in great choruses accompanied by alternating movements with the participants opening and closing the circle they have formed. The choreography very explicitly symbolizes the unity among them all, the participation and euphoria of being together. In the intervals they drink. In these dance sequences there is no hint of a hierarchical arrangement; adults, young people and even children form the circle. The women usually form dance groups apart from the others, but often men and women mix together in the same dance group.

When it is fully day, the festival finishes and the guests return to their homes. They attended because they were obliged to receive; they go away under a duty to give in return.

Other festivals occur throughout the year, with a greater or lesser number of guests, with various amounts of drinking, over the period of several days or just for a few hours after sundown, but there is always drinking and singing with dancing. There is, for example, the festival that develops during the weeks of preparation for the initiation when the boys receive the piercing of their lips and the lip plug. It is the festival of all festivals and, as such, serves as a model for all Guarani rituals; the *chicha*, the dance, the long chant, and the other chants are performed in this festival with more care and intensity. After all, this festival is really a huge invitation to come and "create" the boys, just as though they were invited to work together building a house or preparing a field for planting.

As a metaphor for the reciprocal economy, the Guarani festival goes beyond the economic dimension, and it is more than merely symbolic.

The festival is not the result of a surplus of goods, which can be distributed equally by means of a festival; neither is it the solution that could have been devised by a primitive people for the shared consumption of communal wealth. The festival not only uses and distributes any surplus, it produces an extra amount. It is the specific instrument for the establishment of the relationships required for participative production. The well-known system of shared labour in the communal market gardens and pastureland, so evident in certain rural areas even today, is contextualized in the festival, which promotes levels of satisfactory production to ensure the people of an abundance for new and future festivals. The Guarani festival can be considered as a sacrament according to which the material produce which is consumed is blessed and becomes part of the prayers of the religious chants and dances.

The colonial society looked upon these festivals as drunken orgies with a considerable element of immoral behaviour. More than anything, however, they saw them as a hindrance to accumulation and an exploitation of good produce on the part of the Indians, in spite of the fact that their religious character did not escape the notice of some missionaries. Historically, it was never understood that the justice of proper distribution and the foundations for happy and productive relationships among people revolved around these festivals. All is carried out because Those Above, Our Fathers, desired it to be so. The chant and dance are a means of communicating with these supernatural beings and even imitating them; on earth as in Earth, the Earth of Origin, and that which shall be at last, "without evil."

The dance ritual and its songs symbolize the way in which society is united and working and is celebrated together. The festival, as a special form of ceremonial life, also reveals the "lack of internal differentiation in the social body,"[33] a healthy anarchy and equality that is the foundation of the freedom which is so much reflected in the face of the Guarani.

Although it may seem somewhat contradictory to all that has been said thus far, the festival also gives the people an opportunity to bring into the open their conflicts and tensions, their passions and jealousies. Enemies meet, in a state of inebriation and without self-control because of the celebration, in an appropriate place for telling the whole truth. They remember that Our First Father broke the relationship with his wife and left her when she, out of jealously, accused him of drunken behaviour at a festival. However, these very real and bloody conflicts and fights can be satisfactorily resolved in other festivals, when once again the ties that bind them all together will be reinstated. The real crisis of disintegration takes place when, for a number of consecutive years, the festivals are suspended, as sometimes happens among the families and individuals who are living in isolated circumstances in a non-Guarani environment.

5

The Original Word

As shown on the ceremonial and ritual level, Guarani religion is also expressed through the mythical discourse that tells the story of the origin of the way of being that is peculiarly theirs. In the Guarani's case, as has been noted for other peoples of the Tupi-Guarani family, "symbolic language," which is revealed "on the ceremonial and metaphysical level," is also the most adequate framework for understanding society, in which the rules and social structures are barely distinguished from the cosmological rules and structures, because they create a unique system between them. The underlying principles of this system are the basic structures of reciprocity.[34]

The original word—which is just as we have portrayed the word that tells the myths—is a word that means the reciprocity of knowing how to give this great gift that is the gift of words. Ritualized words and prophetic words are forms of communication and exchange of messages.

THE MYTH OF CREATION

In spite of all that has been said and written about the Guarani, the essential part of their mythological system was unknown until it was brought to light by Nimuendaju in 1914, when he transcribed what he called *The legends of the creation and destruction of the world as the basis of the religion of the Apapokuva-Guarani.*

It is rather difficult to offer a resumé of these myths, because it is in the detail and concrete symbolism where the most expressive intensity is seen. Nevertheless, I shall make an attempt in this regard.

Ñande Ru vusu, Our Great Father, comes first and reveals himself through the original darkness; on his breast is a light like the sun. He gives the earth its beginning, placing it on a firm foundation.

He and the other Our Father, "the one who knows all things," meet a woman, Our Mother, who as wife to both of them, finds herself pregnant with twins. Ñande Ru vusu is angered and abandons Our Mother on earth and leaves the scene, not to return again until the end times and then only in liturgical references.

The pregnant mother begins to walk in search of her husband, but she is eaten by tigers; the twins are born, alas, already orphans.

At first the twins live together with the tigers in their house, but they will take revenge when they learn that the tigers are the ones who killed their mother. The two of them, who are known as older and younger brother, leave to go for a walk. They try to put their mother back together again, starting with her bones. They do not manage it, and death is introduced to this earth definitively. These heroes are the ones who shaped the world to be "Guarani," in nature as well as in the social and cultural order.[35]

Journeying, always walking, the heroes instigate and produce typical cultural situations: They give names to the wild fruits that they collect; they set traps; they free themselves from the tigers; they steal fire from the ravens; they meet others who are like them, both enemies and future brothers-in-law; they get married. At last they meet with their Father again, through the ritual dance and the "voice" of the rattle. The Father leaves them with what he brings in his hands, his shamanist attributes, and then hides himself again. The earth is threatened; the darkness with its Bats can fall on us, and the Blue Tiger wants to devour us. Meanwhile, Our Father made the person of Tupa, who pours out thunder and lightning when he moves around heaven.

And now, in conclusion, the mythical discourse refers to the fact that is danced all year and it is there in the dance that the shaman is revealed, who is an "Our Father," the road. This road leads to the house of Our Mother, where there is always fruit to eat and *chicha* to drink. This is the festival.

This myth of the twins is common to all the Guarani, from the Atlantic coast to the Bolivian mountain ranges. In spite of a few expressions that probably are giving voice to some modern-day concerns, the structure and the symbolic language of the myth are very archaic and definitely prehistoric. The consonance and analogy of this myth, compared with other myths of the tribes of the Tupi people, put the origin of the myth back two or more millennia, when the main branch of the Tupi people was not yet divided into the tribal subbranches which came with the passing of the centuries.

We dare to venture the hypothesis that the persistence of the myth is due to its metaphysical principles and the social organisation remaining the same single entity in such a way that the basic premise of cultural construction and sociological articulation has been kept away from any significant epistemological changes.[36] The Guarani continue to be just as

Guarani as they were in prehistoric times, and this is so because their "social space" has been kept true to itself. There exists "an operational field of a communication structure between communities, that allows them simultaneously to conceive and organise themselves as a coherent and an integrated whole, with a degree of economic reciprocities and basic symbolism in the society under consideration."[37]

As Schaden has already observed, "The myth of the brothers is—for the Guarani, as it is for many other peoples—the fundamental basic text of their religious doctrine and their ceremonial expressions in particular."[38]

THE COSMOS AND ITS MASTERS

The myth of the twins, in its concrete expression, does not completely cover all of Guarani cosmology and mythology. The Guarani cosmos is inhabited by other beings whose natures are divine, spiritual and supernatural. These beings are not differentiated much and are not so individualized that one could draw an ethnographic catalogue of their names, properties or functions.

The Guarani cosmos is not very insistent on a heaven and an earth, according to a vertical axis of one below and one above. The Guarani cosmos presents itself more as a circular platform, whose principal points of reference are the cardinal points of east and west. The gods are situated according to these cardinal points; they prefer to reveal themselves in them and to act from them. The east-west orientation is not just a solar reference; other meteorological phenomena, such as thunder, lightning, rain and wind all have their origin in a place in this space. Thunder, which is generally personified as Tupa, comes from the west and moves towards the east, revealed in the brilliance of the lightning.[39]

What is curious is that this lesser "god," who was made by Our Great Father and is in the service of Our Mother, has become the Christian God. An interpretation error on the part of the first missionaries was the beginning of this semantic adventure through the catechism and years of linguistic usage. The name Tupa was later enriched with other concepts and transferences from Catholic theology and life, until it came to mean the supreme personal God in many indigenous communities—a process which is, in fact, not so rare in the history of religions, in which the name of an ancestral god is empowered by new meanings in a new religion.[40]

Other spaces in the Guarani cosmos are occupied by other beings, who are said to be related to climactic phenomena or with the destiny of the souls after death, who are able both to punish and to help. Sometimes these beings become "servants" to Our Father because of their origin and their behaviour.

Together with an idea that could refer to the horizonal dimension of the cosmos, according to which "heaven" is located at the borders of the earthly platform, there is also an idea of levels superimposed on this plane, as though the cosmos was structured with different floors or heavens, which the ritual dance crosses. This is the cosmological concept that is implicit in the "Ritual Song of Our Great First-born Grandfather," which is a hymn that tells the story of the creation of the earth, the revelation of the gods who made the earth and the story of humanity, "sons of the word." These are ritually adorned and approach, through the medium of song and dance, the gates of the paradises. The gates open, they cross over and enter the dwellings which, in reality, are precisely the place where the true liturgy is celebrated, as it was celebrated by the First Great Grandfather himself.

The Guarani religion also shows some animistic traits. There are "masters" of the hills, of the mountains and rocky crags, of the animals—especially the animals of the hunt—of the cultivated fields and the pathways. These are the "masters" of nature who are invoked frequently, although more on an individual level and less in the big community celebrations. Perhaps these "masters" of nature represent the more archaic religious beliefs, tied to a lifestyle and an economy based on hunting and gathering.

In the Tupi-Guarani world, one class of supernatural beings called Kurupi or Korupira have always held a place of relative importance. They are the spirits of the jungle, always identified with that environment. "The Kurupi protect the animals and punish the hunter who, though already assured of his sustenance, still kills out of malice. They protect the trees in the same manner, not permitting them to be felled without necessity . . . They are spirits filled with mystery, sometimes tyrannical and brutal, sometimes humble, gentle and even naïve, when they can be easily tricked; therefore, it behooves the hunter to makes offerings to them."[41]

Among the Guarani-Isoseño of the Chaco region of Bolivia, the "masters" of the hills (kaa ija) are part of the fundamental creed and are addressed in very real ritual invocations, even among Christian Indians. The ritual practices of these hunters directly express their intention to make themselves agreeable to these tutelary spirits of the animals, as well as to appease them when they must do the "necessary" evil—their very sustenance—which is the death of the hunted animal.

Among the Guarani the world of vegetation is the object of the same devotion, in that they conceive of it as skin or hair on the earth's body.

Some of the aforementioned spirits that seem to be "minor gods" of the Guarani, such as the Kurupi and various types of Pora, ghosts that inhabit dangerous places, are firmly rooted among the Paraguayan people. One should not trifle with nature.

The "demons" also have a place in the Guarani belief system, a fact that Nimuendaju affirmed. They are the primitive Bats, who, being identified with the darkness, seem even to precede Our Great Father himself; they are enemies and devourers of all the light of the stars, the sun and the moon, as well as the ones who cause the feared eclipses. In addition, there are the original Tigers (or Jaguars), ancestors of the present tigers, among whom the Blue Tiger (a demon with shamanist characteristics, capable of ritual chants) is prominent. The Blue Tiger will soon devour all of humanity when Our Father permits it.

In the myth of the twins some figures who are called "Ana" appear, perhaps representatives of enemies from another tribe. They are creatures held in fear and derision, frightening and at the same time ridiculous; these Ana have become associated with the devil among the Guarani Christians. In this case the semantic transference has operated in a similar manner as with Tupa; that is, a mythological figure is adapted to the representative system in the Catholic religion, even though it is somewhat superficial.

If the listing of so many gods, spirits and supernatural creatures gives the impression of a confused and disorderly religious world, observing Guarani religious practice conveys the opposite: the classifications and mythical orders are easily reduced to forms of religious experience in which prayer—as an act of "speaking one's word" through words received by divine inspiration—is the wondrous event and the basic reality. The Guarani religious experience is made up of the forms of relating to the divine, the varieties of song and dance, and the categories of the prophetic word, more than the content of the beliefs. The profusion of representations of gods and spirits is just a device of a metaphoric cosmogony which symbolically orders the ways of speaking. The act of believing is, above all, the act of speaking, which to the Guarani is the speaking one's word through chant and dance, and particularly, in a festival, which in turn speaks of reciprocity and mutual love (*jopoi* and *joayhu*).

THEOLOGICAL REFLECTION

Among the Guarani there is class of persons that specializes in explaining religion or in leading a particular discussion about it. According to the typology presented by Nimuendaju,[42] the three classes of *payé* are distinguished by the possession of greater or lesser number of inspired songs, ritual performance and the control of magical powers. What is common to all, however, is that all are able, in their own way, to give an account of their own knowledge and experience. Prophets and poets in the performance of their inspiration are theologians as well; they can explain the origin of the word and their relationships to one another. This is a given fact in the ethnographical works that have dealt seriously with the Guarani. As Eduardo Viveiros de Castro observes, "The work of Cadogan provides impressive proof of what has already been stated in the essay by Nimuendaju: that Guarani thinking reaches the integral dimension of a philosophy, producing a powerful ethnological discourse which, taking off from their sociological circumstances . . . goes in the direction of poetry in a metaphysical universe."[43]

In *Ayvu rapyta*,[44] the boldness of the metaphors, together with the cohesion of the symbolic system and the presence with which the "authors" of these hymns and poems give account of the sense of their words is striking. Without hyperbole, one must admit that there is a Guarani philosophy and a Guarani theology, with their own more noted protagonists, which cannot be forgotten without doing them an injustice. Nimuendaju records a number of their names, among them Joguyroky, Ñeenguei, Guayrapaiju, Tupaju and Joguyrovyju. Cadogan transcribes what was dictated to him by Pablo Vera, Tomas Benitez, the chief, Che'iro, Kachirito, Tomas and Cirilo . . . Schaden had the privilege of listening to Marcal de Souza, Pa'i Chiquinho, Pa'i José Bourbon and to 'ñanderu' Bastiao in Poydju, who was his adoptive father. Georg Gruenberg, his wife Friedl, and I owe what we know about the Pai-Tavytera to Pa'i Neri, Pa'i Comes, Evangeli Morilla and Agapito Lopez. Among the Chiripa I was acquainted with Zenon Benitez, Ambrosio Carrillo, Alejandro'i Larrosa, and Silverio Vargas. These are the sages of the Amerindians, who have not written books but with their words have created poetry and prophesy for our world. And the list could go on. These theologians are just a small number among the countless many Guarani who have known how to formulate and develop a cosmological discussion that belongs to them in a very special and nontransferable way. This is the secret wealth of this people and—who knows?—it may be the spirit of their resistance.

This quality of the Guarani religious system—staging a discussion that is so open and creative—provokes a number of questions: Is this an individual fantasy? Or is it a collective tradition? What is the place and function of a cosmological and philosophical creation in a given culture?[45]

The pluriformity of discourse and interpretations does not necessarily lead to the conclusion that there is sectarianism or epistemological chaos among the Guarani. It is true, however, that this fact makes the systematization and exact description of the Guarani religion enormously difficult. There is not just *one* Guarani religion, if by that definite dogmatic formulations are understood, as Schaden has noted in his *Aspectos fundamentais da cultura guarani*.[46] However, there exists a network of relationships between the Guarani society and the supernatural realm which is seen through individual persons.

> One must not despise the extraordinary role of individual religious experience, for in any circumstance a person can enter into contact with the supernatural, receiving consolation, advice or revelations from the deities or from the protecting spirits. In this way, all individuals have their own religious experiences, in accordance with their character and the mystical predilection of their personality. Thus, with the passing of the years, they continue to develop—apparently built upon a common doctrinal basis—their own idea of the world, their own interpretive system, with innovations and "aberrations" which are more or less heterodoxical in character, according to their personal inclinations and experiences.[47]

The Guarani religious experience leads to the following paradox: the ideas about the supernatural world, whether psychological or mythological in nature, are expressed and communicated by real individuals who are believed to be inspired; what is peculiar to these individuals is that they feel, every one of them, that they are the creators of their own mythologies. When they explain something, they are not explaining a text that has been accepted as normative before their time, but what they have just heard and sung as an inspired word.

The open character of the Guarani word and the resulting multiplicity of cosmological discourses and psychological theories among the various *pa'i, ñande ru*, or any other Guarani who speaks about religious experience, aroused a certain uneasiness among the early missionaries and even scorn for a religious discourse that appeared to be so irrational. Present-day anthropologists also feel lost when they try to develop a theoretical and ideological system. This same reality, however, puts the Guarani religion in a place beyond the reach of the dogmatists and doctrinal repetition, in which the freedom of the word actually proclaims the freedom of life. "The Guarani abhor anything that seems to curtail their freedom, which they value above all else."[48]

For these same reasons, the Guarani incorporate elements from other religious systems into their own without difficulty—whether they be sacred objects such as a cross, or religious personages like the great Noah

(Noendusu), or Jesus Christ (Pa'i Tani) with the name of St. Stephen, the proofs of the journey after death, with echoes of a Catholic purgatory, certain ritual signs of baptism, and still other borrowed elements. In all of these cases, though, the "re-Guaranisizing" of these elements is so strong that the Christian significance is hardly noticed, while meaning is imputed to them by the Guarani system. It is always the Guarani meaning that prevails.

In any case, a question remains. In the texts which Cadogan collected, the marked Platonism of the chants and poems brings surprise and arouses admiration, mixed with suspicion. No matter how many times the poem about the "basis of the word" has been read or heard, the theologically educated Christian is impressed by that which seems resonant of the prologue in the gospel of St. John.[49] This kind of thinking is especially striking when dealing with the Mbya, and is common to all the modern Guarani. This "Platonism," charged with utopian ideas, informs the theology of the Guarani word, the psychological theory of the soul-word, the philosophy of the earthly dwelling as an imperfect copy of an ideal perfection, the fascination with the new earth and, more than all the above, the preeminence of mutual love, whose symbol is the ritual festival with drink and song in the style of an unending feast.

Was the "savage" thought of the Guarani always so Platonic? Is to call it Platonic not an improper or badly translated —ethnocentric—reduction of thinking that is after all Guarani? It certainly arouses suspicion about the Platonic modernity of Guarani thought. However, this very fact obliges us to look at the situation from another perspective: the analogical relation to our philosophy or theology is not the norm of their progress and perfection; neither is their eventual conversion to our system the measure of their excellence. In other words, Guarani thought does not need to define itself by its Platonism; rather, Platonism is merely an occasional explanatory resource that can help the efforts of translation.

For the theologian, it is of primary importance to bear in mind the distinct character and irreducibility of Guarani thought (likewise forms of expression), to take it seriously and regard it as worthy of true dialogue. This is a step that goes beyond just listening and recording the words of another—the limits of some anthropology—and allows this word to enter the conversation about the universally valid religious experience.

If the Guarani today are seen as mystics and theologians, they owe it to Christian influence. Recognition must be given to the fact that Christianity was almost always introduced among the Guarani by means of catechisms and liturgies, as well as moral prescriptions, which in themselves favour neither the development of theological discussion nor the charismatic liberty of the mystic. If these two dimensions of the Guarani religious way of being are so genuine, then we must postulate another origin for them, and it seems that this origin can be none other than the practice of their own "primitive" social and religious experiences. This experience embraces a body of cosmological myths as the ideals to be possessed by the Word and to be spoken by for it in prayer (ñembo'é). In the actual circumstances in which we see them handling religious ideas, is it not every Guarani who has a "consciousness of divinity," a sense of being true "god-people"? Basic to the Guarani theory of humankind is

> an idea that it is possible to surpass the human condition in a radical manner, since the distance between people and the gods is at the same time, both infinite and nonexistent . . . The secret of the Tupi-Guarani philosophy seems to be exactly this: the affirmation of one is not necessarily the best to posit the immanence of the divine in the human.[50]

6

The Land without Evil

One cannot speak about the Guarani today without making a definite reference to their search for the "land without evil." Their image as untiringly and prophetically seeking this "land without evil" has been widely popularized. The reality and significance of this land has not only been the subject of anthropological studies, but also a fascinating theme for sociologists, historians, theologians and poets. In this way, an indigenous experience has become a model and a paradigm for thinking and developing a broader and more general reality, which is the goal, or the ideal, of a more cohesive and human society.

> The poor of this land
> we want to invent
> this "land without evil"
> which comes every morning.[51]

Ethnologist Judith Shapiro sees in the establishment of the theme of a "land without evil" within the discussion of modern theologians and missionaries not just a simple metaphor to help us make the doctrine of the Christian paradise understandable to the Indian, but a "theological place" which providentially serves the understanding and makes real the search for the true Kingdom of God. Those who go towards the "land without evil" will not miss paradise, but, on the contrary, will make this ideal begin here and now, on a vigorous and free road, without alienation or oppression. "The 'land without evil' of the Guarani is nothing more and nothing less than a land of liberty for all mankind."[52] The search for this land, in the way it is envisioned and lived by the Guarani, will embrace important elements for a theology of the earth, this earth on which and of which the Kingdom of God is established.

But does this theological projection agree with the ethnic reality and the historical process of the Guarani? This is what we shall try to see.

THE GOOD EARTH

Archaeology of the Guarani carried out through the examination of pottery and the locations of ancient villages offers evidence that the Guarani are a people who move about within a large geographical context, with temporary migrations into very distant regions and with frequent displacements within the same region. They are not really nomadic, but rather dynamic colonists. The Guarani occupy territories with consistent ecological characteristics, that is, lands suitable for growing corn, manioc, sweet potatoes, yucca and squash. These lands offer a well-defined ecological horizon, whose limits are exceeded only with difficulty. One can speak quite properly of a "Guarani land" and rarely be contradicted.

The Guarani choose humid climates, with a temperature between 18 and 22 degrees centigrade, preferably situated on the banks of rivers or lakes, in areas that are not higher in altitude that some four hundred metres above sea level, covered by forests and jungles that are typical of the subtropical region.

This land, however, is not an inflexible or unchangeable factor. If the land imposes its conditions, it is still the Guarani who make it theirs. The Guarani land coexists with the Guarani who live on it. The Guarani ecology is neither nature on its own nor defined exclusively by its productive worth. The Guarani refer to their land with an expression that is typically theirs, calling it *tekoha*; however, if *teko* is the way of being, the system, the culture, the law and the customs, then *tekoha* is the place and the environment that provide the conditions which make possible the Guarani way of being, or the Guarani lifestyle. "*Tekoha* signifies and at the same time produces economic relationships, social relations, and politico-religious organisation that are essential for Guarani life. Although it seems to be redundant, it must be stated that even in the case of the Guarani leadership, if there were no *tekoha* there would be no *teko*."[53] *Tekoha* with all its earthly materialism is primarily an interplay of cultural space: economic, social, religious and political. It is the place, as the Guarani say, where we live according to our customs.

> This industrious people, always planting on the hills and moving their fields every three years . . . Live in well built houses . . . Some have eight to ten pillars that support the roof, and others more or less, depending on how many vassals serve the chief, because usually they all live in one house . . . Their villages are small, because as they always plant in the hills, they prefer to be few in number, so that they will not run out of food, and also to accommodate their fishing and hunting.[54]

The way in which the Guarani communities live, or want to live now that they are subject to many obstacles that impede their desires, agrees with this description of the Guarani habitat, written by a Jesuit missionary in 1620. The fundamental structure of *tekoha* and how their spaces interrelate can be described in this manner: a hill that has been preserved as it is without being disturbed, reserved for hunting, fishing and the collection of honey and wild fruit; some especially fertile spots of land for them to grow roses and other crops; and finally, a place where the big communal house is erected, with a large open patio around which grow some banana stalks, some taro, some cotton and a type of betel-nut (*ururcu*). These are the three spaces—hills (or jungle), fields and hamlet—that provide the proper environment for a good Guarani land.

The concept of regarding the earth as a mother—the bosom of fertility and breasts of abundant supply—is usually attributed to the Indians in general. This image is neither common nor typical of the Guarani; to them the land is more like a body covered with skin and hair, dressed up and adorned. To judge from certain idiomatic expressions, the Guarani have a rather visual and flexible view of the earth, and perhaps even see it as receptively acquiescent. How beautiful to see and hear the earth with its multitude of colours and its countless voices! The hill is tall (*ka'a yvaté*); it is big (*ka'a guasu*); it is lovely (*ka'a pora*); it is golden and perfect (*ka'a ju*); it is like a resplendent llama (*ka'a rendy*); it is a brilliant thing (*mba'e vera*). The rivers are clear (*y sati*), white (*y moroti*), black (*y hu*), red (*y pyta*), or like a current of water crowned with feathers (*paragua y*). And finally, the sea is the colour of all colours (*para*).

It does not seem strange that Guarani poetry feeds its metaphors with experience of this brilliant universe that is resounding with voices.

You yourself are the Creator.
Now we are treading on this shining earth, said the
    Creator.
Now we are treading on this evocative earth, said the
    Creator.
Now we are treading on this thundering earth, said the
    Creator.
Now we are treading on this perfumed earth, said the
    Creator.
Now we are treading on this shining, perfumed earth,
    said the Creator.
Now we are treading on this evocative, perfumed
    earth, said the Creator.

. . . .

Beautiful they are when they open
the flowers of the gates of paradise;
the flowers of the brilliant gates of paradise;
the flowers of the evocative gates of paradise;
the flowers of the thundering gates of paradise.

Until a short time ago, before the onset of the rapid ecological deterioration in the region, walking the paths of the Guarani *tekoha* and resting in their homes was a spectacular experience with a kind of symphonic accompaniment. A people that has lived in such an environment for centuries has had to think of its true land in terms of light and sound, for not only the birds, the insects and the waters talk, but also the trees, like the cedars from which "the word flows" (*yvyra ñe'ery*).

This is the good land that the Guarani—travelers, horticulturists, and villagers—have indefatigably endeavoured to cultivate and, on it, to live.

THE FOUNDATION OF THE LAND

The Guarani good earth is very real, because it is not founded on nature as such, but on the religious act which gives it its beginning and preserves it. Each of the Guarani groups has its own concepts and symbols to convey this foundation and centre of the cosmos, but all agree that it is dependent on the goodness of the earth and its conservation, its perfection and stability, on the safeguarding of this central base.

For the Mbya, the earth engenders within this foundation the ritual baton of Father Ñamandu himself. In the centre of this land, where it is forming, there grows a blue-green palm; other palms come up, marking the cardinal points, the dwelling place of the divine beings and the place where primitive time and space originated. For the Pai-Tavytera, Our Great Grandfather established the earth on a base of two crossed poles in the form of a cross, and from this centre he extended it and took it to its farthest limits. These same Guarani recognise the area where they live as "the centre of the earth" and they call it precisely that (*Yvypyte*). The Pai think of themselves in this way and they call themselves "the people who live in the centre of the earth (*Tavytera*)"; this is their lot and destiny.[55]

The earth receives its beautiful fullness from its religious foundation, based in turn, on the performance of a liturgical act by Our First Father. The conservation of the world, then, consists in keeping this liturgy alive and up-to-date. Chanting and praying, holding the ritual baton, some-times in the shape of a cross which is stuck into the ground, sustain the world and continually establish it anew. To cease praying and disregard the ritual are to take away the very support of the earth, instigating its instability and its immanent destruction.

Nevertheless, Guarani land is ordered and made part of the cosmos not as a church or a sacred place, but in relation to a song and a festival, the sacramental context of the word and the ritual act; at the same time, the festival is primarily the sacrament of mutual love and participation.

After we have reaped the fullness of your fruits, give them to us to eat, to all of your fellows without exception. The perfect fruits are produced so that all may eat of them, and not to be an object of stinginess. In giving food to everybody, only in this way, only when Our First Father sees our love for everybody, will he grant us happy days so that we can go on planting repeatedly.[56]

The foundation of the Guarani land, as a result, is the festival where they share the happiness: drinking the *chicha* (*kawi*), eating the fruit of the earth and the work of many, sharing together in the communal work in the fields (*potyro*). This is where they create the divine word and this word is shared by all.

Where there is a Guarani festival, there is found the actual centre of the land, and the good and perfect land they strive to attain.

IN SEARCH OF PERFECTION

The good earth which is the result of the festival and the communi-cated word is the same as that which brings perfection and completeness (*aguyje*). Both the fruits which reach their full maturity and the persons who attain the desired perfection have *aguyje*.[57]

This perfection, with its virtues and models, embodies the ideal for a human person. According to the present-day expressions, the great Guarani virtues are goodness (*teko pora*), justice (*teko joja*), good words (*ñe'é pora*), just words (*ñe'é joja*), reciprocal love (*joayhu*), diligence and availability (*kyre'y*), deep peace (*py'a guapy*), serenity (*teko ñemboro'y*), and inner purity without duplicity (*py'a poti*).

These practices and ways of being do not actually refer to individual or personal behaviour, but to relationships with others. These virtues are mainly envisioned and given their social context in political meetings and in the religious feasts. They are closely connected to speech: the word that is heard, the spoken word and the prophetic word. These words are made possible by the practices of reciprocity. What the Guarani, who searches for the good land, seeks is this state of perfection, which is produced by the convergence of various desired conditions, the use of different means and even the practices of certain psycho-religious techniques. In such a state of perfection the Guarani is able to leave the earth full of evil, arrive at a place of abundance, offer invitations and festivals, and attain extraordinary mystical experiences. These are the means that make perfection possible and lead to the complete fulfilment of a human being, heroic in its ideal imagery and in its model reality.[58]

Two types of persons achieve this Guarani perfection, although they reach it by different, but not necessarily opposite, means: the *pa'i* and the *karai*. The *pa'i* is the father of an extended family, a respected man, perhaps an elder, with some abilities as a shaman and a prophet. He is a master of the word, able to invite many guests, and does not lack the means of offering them an abundance of food and drink. With him together in his house are many sons-in-law and other relatives. He is a calm and serene man; his internal organs do not get agitated or beat around disjointedly like a frightened chicken—to use the Guarani expression—when some difficulty arises or a conflict erupts. He does not get angry; if he has to deliver a reprimand or administer a punishment, he has other younger people at his side to carry out the deed on his behalf. Calmly, when he feels the urge, he takes the rattle in his hands, shakes it, listens to its "voice," and then he himself makes the word with this voice. He can spend the whole night in this manner, singing and praying, accompanied by just his wife, who makes the rhythm sound with the beat of the bamboo grinding pole against the ground.

The religious experience which makes this head of the family also a shaman is essential to the make-up of the Guarani person, the *avá*, the male par excellence. The *pa'i* is, to some degree, also a shaman (*payé*), as we have already seen in the section "The Prophetic Word," above.

It is easy to understand that the traditional tribal mythical hero, who represents the concept of the ideal in its completeness, is not, for example, a great warrior, but is, of necessity, a great shaman, a wise man with exceptional powers.[59]

The other figure is the *karai*, the traveling shaman, whose function is almost exclusively religious, which seems to set him apart from the community. As prophets of catastrophes and interminable evils, they were the main instigators of migrations and movings, of warring actions and unending ritual dances that lead the community to the brink of exhaustion. These are the sorcerers and magicians, the "semi-gods," that are spoken about in the historical documents from the early days of the Conquest. They are the god-men, in whose power are the forces of nature: rain, wind, fire and plagues of all kinds. In these *karai* at least one person has recognized prophets of society over against the State[60], at a time when a greater population density of Guarani people has led to a greater concentration of power in the hands of a few chiefs. However, these *karai* scarcely intensify some elements of the Guarani character, such as cannibalism, the dances, and the migrations, in a movement that somewhat destabilizes society. In fact, their presence was as much respected as feared, as though they exhibited a surplus of power, even in religious matters. Clairvoyant denouncers of evils, but living on the fringe because of their position, they made a profession out of crisis and prophecy out of anarchy. It does not seem strange that for a missionary in the seventeenth century such as Father Antonio Ruiz de Montoya, these *karai* were taken to be "sly and crafty men."[61]

In spite of everything, the two figures—*pa'i* and *karai*—are not necessarily opposites; together they represent a societal organisation and a personal ideal in which the reciprocal economy is commonly upheld and complete, and each one is able to reach a state of perfection in a land where there is no evil and no death.

The Guarani know that they must die and they are not afraid of death, but their ideal is found in those who reach such a degree of perfection that, without dying, they cross over to live in that "land without evil" where the plants grow by themselves in abundance and where the feast and the dance know neither an ending nor weariness.

Among the Guarani, numerous stories about *payés* (including one about two sisters) circulate, who, inspired by dreams and visions, separate themselves from their tribe and take up a solitary life of fasting and ritual dances. Fasting here should be understood as abstinence, as practised by these *payés*, of any food of European origin—in other words, nothing but corn. Furthermore, the *payé* must also abstain from meat, and any heavy vegetable nourishment, living solely on certain fruits, maize and honey. He miraculously finds the food in his clearing, or under his net in the morning, when he finishes his ceremonial dances . . . Owing to this kind of life, his body becomes light; his animal-soul (*acyguá*) dominates him, while it travels around where it wishes. During the ceremonial dances, his souls abandon the earth and return to Ñandecy, Ñanderyquey or Tupa. Sometimes he finds himself with a dead body, and at other times he ascends in his living body. Generally he goes out alone, but sometimes he takes his disciples. There are instances when he dances with the whole household, with everybody who is gathered there, under its roof.[62]

With these stories, which undoubtedly have some moral and ethical lesson, we also find the ones that the Mbya attribute to their deified heroes, those who by various means have reached perfection (*aguyje*). I give you the saga of Chiku as an example.

Kuarachy had given a seat to Chiku in the house of prayer. Chiku set about to attain mercy. He sang, danced and prayed; he asked for the condition in which he would suffer no evil . . . Chiku went to Asunción (the capital of Paraguay), and mixed with the people who are not our own kind . . . After these things, the Tupa took him to the jungle where they installed him again. Only after this happened did he attain *aguyje*. Chiku attained perfection: from the palms of his hands to the soles of his feet llamas sprang forth; his heart shone with the reflection of his wisdom; his divine body was changed into incorruptible dew, his crown of feathers was covered with dew; the flowers from the crown of his head were llamas and dew.[63]

For the Guarani there is a direct connection between the "land without evil" and the perfection of the person; the road to one leads to the other. Thus, as the "land without evil" is real and is in this world, perfection, which in its highest degree of excellence includes not dying, which is not merely immortality, is also real and attainable on the earth. The "land without evil" as a new earth and the land of the festival, the place of reciprocity and mutual love, also produces perfect persons, who do not die. With their feet firmly on the ground, generations and generations of

Guarani have gone in pursuit of this goal, which is not utopian in nature. Their migrations have taken them to the furthest reaches of their geography, have dispersed them and have caused them to speak with different dialects and practice different cultural activities—handicrafts, rituals, social organisation—yet still they have perpetuated the myth, the conceptual force and symbol that embodies the whole, that the perfection of the person is found in the "land without evil," not beyond this life, but this side of death. This happens because here in this life, with the word that comes from Those Above and is sung and prayed in the festival here below, *aguyje* is achieved, the perfection of fruits and the perfection of persons, all at the "mercy" of the Guarani. Ethnographers who have studied the Guarani assert with great certainty the *aguyje* tradition, the tradition of perfection and maturity.[64]

THE EVIL IN THE LAND

Historically, the Guarani have an undeniable experience of evil in the land; it is the impossible festival, unattainable perfection. Pessimism has even been spoken of as an essential component of their life in the world.[65] It is a fact that Guarani talk about fatal and harmful things (*mba'e megua*), which are always immanent and threatening, more often than they talk about the good and perfect land. There are countless traditions that speak of catastrophes and cataclysms which have already occurred or always can occur. The most persistent and widely spread of these traditions is that of the flood (*yporu*).[66] However, there is also the instability of the earth which, for lack of support, disintegrates and falls; at the same time the devouring fire advances from the west towards the east (*yvy okai*). There are still other catastrophes which in different ways announce the end of the world: an invasion of darkness or the arrival of the Blue Tiger (*Jaguar rovy*), who devours people. These are the things which break up the cosmos and instigate chaos, like games played with malicious motives or bad jokes that make this world into something ridiculous and inane. This is the realm of the *mba'e megua*. For the Chiriguano of Bolivia, the *mba'e megua* par excellence is war.

The various metaphors for the destruction of the earth and its evils can be the subject of a natural lecture, free of mythology: it has to do with prolonged droughts, the exhaustion of the soil, various plagues of diseased animals, eclipses of the sun and the moon, floods, enemy attacks . . . This, however, is not the Indian interpretation. The evil in the earth, this "deformed thing," is never a natural occurrence or a merely ecological circumstance, but reason or logic (*teko*). The good way of being (*teko pora*) and the religious way of being (*teko marangatu*) for many reasons have deteriorated and have acquired an excess of evil (*teko vai*), which make the very act of singing any kind of a song, of producing any prayer or, even more so, the convocation of any festival impossible. The contemporary Pai indicate the following as the causes that can bring about the destruction of the earth: violence, especially murder; wrongs committed against the moral order, which negate communal collaboration and mutual love; and also personal offence, which happens when a person closes himself or herself off from the necessary step of reconciliation.

It is impressive to listen to the "fathers and mothers" (*ñande ru and ñande sy*) when, in a break in their song and their ritual dances, they explain what evil they are attempting to bind by their prayers. The actual evil is seen in hills that are stripped of their forests, in ranch fences that cut across the paths and reduce to nothing the indigenous territories, in the selfishness of the white men and in their lack of religion. In the face of this state of affairs, the ever-present cataclysms are lying in wait to hurl themselves upon the world: hurricane winds, tempests, fires, floods, misfortunes of all kind, in the form of sudden deaths, incurable diseases, famines, and social unrest.

The evil in the land is not of this present age. Probably the perception of "deformities" of the cosmos was the principal motivation behind the prehistoric migrations. From ancient times the Guarani society has been acquainted with serious crises which have affected their life and their way of being. However, there is no doubt that it was with the introduction of the colonial system that evil burst forth with unusual force and in ways hitherto unknown. Plagues, slavery, captivity and persecutions were the four horsemen of the colonial apocalypse. When the *encomienda* system was imposed in 1556, the obligatory rotation of personal service was also established. This destroyed the Guarani system, breaking the rule of reciprocity. The Guarani replied with repeated rebellions and other methods of resistance. Even the establishment of the famous reductions by the Jesuits, from 1610 on, were considered, not without good reason, to be a kind of "simulated captivity," and there was resistance against them.[67]

Colonial history is a progression of evils which seems to the Guarani to have no end. Worst of all the colonial evils is denying the Guarani their land. Where can they go? Both to the east and to the west there is the same devastation, the same fences. Land that has not yet been traversed or exploited, which has not be violated or built up—which was one of the ideal projections of the "land without evil" (*yvy marane'y*)—no longer exists. The jungles and the hills are disappearing, everything is turning into fields and the fields are claimed by the white man for his cows. The whole earth has gone bad; the *mba'e megua* covers everything.

Though a migrant people, frequently moving from one territory to another, never before has the Guarani been left without a land. Now, in their search for the "land without evil," they fear the day when there will only be evil without land. It will be the final exile.

IN SEARCH OF THE "LAND WITHOUT EVIL"

[If all this had not occurred] would the search for the "land without evil," which in its primary sense was a very real goal energized by an economy based on a continually active reciprocity and a desire for the perfection of the person which was constantly renewed have become a mere ritual, "the fruit of psychic, pessimistic, and visionary anxiety"?[68]

The myth, in so far as it is a myth, in this way would have lost all its force, no longer able to provide a critical awareness of the actual situation which forces them to leave or makes them feel like strangers in their own land. This myth of the "land without evil," even correctly interpreting reality, would not have achieved its transformation, let alone voiced it or given it ritual significance.[69] Was this always the case? Or are we dealing with a reduction of the field of action brought about by a history of oppression which compels the ritualization of that which it cannot change? The Guarani, without the means of self-edification through the gift which is amply communicated in a reciprocal economy, would have moved to symbolize this gift, communicating only words and establishing the dance.

It is very probable that among the modern Guarani, the search for the "land without evil" has been reclothed by a more accentuated mysticism than that of ancient times. In the *Tesoro de la lengua guaraní*, published by Ruiz de Montoya in 1639, the expression *yvý marane'y*, which modern ethnographers translate as "land without evil," means simply "the earth intact, that has not been built up," and *ka'á marane'y*, "hills where no trees have been felled nor has anyone passed through."[70] As we can see, these meanings are sufficiently distant from the ritualized "land without evil" to insist on their ecological and economic aspect. A search for an economic land and the longing for a prophetic land, however, are not contradictory. The one does not exclude the other.

Colonial history, from centuries back, has discouraged any attempt at migration or occupation of good lands by the Guarani; with the successive and implacable settlements, the states have wanted to annihilate borders and take over any free spaces. Is not the Guarani's real search, with their migratory rituals and their displacement when they were given up a means of recourse for maintaining a new kind of space, this time a space that is as much a part of the economy as it is religious and political? Thanks to their religious experience and their system of life, the Guarani have resisted up to the present and have maintained their *tekoha*, the place of their way of being. Their kind of economy and their personal ideal represent a great liberty when standing up to the State. If the road to personal perfection seems to be more individualized today and the search for the "land without evil" more ritualized, this is not due to a renunciation of the real goals, but rather, introducing into practice new resources for maintaining what is essential to their liberty. The search for the "land without evil," even in its most ritualized form, is not merely a conservative return to traditional social and religious structures, but rather a way of responding to the evolving neo-colonial system. Maintaining the principles of a reciprocal economy and remaining faithful to their own peculiar way of thinking and edifying the human person, the Guarani are freeing themselves from being reduced to generic citizens. Is not the very existence of the Guarani a continual criticism of the dominant structures, which try at all costs to make them an object of the market economy, owners of private property and supplicants seeking a personal salvation in the world to come?

As Don Pedro Casaldaliga has poetically stated it, to invent a "land without evil" along the Guarani lines is to create a land of liberty for all people each new morning.

What is astonishing about this Guarani "*teko*-logy," in which the search for the "land without evil" is an important theme, is its enormous theological reach in religious dialogue with Christians. Fundamental concerns, such as the relationship between economy and prophecy, society and the individual, the word of God and human word—which arouse so many doubts and perplexities in all our lives—in the Guarani religious vision provide issues to ponder and horizons that open out toward action.

Notes

Introduction

1. *A moralised history of the order of St. Augustine in Peru.*
2. This refers to any inhabitant of the Iberian peninsula.
3. "Discussions on the truth: Causes and difficulties that hinder the conversion of the Indians."
4. *A brief history of the destruction of the Indies.*
5. *A historical apologetic.*
6. *On the sole method of bringing all peoples to the true religion.*
7. *The spiritual conquest of Paraguay.*
8. The title of this book translated literally means "the flint of divine love," but I would suggest that the intention leans more towards a reading of "the spark of divine love."

Part 1: Tseltal Christianity

1. The root *al* means child of a woman, and *nich'an* child of a man.
2. A Ladino is any person who is not an Indian.
3. Atole is a drink made from maize flour.
4. We note that frequently one speaks of "syncretism" in the indigenous religions. To my mind, this is a misuse of the term or an ethnocentrism by which we judge them incapable of having arrived at a synthesis of the pre-Hispanic elements and those of Western Catholics. It is certain that during the process of acculturation, many times there is syncretism, but this is dealing with a process which usually leads to a synthesis (that is, an ordered and harmonious whole) of the elements of the cultures that are in contact (cf. Maurer 1983).
5. *Translator's note*: I have endeavoured to retain some of the rustic flavour of this quotation, as in some of the others where the Indian thought forms have been portrayed in the Spanish of the text.
6. To bring this quote into the present, the author has taken the liberty of changing the verbs into the present tense.
7. I am going to limit myself to the area in which the Jesuits work.
8. The wife of the candidate is asked if she accepts the proposal that her husband take on this responsibility, because she will help him, for example, in taking communion to the sick when he is unable to do so, and so forth.

Part 2: The Religion of the Andean Quechua in Southern Peru

1. Montoya says: "The first is a recreated pre-Hispanic component; that is, an inheritance from the Inca empire which has survived down through almost five centuries, though continually recreating itself . . . The Andean Quechua cul-

ture is, in the first instance, a culture founded on the principle of reciprocity, that is to say, in the organisation of the state, the society and the communities are related around the interchange of communal units, between domestic units within the 'ayllu,' and between the 'ayllus' and the Inca state . . . In the second place, there is that which we might call the principle of competitiveness between the members of an 'ayllu' and between 'ayllus.' This element of competition appears in the chronicles of all the literature that tells about the nature of the Inca empire, as well as in the anthropological texts and literature that describes Andean life in the present day . . . In the composition of the 'Quechua self,' the collective component is decisive . . . This is the third element of the Quechua culture. The collective self is expressed in 'we' (ñuqanchis), in 'the people did it,' 'we went,' and in the absence of individualisation with respect to merit or benefit" (Montoya 1987, 9-12).

2. Lord of Earth Tremors.

3. Among the Quechua people of Q'ero and Lauramarca there is a relationship between Jesus Christ (the Taytacha at Qoyllur Riti) and the Apu Ausangate. Flores refers to the testimony of Domingo Pauccar, according to which, although Jesus Christ and Ausangate watch over us and can influence our life, the former is in Hanaqpacha and has more power, and the latter is in Kaypacha and must obey the commands of Jesus Christ (1984, 215-216). Felix Machacca adds: "The 'little father Qoyllur Riti' appeared (a miracle apparition) in the body. Taytacha and Ausangate are together. The messenger who was sent became the 'little father' and Ausangate . . . They say that when the snow disappears from the mountains, the end of this time will come. For sure the Apus will disappear too. God knows when this time will end. They say, according to God's testament, the world will end in the year two thousand, which is counted from the birth of Jesus. All is in vain: gold, silver, things" (1984, 214).

Concerning the Ukukus' climb to the snowcap and the procession, the Müllers opine: "To us it seems to be a symbolic repetition of the creation of the present cycle, of the era in which we live, according to the myth of the Naupa Machu, who live by the light of the moon alone in the time of chaos before the arrival of the sun and before they were burnt. Only those who fled to the jungle were able to survive; these are the Chunchos today. The Ukukus ascend to the snowcap in the darkness of night. There they greet with devotion the sunrise, the sun which symbolizes our time and the world order, according to the Andean view and that which is most common. It is difficult to determine the significance of the Ukukus, but it is certain that these costumed figures have more than one connotation. The 'Chunchos' dancers, who do not ascend to the snowcap but rather wait below for the sunrise, are connected to the inhabitants of the jungle and also symbolize, through the mythology, the origin, the ancestors, and the other life. When the Ukukus descend with the cross—Taytacha of the snowcap—and they carry it to the church in procession with the 'Chunchos,' they express the inseparable relationship of Taytacha with the Andean deities" (1984, 174).

4. One can consult the Müllers (1984a) and Flores (1984) on this point. They analyze several myths about Inkarri and make an interesting comparison between Jesus Christ and Inkarri, without trying to make it extend to other Andean regions outside the communities under study. I cite Flores because it

seems interesting to me in connection with the problem of Quechua Christianity in the marginal Andean areas: "Jesus Christ does not appear clearly as the Son of God the Father, but as a semi-independent God with a marked likeness to Inkarri. Inkarri belongs to the time of the Son, but he is distinct and independent in his actions from Taytacha. In the region of Q'ero he appears as the modeller for the shape of the earth. He is the father of culture, of agricultural activity and of the animal kingdom when he appears with his feminine consort; with his sling he brings down the mountains, he levels the earth, lays the rivers, walks and sits leaving his marks. Sometimes he acts alone; at others he is accompanied by his feminine mate, Qoya, or in competition with Qollariy or Qollkhapq. Inkarri always comes from La Raya, that is, the source of the River Vilcanota or Wilkamayu, and walks towards the valley of Cusco, where he performs exploits such as stopping the sun so that the city can be finished, erecting the cathedral or playing Sacsawaman, placing Maria Angola, setting the clock and then continues on his path of creation into the sacred valley. He will come to Q'ero, where he will walk, rest, bathe, and finish by entering the jungle where he continues to live with his wife and his children . . . The similarity to Jesus Christ shows in his course of action. Both are creators who put things in order; they walk on this earth, which is the same as living; and they are persecuted. Jesus dies, but rises from the dead and now lives in heaven. Inkarri flees from the Spaniards and priests and finds refuge in the mountain, where he is alive also. Both have the sun as a symbol of their time" (Flores 1984, 150-152).

5. I do not know what the coming of John Paul II to Cusco in 1985 meant for the Quechua, when they gave him a grand reception in the impressive setting of Sacsawaman. The majority of them did not have the insight of Guaman Poma de Ayala, who, in his chronicles, insisted on the presence of a papal nuncio for Peru, a man who could pass information to the pope directly, independent of the king, who never wanted to accept the existence of any other apart from the nuncio of Madrid (Guaman Poma 1987, 1068). Neither, perhaps, did they share the syncretism of certain informants from Q'ero, whom Flores cites: "Holy-Roman-Father is the Apu of the potatoes and corn; in that place Taytacha lay down for a rest: from the beginning of the world the Apu exists. This one has life. With him the bishops talk about what God has written. He is far away, beyond Arequipa" (1984, 219). Despite the syncretistic redaction because of the similarity between the Quechua word for potato (*papa*) and the Spanish word for pope (*papa*), the distant Apu has become a protector of vital crops; a trait from the early catechism is preserved in the role of the pope and the bishops, who meet in order to bring the content of the divine revelation to the attention of the church.

6. I have made a study of these three paths in El Agustino, a marginal parish of greater Lima, in *Los caminos religiosos de los inmigrantes de la Gran Lima* (1988). El Agustino is a parish of some ninety-four thousand persons, the majority of provincial origin. In a sample comprising the parents of the 4,019 children whose births were registered in the district council in 1984, three out of every four were from the provinces, and 38.4% were from one of the five zones of the Andean Trapezoid. In a survey carried out by the heads of families in the parish, 38.7% stated that Quechua was their mother tongue.

Part 3: The Aymara Religious Experience

1. The sources for this work are of two types: first, fifteen years of work living in various Aymara regions; second, the respectful research of other scholars interested in the Aymara and Andean religious dimension. Anticipating the writing of this article, the discussions in two seminars about Aymara religion organised in La Paz by the Centre of Popular Theology in 1986-87 have been very helpful; these seminars formed the basis for *Fe y Pueblo* nos. 13 and 18. A first writing, done in Chucuito with the support of the Institute of Aymara Studies, was read and commented on by Olivia Harris, Diego Irarrazaval, Domingo Llanque, Manuel M. Marzal, and Calixto Quispe. I thank them for their interest and support; their insights have been incorporated into this final version. The main contributions of other authors are indicated in notes, but there are many more names and works that are implicitly referred to between the lines. In an effort to provide a synthesis for people who are not familiar with the Aymara world, without making it a heavy piece of erudition, it has been impossible to attirbute all my accrued knowledge. For a more global approach to the Aymara people and their culture, see the collected work of Albó (publishing editor) with its bibliography, and on a more popular level, the *Bulletin* periodically published since 1974 by the Institute of Aymara Studies (Chucuito, Puno), which includes a parallel series in Aymara. Among the many monographs on specific communities, that of Carter and Mamani (1982) is the one with the broadest and most understandable vision of communal life, in this case that of Irpa Chico quite close to the city of La Paz. Specifically on the religious aspect, see the dictionary of Hans van den Berg (1985) with its bibliography, and his most complete bibliography about the Aymara world in four volumes (1980-84). Although its focus is now out of date, see also a detailed study of the religion in Chucuito covering the years 1940-1950 in Tschopik (1951). The doctoral thesis of Enrique Jorda (1981) is currently the best and most documented theological reflection in depth of the Aymara religion.

2. Robert Redfield has developed more thoroughly this double view in the years 1950 to 1960. He gives a similar weight to the role of the Qilqa (Bouysse and Harris 1987), though in the Andes they failed to develop "sacred scriptures."

3. This is the motto for the Confederación Sindical Única de Campesinos de Bolivia (CSUTCB), which brings together almost the entire rural population in the country.

4. Carter and Mamani 1982; *Bulletin* of IDEA, passim: Allen 1972.

5. Monast (1972) portrays the reaction of a missionary who discovers the religious universe of the Aymara without being prepared for it. See comparable personal experiences of daily development in the personal diaries of Garcia among the Quechua in Cusco (1983).

6. This approach has been developed mainly by Harris and Bouysse (1988), particularly on the basis of their data from the northern sector of Potosi.

7. Palacios (1982) has an excellent description of the symbolism of the house among the shepherds of Puno. See Martinez (1976) concerning customs on the Chilean high plateau.

8. The religious dictionary of Hans van den Berg (1985) cites eighty-nine supernatural beings in the Andean tradition, and undoubtedly it falls short because of insufficient coverage of the more traditional regions of Oruro and Potosí. During just one ceremony for the cattle belonging to a particular family in Oruro, Abercrombie (1986, 169-170) noted sixty libations to the same number of other protectors, which included the direct protectors of the home, the spirits of the cattle and even the spirits of the dung.

9. See illustrations of Illa and other complementary ritual objects (*mullu*, *chiw chi*, *misterio*, etc.) in the dictionary by Berg (1985). This author only underlines their role as amulets and not as engendering spirits.

10. Berg (in preparation) is the most complete resource of the Aymaran agricultural rites with regard to time and regions. The correlation between the agricultural, ceremonial and musical cycles is demonstrated by Mamani (1988) on the northern plateau and by Harris (1983) in the northern sector of Potosí.

11. See reports about the mountain Pachajiri near Lake Titicaca in *Fe y Pueblo* 13 and 18.

12. Berg (1987) and Harris (1983) emphasize the role of the dead throughout the productive period of the rains.

13. In Dillon and Abercrombie 1984. Note that in the northern hemisphere the dates for Christmas also coincide with the winter solstice, when the sun is reborn.

14. In *Fe y Pueblo* 18 there are other testimonies from priests, pastors and *yatiris*.

15. "It seems to us that Jesus Christ is little known as the only Mediator and Saviour" (Jorda 1981, 204; see also 330-338).

16. We cannot explore the process here. See the chapters by Carter and Albó, both about the high plateau of La Paz, in Mayer and Bolton 1980. For the rites associated with roof covering, see Ochoa 1976b (for Puno); and Platt 1976 (for the area north of Potosí).

17. Although in practice a portion of ground is treated as a family inheritance and agrarian reform that has encouraged the division of property into family holdings, the community often maintains ultimate control and access to the land. A community usually will not accept the sale of a piece of property to a stranger, for example, and it reserves the right to expel anyone who does not keep communal commitments or who commits a serious communal crime.

18. For example, the imposition of fines for damage done to the newly planted fields by cattle and performing rituals against hail storms.

19. In the northern region of the plateau a whip inlaid with silver is a common symbol. It is also a ritual object, but not as elaborate as those found on the southern plateau. See Rasnake (1982) for the central role of the rods in the symbolic universe of the Yura, a group of Aymara who have mixed with the Quechua in Potosí.

20. Different from the *yatiri* and even the Protestant pastors, the priest is neither a member of the community nor usually a peasant. Frequently he is even a foreigner. He is only seen in the community on rare occasions, when he visits or when the people visit him at his residence. Furthermore, because he is celibate this puts him in a very special situation, which Rome has difficulty in under-

standing (Jorda 1981, 432-435), for this means that he has never attained the maturity of personhood (*jaqi*). He is, however, considered to be a necessary religious mediator. Luckily the image of the priest as exploiter, aligned with banks and mestizos is diminishing. Where new pastoral schemes have been developed, the prevailing view is more one of the priest as promoter of new projects beneficial to the region. Nevertheless, they often continue to distance themselves from communal schemes, and their association with the *kharisiri*, who takes the fat of his victims for the baptismal oil, has not disappeared.

21. Ochoa (1977) and Cadorette (1980) describe in detail the ceremony in Chucuito, Puno. Similar rites also exist in the north of Potosi, in Oruro, and even among the Urus of Chipaya. According to Platt (1985), the rite could also be related to a well-known myth in which the fox, after eating his fill in the heavens, fell to earth. When he burst open, he fertilized the earth with all types of seeds.

22. See Monast 1972, 152-168. The discussion is based on several examples taken from different contexts.

23. Garcia (1983, 74-76), in his diary of a rural priest serving the Quechua communities of Cusco, relates a personal experience of this type. A common thief decided to return to the community from which he had been expelled, and there, in effect, he was sacrificed. The pastor meditated in this way: "A sense of living and belonging in a manner of dying to live and living to die. Was this not what the thief already knew and sought after? Was this not his redemption? To return and belong to his community, from the mother earth and through the atoning punishment?"

24. Platt 1982, 145-146. See the larger context of the revolt of Chayanta in Harris and Albó 1984, 59-71. Blood that is spilt for just causes fertilizes the earth; unjust wars bring calamities. Two of the major disasters on the high plateau in this century have been attributed to the number of unburied dead in two wars in the same corresponding years: the war in Chaco (1932-1935) and the war in the Malvinas (1982).

25. "Testimonio y reflexion aymara," *Fe y Pueblo* 18 (1988).

26. In the general uprising of 1780-1783 many similar cases occurred which were taken up by Hidalgo (1982). In Chucuito, for example, they took out the hearts of all of the white victims. I have heard tales of *wilanchas* in other rebellions which, like the story told, happened in the years immediately preceding the agrarian reform of 1953. See also note 2.

27. This is the current metaphor used to refer to authorities and leaders. In some places there even exists a tradition of an annual occasion when the person in authority invites all the people from the community, referring to it as "taking his flock to pasture."

28. "Testimonio y reflexion aymara," *Fe y Pueblo* 18 (1988).

29. Berg (in preparation) summarizes and compares much information about the rituals and beliefs of the Aymara in relation to death. See an interpretive preview in Berg 1987. See the more local studies in Carter and Mamani (1982) for Irpa Chico, near La Paz; Harris (1983) for *ayllu* Laymi, north of Potosi; and Kessel (1978) for northern Chile.

30. The "little angels" or dead children have another kind of symbolism with closer ties to "heaven."

31. In several areas of the Aymara territory they continue to bury the dead beside the house, preferably close to the cultivated fields. Harris and Bouysse (in press) comment that for the Andeans the Christian cemeteries may have had the implication of too much dangerous power concentrated in one place.

32. Duviols 1978; Taylor 1980.

33. Personal communication from Veronica Cereceda.

34. Principally Harris and Bouysse (in press). See also Abercrombie 1986.

35. Ochoa 1976a. His fellow countryman Llanque (1986) expresses the same idea in very similar terms. For a summary of the contemporary Aymara worldview, see Jorda 1981, 147ff., which is also based on Ochoa.

36. Personal communications and notes on Aymara religion from I. Taller of the Centre of Popular Theology (1986). See *Fe y Pueblo* 18.

37. Barstow (1979) analyzes these contrasts in Carabuco; Ochoa (1977) and Cadorette (1980) in Chucuito.

38. Sandoval, Albó, and Greaves (1978) analyze the relationships between residents and their community of origin. Buechler (1980) details the new symbolic terms of reference developed through participation in the festivals.

39. Notes from two workshops on Aymara religion. See *Fe y Pueblo* 13 and 18.

40. *Translator's note:* The original word here is very strong and crude.

41. *Fe y Pueblo* 18; Riviere 1982, chap. 7; Riviere 1987.

42. Platt 1983, 1986; "Religiosidad Popular," a bulletin in the diocese of Oruro (1986).

43. Platt 1983. On the island of Amantani in Lake Titicaca (which is inhabited by Quechua today), the prominent hills are also called Pacha Tata and Pacha Mama. It is common to have female and male hills; there are even Pacha Mamas which are both male and female (Martinez 1987, 112). However, the name Pacha Tata is not found in general usage.

44. Wachtel 1976. For more about Carnival and the Tiu in Oruro, see Guerra 1970, 1977. In the main mining district of Bolivia there are comparable festivals on the Day of Assumption (*Llallagua*) and in particular on the day of St. Michael the Archangel (*Uncia*).

45. Quoted in Platt 1986, 35. Nash (1970) emphasizes the political dimension in the mining rituals.

46. Albó, Greaves and Sandoval 1982-1987 (for the religious dimension, see in particular vol. 3); Buechler 1980.

47. Albó and Preiswerk 1986.

48. *Fe y Pueblo* 13, 42-48.

49. Temple 1986. This is not dealing with anything that is exclusively Aymaran or Andean. It is rather an alternative proposal that can be seen in many societies where the penetration of capitalism has not yet managed to develop the opposite tendency to accumulate wealth for the benefit of just the few.

50. See the explanation for *kuskachasiña* in *Fe y Pueblo* 13, 10, and Platt (in press).

51. Some people ask whether a religion like that of the Aymara, so dominated by a cosmic conception of God, can take on the idea of a liberating God. Usually it is said that a cosmic vision is more likely to lead to a "myth of eternal return." In the Aymara religion there is definitely a cyclical element, expressed,

for example, in the relationship between reciprocity and restoration of balance, in the idea of *kuti*, or in the importance placed on the dead as seeds of the future. However, as we have seen when we referred to the dialectic of gifts, in these comings and goings they never return to the point of departure. As in any dialectic, there is a steady progression forward. Thus, the idea of a liberating God fits.

52. Jorda (1981) had good insight into this concern, and as a central point in his thesis, he stressed the need to complement the theology of political liberation with a theology of cultural liberation. In this manner he engages in the old debate of the social sciences about the relationship among class, ethos, nation, and state.

53. An abbreviated articulation of the conclusions in "Testimonio y reflexion aymara," *Fe y Pueblo* 18.

54. In Albó (1985a) various examples of this ambiguity and of the social conditionings that favour one or the other solution are developed.

Part 4: The Guarani Religious Experience

1. See Melià 1969, I: 53-55.
2. See Melià 1986, 90.
3. Metraux 1967, 23; Melià 1986, 33.
4. *Aconteceu*, Special edition 15 (Sao Paulo: CEDI, 1984), 198-300.
5. Hernandez 1913, I:79.
6. Lozano 1754, I:110.
7. Barzana 1970, 589-590.
8. Ruiz de Montoya 1639/1892, 50.
9. Charlevoix 1756/1910, I:327.
10. Nimuendaju 1914/1987, 28. *Translator's note*: This quotation is given in Portuguese in the original Spanish text.
11. See Schaden 1966 and Melià 1973.
12. Cadogan 1959a, 19-23.
13. Cadogan 1959a, 40,
14. Ibid.
15. Schaden 1974, 108.
16. Ibid., 107.
17. Ibid., 107-108; Susnik 1984-1985, 111-116; Melià and Grünberg 1976, 248-249.
18. Cadogan 1959a, 187.
19. Nimuendaju 1914/1987, 31-32.
20. Cadogan 1959a, 40-42.
21. Ruiz de Montoya 1639/1892, 49.
22. Nimuendaju 1914/1987, 77.
23. Ibid., 34-35, 78.
24. Cadogan 1959a, 91-92.
25. Schaden 1954, 248-249.
26. Schaden 1974, 119.
27. Ibid., 126.
28. Cadogan 1959a, 90.
29. Schaden 1974, 118-120.

30. Riester 1984.

31. Cadogan 1959a, 95.

32. Clastres 1974, 141.

33. Viveiros de Castro 1986, 364.

34. Gallois 1988, 51-53.

35. Schaden 1976, 841.

36. Gallois 1988, 52.

37. B. Albert, *Temps du sang, temps des cendres: représentation de la maladie, système rituel et espace politique chez les Yanomani du sud-est.* Thèse doct. Université Paris X, mimeo, 883 pp, p. 684. Quoted by Gallois 1988, 53.

38. Schaden 1976, 852.

39. Nimuendaju 1914/1987, 55

40. Melià 1969, I:151-156.

41. Schaden 1976, 858-859.

42. Nimuendaju 1987, 75.

43. Viveiros de Castro, in Nimuendaju 1987, xxxi. *Translator's note:* This quotation was given in Portuguese in the original Spanish text.

44. Cadogan 1959a

45. Viveiros de Castro, in Nimuendaju 1987, xxxi.

46. Schaden 1974, 106-107.

47. Ibid.

48. Ibid., 105.

49. See the section "The Word Is Everthing" earlier in this chapter.

50. Viveiros de Castro, in Nimuendaju 1987, xxxiii.

51. Casaldaliga 1980, 67.

52. Ibid., 23; Shapiro 1987.

53. Melià 1986, 105.

54. MCA 1951, I:166-167.

55. Melià and Grünberg 1976, 217.

56. Cadogan 1959a, 131.

57. Ibid., 49; Susnik 1984-1985, 96-102.

58. Melià and Grünberg 1976, 188.

59. Schaden 1959, 119.

60. Clastres 1974.

61. Ruiz de Montoya 1639/1892, 90.

62. Nimuendaju 1987, 61-62.

63. Cadogan 1959a, 145-148.

64. Ruiz de Montoya 1639/1892, 20; Cadogan 1959a, 51.

65. Nimuendaju 1987, 67-71.

66. Ruiz de Montoya 1639/1892, 53.

67. Melià 1986, 176-177.

68. Susnik 1984-1985, 97.

69. Queiroz 1973, 49.

70. Ruiz de Montoya 1639/1892, 209.

Bibliography

ABERCROMBIE, Thomas A.
1986   *The Politics of Sacrifice. An Aymara Cosmology in Action*. Chicago, University of Chicago, tesis doctoral en antropologá, ms.

ACOSTA, José de
1588   *De procuranda indorum salute, en Obras*. Madrid, Biblioteca de Autores Españoles, 1965.
1954   *De procuranda indorrum salute*. Madrid (originally published in 1558. Translated in 1994 by G. Steward McIntosh and privately printed by MAC Research, 50 Nelson St. Tayport, Fyfe DD6 9DS, Scotland).

ALBÓ, Xavier
1985a   *Desafíos de la solidaridad aymara*. La Paz, CIPCA.
1985b   "Pacha Mama y Q'ara: el aymara ante la opresión de la naturaleza y de la sociedad" en *Estado y sociedad*. La Paz, n. 1/1: 73-88.
1988   *Raíces de América: el mundo aymara*. Madrid, Alianza Editorial y UNESCO.

ALBÓ, Xavier, GREAVES, Tomás y SANDOVAL, Godofredo
1982-87   *Chukiyawu, la cara aymara de La Paz*. La Paz, Cuadernos de Investigación CIPCA, n. 22, 23, 24 y 29.

ALBÓ, Xavier y PREISWERK, Matías
1986   *Los Señores del Gran Poder*. La Paz, Centro de Teología Popular.

ALLEN, Guillermo
1972   "Costumbres y ritos aymaras en la zona rural de Achacachi (Bolivia)" en *Allpanchis*, Cusco, Instituto de Pastoral Andiana, n.4: 43-68. Republicado en *Búsqueda Pastoral*, La Paz, n. 18:17-38.

ALLIER, Raoul
1925   *La psychologie de la conversion chez les peuples noncivilisés*, Paris (citado por Ricard).

ANSION, Juan
1987   *Desde el rincón de los muertos: el pensamiento mítico de Ayacucho*. Lima, Gredes.

ARMAS, Fernando de
1953   *La cristianización del Perú* (1532-1600), Sevilla, Escuela de
          Estudios Hispanoamericanos.

ARRIAGA, Pablo José de
1621   *La extirpación de la idolatría en el Perú, en Crónicas peruanas de
          interés indígena,* Madrid, Biblioteca de Autores Españoles, 1968,
          editor Francisco Esteve Barba.

AVENDAÑO, Hernando de
1649   *Sermones de nuestra santa fe católica en lengua castellana y gen-
          eral del Inca,* Lima, Jorge López de Herrera.

AVILA, Francisco de
1987   *Ritos y tradiciones de Huarochirí del siglo XVII.* Lima, Instituto
          de Estudios Peruanos, editor Gerald Taylor.
1646-48   *Tratado de los evangelios en lengua castellana y general de los
          indios,* Lima, 2 tomos.

AVILA, Santa Teresa de
1957   *Obras completas.* Madrid, Aguilar.

BARSTOW, Jean R.
1979   *An Aymara Class Structure, Town and Community in Carabuco,*
          Chicago, University of Chicago, tesis doctoral en antropología, ms.

BARZANA (see INSTITUTUM HISTORICUM SOCIETATIS JESUS)
1970   *Monumenta Peruana,* Roma V (1592-1595).

BERG, Hans van den
1980-84   *Material bibliográfico para el estudio de los aymaras, callawayas,
          chipayas y urus.* Cochabamba, ISET, 4 vols.
1985   *Diccionario religioso aymara.* Iquitos, CETA, IDEA.
1987   "Día de difuntos, fiesta a la vida" en *Cuarto Intermedio,* La Paz,
          n. 5:3-17.
(en preparación) *La Tierra no es así nomás...,* Cochabamba, ISET.

BERGER, Peter
1973   *The Social Reality of Religion.* Penguin Books, England.

BLOM, Franz
1956   "Vida precortesiana del indio chiapaneco de hoy," en *Estudios
          antropológicos...en homenaje al Dr. Manuel Gamio.* México,
          UNAM.

BOUYSSE-CASSAGNE, Théresè y HARRIS, Olivia
1987   "Los tres pacha en el pensamiento andino del siglo XX" en
          BOUYSSE et al. *Tres reflexiones sobre el pensamiento andino.*
          La Paz, HISBOL.

BOUYSSE-CASSAGNE, Thérèsè y HARRIS, Olivia, PLAT, Tristan y
    CEREDECDA, Verónica
1987   Tres reflexiones sobre el pensamiento andino. La Paz, HISBOL.

BUECHLER, Hans
1980   The Masked Media. The Hague, Mouton.

CABELLO DE BALBOA, Miguel
1586   Miscelánea antánea antártica. Lima, Universidad Nacional Mayor
            de San Marcos, 1951.

CADOGAN, León
1959a   Ayvu rapyta. Textos míticos de os Mbyá-Guaraní del Guayrá.
            São Paulo, Univ. de São Paulo, Fac. de Fil, Cienc. e Letras, Boletim
            227, Antropologia 5.
1959b   "¿Cómo interpretan los Chiripà (Ava-Guaraní) la danza ritual?,"
            en Revista de Antropologia, VII, 1-2; 65-99, São Paulo.
1962   "Aporte a la etnografía de los Guarani del Amambaí, Alto
            Ypané," en Revista de Antropología, X, 1-2; 43-91, São Paulo.
1968   "Ñane Ramoi Jusú Papá Ñengaraté. Canto ritual de Nuestro
            Abuelo Grande (el Creador)" en Suplemento Antropológico de
            la Revista del Ateneo Paraguayo, Asunción, III, 1-2; 425-450.

CADORETTE, Raimundo
1980   "La diosa bondadosa: la fiesta de la Asunción en Chucuito," en
            Boletín del Instituto de Estudios Aymaras, Chucuito, serie 2, n.
            7:21-47.

CALANCHA, Antonio de la
1639   Crónica moralizada de la Orden de San Agustín en el Perú,
            Barcelona, Pedro Lacavallería, tomo I.

CARTER, William y MAMANI, Mauricio
1982   Irpa Chico. Individuo y comunidad en la cultura aymara. La Paz,
            Juventud.

CASALDALIGA, Pedro
1980   A missa da terra sem males. São Paulo, Paulinas.

CASO, Alfonso
1958   Indigenismo. México, Instituto Nacional Indigenista.

CELESTINO, Olinda y MEYERS, Albert
1981   Las cofradías en el Perú: región central. Frankfurt, Verlag Klaus
            Dieter Vervuest.

CHARLEVOIX, Pierre Francois Xavier de
1756   Historia de Paraguay..., Madrid, 6 tomos, Lib. General de
            Victoriano Suárez, 1910-1916.

CLASTRES, Hélène
1975   *La terre sans mal: el prophétisem tupi-guarani.* Paris, Editions de
            Seuil. Versión portuguesa: *Terra sem mal*, São Paulo, Brasiliense,
            1978.

CLASTRES, Pierre
1974   *La societé contre l'Etat. Recherches d'anthropologie politique.*
            Paris, Les Editions de Minuit. Versión portugesa: *A sociedade
            contra o Estado.* Rio de Janeiro, Francisco Alves, 1978.

COBO, Bernabé
1653   *Historia del nuevo mundo, en Obras*, Madrid, Biblioteca de
            Autores Españoles, 1964, 2 tomos.

CONSEJO NACIONAL DE POBLACION
1984   *Peru: hechos y cifras demográficas*, Lima.

CORTES Y LARRAZ, Pedro
1770?   *Descripición geográfico-moral de la diócesis de Guatemala.*
            Tipografía Nacional de Guatemala, 1958.

DEPARTAMENTO DE MISIONES
1987   *De una pastoral indigenisia a una pastoral indígena.* Bogotá,
            CELAM.

DIEZ, Manuel
1675   *Conciones in lingua tzeldaica*, ex collectione americana domini
            Brasseur de Bourbourg, Bibliothéque Nationale de Paris,
            Departamento de manuscritos R31, 978, (4052).

DILLON, Mary y ABERCROMBIE, Thomas
1984   *The Destroying Christ: An Aymara Myth of Conquest.* Trabajo
            presentado en el simposio: "From History to Myth in South
            America," American Anthropological Association.

DIOCESIS DE ORURO
1985   Religiosidad Popular, IV Encuentro de Agentes de Pastoral,
            Oruro, policopiado.

DOCUMENTO
1838   *Informe de los párrocos del Estado al gobierno del mismo sobre
            la situación de los pueblos...*, San Cristóbal, Secundino
            Orantes..

DURKHEIM, Emilio
1912   *Las formas elementales de la vida religiosa.* Buenos Aires, Edit.
            Schapire, 1968.

DUVIOLS, Pierre
1978   *Camaquen, Upani: un concept animiste des anciens Péruviens,*
            en HATMANN, R. y OBEREM, U (ed.), *Amerikanistische*
            Studien. Festschrift für Hermann Trimborn. St. Augustin
            Collectanes Instituti Anthropos, n. 20.

ELIADE, Mircea
1954   *Tratado de historia de las religiones.* Madrid, Instituto de Estudios
            Politicos.

FE Y PUEBLO. Revista del Centro de Teología Popular.
1986, Agos.: Religión aymara y cristianismo, n. 13.
1986, Nov.: Sectas, pentecostalismo y religiosidad popular, n. 14.
1987, Nov.: Religión aymara liberadora, n. 18.

FLORES, Carlos
1984   *Una interpretación teológica del sincretismo andino de O'ero y*
            Lauramarca, México, Universidad Iberoamericana, tesis de
            licenciatura en teologia, ms.

FUENTES Y GUZMAN, Antonio de
1693   *Recolección florida, discurso historial y demostración material,*
            militar y política del Reyno de Guatamala, Tipografía Nacional
            de Guatemala, 1932.

FUENZALIDA, Fernando
1977   "El mundo de los gentiles y las tres eras de la creación," en *Revista*
            de la Universidad Católica, Lima, n. 2:59-84.

GALLEGO, Andrés
1984   "El Instituto de Pastoral Andina: un servicio a la Iglesia del Sur
            Andino," en *Allpanchis,* Cusco, Instituto de Pastoral Andina, n.
            24: 9-26.

GALLOIS, Dominique
1988   *O movimento de cosmologia waiâpi. Criacaô e transformacaô.*
            São Paulo, Univ. de São Paulo, FFLCH, mimeo.

GARCÍA, José María
1983   *Con las comunidades del Ausangate,* Lima, Centro de Proyección
            Cristiana.

GARCILASO DE LA VEGA, el Inca
1609   *Comentarios reales de los incas,* Buenos Aires, Emecé, 1944.

GARR, Mateo
1972   *Cristianismo y religión quechua en la prelatura de Ayaviri,* Cusco,
            Instituto de Pastoral Andina.

GEERTZ, Clifford
1968   "Religion as a Cultural System," A.S.A. *Monographs*, n. 3.

GIBSON, Charles
1975   *Los aztecas bajo el dominio español* (1519-1810), México, Siglo XXI.

GOSSEN, Gary
1947   *Chamulas in the World of the Sun.* Cambridge, Mass., Harvard University Press.

GOW, Rosalind y CONDORI, Bernabé
1976   *Kay Pacha: tradición oral andina*, Cusco, Centro de Estudios Rurales Las Casas.

GUAMAN POMA, Felipe
1615   *Nueva crónica y buen gobierno*, Madrid, Historia 16, editor J. Murra, 3 tomos, 1987.

GUERRA, Alberto
1970   *Antología del carnaval de Oruro*, Oruro, Quelco, 3 tomos.
1977   *El tío de la mina. Una sobrevivencia de la mitología andina.* Oruro, Imprenta Indgraff.

HARRIS, Olivia
1983   "Los muertos y los diablos entre los laymi de Bolivia," en *Chungará*, Arica, n. 11: 135-152.

HARRIS, Olivia y ALBO, Xavier
1984   *Monteras y guardatojos. Campesinos y mineros en el norte de Potosí.* La Paz, CIPCA (Cuadernos de investigación n. 26, reedición ampliada del original de 1974).

HARRIS, Olivia y BOUYSSE-CASSAGNE, Thérèse
1988   "Los tres pacha en el pensamiento andino del siglo XX," en ALBO, Xavier EDIT. *Raíces de América: el mundo aymara*, Madrid, Alianza Editorial y UNESCO.

HERNANDEZ, Pablo
1913   *Organización social de las doctrinas guaraníes de la Compañia de Jesús*, Barcelona, Gustavo Gili, 2 tomos.

HIDALGO, Jorge
1983   "Amarus y Cataris: aspectos mesiánicos de la rebelión indígena de 1781 en Cusco, Chayanta, La Paz y Arica" en *Chungará*, Arica, n. 10.

HOLLAND, William
1963   *Medicina maya en los Altos de Chiapas*, México, Instituto Nacional Indigenista.

INSTITUTUM HISTORICUM SOCIETATIS JESUS
1970   *Monumenta Peruana*, Roma V (1592-1595).

JORDA, Enrique
1981   *La cosmovisión aymara en el diálogo de la fe. Teología desde el Titicaca*. Lima, Facultad de Teología, tesis doctoral, ms.

KESSEL, Juan van
1978   "Muerte y ritual mortuorio entre los aymaras," en *Norte Grande*, Santiago de Chile, n. 6: 77-91.

KLEIN, Herbert
1970   "Rebeliones de las comunidades campesinas: la república tzeltal de 1712" en *Ensayos de Antropología en la zona central de Chiapas*, México, Instituto Nacional Indigenista, Norman McQuown y Julian Pitt-Rivers edit.

LAFAY, Howard
1975   "Los mayas, los hijos del tiempo" en *National Geographic*, reimpresión.

LAFAYE, Jacques
1974   *Quetzalcóatl y Guadalupe*, Paris, Gallimard. Traducción castellana en México, Fondo de Cultura Económica, 1977.

LANDA, Diego de
1560-70 *Relación de las cosas de Yucatán*, México, Porrúa, 1959.

LAS CASAS, Bartolomé de
1537   *Del único modo de atraer a todos los pueblos a la verdadera religión*, México, Fondo de Cultura Económica.
1552   *Brevísima relación de la destrucción de Indias*, en *Obras*, Madrid, Biblioteca de Autores Españoles, tomo V. In English, *In Defense of the Indians*, trans. Stafford Poule, DeKalb, IL, Northern Illinois University, 1992.
1559   *Apologética historia*, en *Obras*, tomos III y IV.

LAUGHLIN, Robert M.
1977   *Of Cabbages and Kings*, Washington, Smithsonian Institution Press.

LOZANO, Pedro
1754-55 *Historia de la Compañia de Jesús en la Provincia del Paraguay*, Madrid, Viuda de Manuel Fernández.

LLANQUE, Domingo
1972　　　"Mamatan Urupa, rito de acción de gracias" en *Revista Teológica Limense*, Lima, p. 239-254. Nueva versión revisada en *Boletín del Instituto de Estudios Aymaras*, Chucuito, serie 2, n. 10: 6-27.
1986　　　"Producción alimenticia y ritos agrícolas enttr los aymaras" en *Boletín del Instituto de Estudios Aymaras* serie 2, 23: 4-26.

MCA
1951　　　*Manuscritos da Colecâo de Angelis/ I. Jesuitas e Bandeirantes no Guairá* (1549-1640), Rio de Janeiro, Biblioteca Nacional.

MADARIAGA, Salvador de
1959　　　*El corazón de piedra verde*, Buenos Aires, Sudamericana.

MAMANI, Mauricio
1988　　　"Agricultores a los 4000 metros" en ALBO, Xavier edit. *Raíces de América: el mundo aymara*, Madrid, Alianza Editorial y UNESCO.

MARTINEZ, Gabriel
1976　　　"El sistema de los uywiris en Isluya" en *Homenaje al Dr. Gustavo Le Paige*, Antofagasta, Universidad del Norte.
1987　　　*Una mesa ritual en Sucre. A proximaciones semióticas al ritual andino*, La Paz, HISBOL-ASUR.

MARZAL, Manuel M.
1971　　　*El mundo religioso de Urcos*, Cusco, Instituto de Pastoral Andina.
1977　　　*Estudios sobre religión campesina*, Lima, Pontificia Universidad Católica.
1983　　　*La transformación religiosa peruana*, Lima, Pontificia Universidad Católica.
1985　　　*El sincretismo iberoamericano*, Lima, Pontificia Universidad Católica.
1988　　　*Los caminos religiosos de los inmigrantes de la Gran Lima*, Lima, Pontificia Universidad Católica.

MATOS MAR, José
1986　　　*Taquile en Lima: siete familias cuentan*, Lima, Banco Internacional del Perú y UNESCO.

MAURER AVALOS, Eugenio
1983　　　*Los Tzeltales*, México, Centro de Estudios Educativos.

MAYER, Enrique y MASFERRER, Elio
1979　　　"La población indígena en América en 1978" en *América Indígena*, México, Instituto Indigenista Interamericano, XXXIX-2: 217-337.

MAYER, Enrique y BOLTON, Ralph, edit.
1980   *Parentesco y matrimonio en los Andes*, Lima, Pontificia Universidad Católica.

MEDINA, Andrés y SEJOURNÉ, Laurette
1964   *El mundo mágico de los mayas*, México, Museo Nacional de Antropología e Historia.

MELIÀ, Bartomeu
1969   *La création d'un langage chrétien dans les réductions des Guarani au Paraguay*, Univ. de Strasbourg, 2 tomos, tesis.
1973   "El pensamiento 'guaraní' de León Cadogan," en *Suplemento Antropológico*, Asunción, Universidad Católico, VII: 1-2 7-14.
1986   *El guaraní conquistado y reducido. Ensayos de etnohistoria.* Asunción, Centro de Estudios Antropológicos.

MELIÀ, Bartomeu y GRÜNBERG, J. y F.
1976   "Los Pai-Tavytera: etnografía guaraní del Paraguay contemporáneo" en *Suplemento Antropológico*, Asunción, Universidad Católica, XL, 1-2: 151-295.

MELIÀ, Bartomeu, SAU, Marcos Vinicios de A. y MURARO, Valmir F.
1987   *O guarani: uma bibliografía etnológica.* Santo Angelo, Fundames, Fundacaô Nacional Promemória.

MOLINA (el cusqueño), Cristobal de
1574   *Fábulas y ritos de los incas*, en *Las crónicas de los dos Molinas*, Lima, Edit. F.A. Loayza, 1943.

MONAST, Jacques
1972   *Los indios aymaras*, Buenos Aires, Lohlé.

MONTOYA, Rodrigo
1987   *La cultura quechua hoy*, Lima, Mosca Azul.

MÜLLER, Thomas y Helga
1984a   "Mito de Inkarri-Qollarri: cuatro narraciones" en *Allpanchis*, Cusco, Instituto de Pastoral Andina, n. 23: 125-143.
1984b   "Cosmovisión y celebraciones del mundo andino." *ibid*, p. 161-176.

NACHTIGALL, Horst
1975   "Ofrendas de llamas en la vida ceremonial de los pastores" en *Allpanchis*, Cusco, Instituto de Pastoral Andina, n. 8: 133-142.

NASH, June
1970   "Mitos y costumbres en las minas nacionalizadas de Bolivia" en *Estudios Bolivianos*, 1/3: 69-82.

NEWPOWER, Paul
1974   "Pachjiri: montaña sagrada de los aymaras" en *Boletín Ocasional*, Chucuito, Instituto de Estudios Aymaras, n. 7: 1-5. Nueva versió abreviada en 1986 en *Fe y Pueblo*, n. 13: 18.

NIMUENDAJU, Curt Unkel
1914   *As lendas da criacao e destrucao do mundo comofundamentos de la religiao dos Apapocúva-Guarani*, São Paulo, Hucitec, Edusp. 1987.

NUÑEZ DE LA VEGA, Francisco
1702   *Constituciones diocesanas del Obispado de Chiapas*, Roma, Caietano Zenobi.

OCHOA, Victor
1976a   "Un Dios o muchos dioses" en *Boletín del Instituto de Estudios Aymaras*, Chucuito, n. 29.
1976b   "Ritos para la construcción de la casa" en *Boletín del Instituto de Estudios Aymaras*, Chucuito, n. 36.
1977   "La fiesta de la Virgen de la Asunción en Chucuito" en *Boletín del Instituto de Estudios Aymaras*, Chucuito, n. 50.

PALACIOS, Félix
1982   "El simbolismo aymara de la casa" en *Boletín del Instituto de Estudios Aymaras*, Chucuito, n. 82: 37-57.

PEÑA Y MONTENEGRO, Alonso de la
1668   *Itinerario para párrocos de indios*, Amberes, Hermanos de Tournes, 1754.

PITT-RIVERS, Julian
1971   "Thomas Gage parmi les Naguales" en *L'Homme*, vol. IX.

PLATT, Tristan
1976   *Espejos y maíz: temas de la construcción simbólica andina*, La Paz, CIPCA, Cuadernos de Investigación, n. 10. Nueva versión en MAYER y BOLTON edits. 1980 *Parentesco y matrimonio en los Andes*, Lima, Pontificia Universidad Católica, p. 139-182.
1982   *Estado boliviano y ayllu andino. Tierra y tributo en el norte de Potosí*, Lima, Instituto de Estudios Peruanos.
1983   "Religión andina y conciencia proletaria. Qhuyaruna y ayllu en el Norte de Potosi" en *HISLA*, Revista Latinoamericana de Historia Económica y Social, Lima n. 2:47-74. Versión abreviada en 1986 en *Fe y Pueblo*, n. 13: 31-35.
1985   "Ayllu and confradía in a Macha parish," ponencia presentada en la reunión annual de la American Society for Ethnohistory, Chicago.
1988   "Pensamiento político aymara" en X. ALBO edit. *Raíces de América: el mundo aymara*, Madrid, Alianza Editorial y UNESCO.

POBLETE, Renato y GALILEA, Carmen
1984   *Movimiento pentescostal e Iglesia católica en medios populares.*
            Santiago de Chile, Centro Bellarmino, mimeografiado.

QUEIROZ, Maria Isaura de
1973   "O mito da terra sem males: uma utopia guarani?" en *Vozes,*
            Petrópolis, ano 67, 1: 41-50.

QUIROGA, Pedro
1563?   *Coloquios de la verdad,* Sevilla, Centro Oficial de Estudios
            Americanistas, 1922.

RAMOS GAVILAN, Alonso
1621   *Historia del célebre santuario de Nuestra Señora de Copacabana*
            y sus milagros, Lima, Ignacio Prado Pastor, 1979.

RASNAKE, Roger
1982   *The kurahkuna of Yura: indigenous authorities of colonial*
            Charcas and contemporary Bolivia, Ithaca, Cornell University,
            tesis doctoral en antropología, ms.

REDFIELD, Robert
1934   "Culture Changes in Yucatan" in *American Anthropologist,* vol.
            XXXVI.

RICARD, Robert
1947   *La conquista espiritual de México,* México, Jus.

RIESTER, Jürgen
1984   *Textos sagrados de los Guaraníes en Bolivia. Una cacería en el*
            Izozog, La Paz-Cochabamba, Ed. Los Amigos del Libro.

RIVIERE, Gilles
1982   *Sabaya: structures socio-économiques et représentations*
            symboliques dans le Carangas, Bolivie, Paris, Ecole des Hautes
            Etudes des Sciences Sociales, tesis doctoral, ms.
1987   "Cambios sociales y pentecostalismo en un comunidad aymara"
            en *Fe y Pueblo,* n. 14: 24-30.

ROHEIM, Geza
1973   *Psicoanálisis y antropología,* Buenos Aires, Sudamericana.

ROSTWOROWSKI, María
1983   *Estructuras andinas del poder,* Lima, Instituto de Estudios Peruanos.

RUIZ DE MONTOYA, Antonio
1639   *La Conquista espiritual hecha por los religiosos de la Compañía*
            de Jesús en las provincias del Paraguay, Paraná, Uruguay y Tapé,
            Bilbao, Mensajero, 1892.

SANDOVAL, Godofredo, ALBO, X. y GREAVES, T.
1978   *Ojje por encima de todo. Historia de un centro de residentes excampesinos de La Paz.* La Paz, CIPCA, Cuadernos de Investación, n. 16.

SANTO TOMAS, Domingo de
1560   *Gramática o arte de la lengua general de los indios del Perú*, Lima, Universidad Nacional Mayor de San Marcos, 1951.

SCHADEN, Egon
1954   "O estudo do indio brasileiro: ontem e hoje," en *América Indígena*, México, Instituto Indigenista Interamericano, XIV, 3: 233-252.
1959   *A mitologia heróica de tribus indígenas do Brasil*, Río de Janeiro, Ministerio de Educacâo e Cultura.
1966   "A obra científica de Kurt Nimuendajú," en *Suplemento Antropológico de la Revista del Ateneo Paraguayo*, Asunción, II, 1: 27-29.
1974   *Aspectos fundamentais da cultura guaraní*, São Paulo, Editora Pedagógica e Universitária; Edusp.
1976   "Les religions indigénes en Amérique du Sud" en *Encyclopédie de la Pléiade, Histoire des religions*, Paris, Gallimard, III: 836-886.

SECRETARIADO DEL EPISCOPADO PERUANO
1987   *Directorio eclesiástico del Perú*, Lima.

SERNA, Jacinto de la
1656   *Manual del ministro de indios para el conocimiento de sus idolatrías y extirpación de ellas*, México, Imprenta del Museo Nacional, 1892.

SHAPIRO, Judith
1987   "From Tupa to the Land without Evil: the Christianization of Tupi-guarani Cosmology" in *American Ethnologist*, Washington, XIV, 1: 128-139.

SUSNIK, Branislava
1984-85   *Los aborígenes del Paraguay, VI. A proximación a las creencias de los indigenas*, Asuncón, Museo Etnográfico-Andrés Barbero.

TAYLOR, Gerald
1980   "Supay" en *Amerindia*, Paris, n. 5: 47-63.

TEMPLE, Dominique
1986   *La dialéctica del don*, La Paz, HISBOL.

THOMPSON, Eric J.
1975   *Historia y religión de los mayas*, México, Siglo XXI.

TSCHOPIK, Harry
1951   *Magia en Chucuito*, México, Instituto Indigenista Interamericano, 1968.

URBANO, Henrique
1981   *Wiracocha y Ayar: Héroes y funciones en las sociedades andinas*, Cusco, Centro de Estudios Rurales Las Casas.

VILLAGOMEZ, Pedro
1649   *Exhortaciones e instrucción acerca de las idolatrías de los indios*, Lima, Edic. Urteaga y Romero, 1919.

VILLANUEVA, Horacio
1982   *Cusco 1689: economía y sociedad del surandino peruano*, Cusco, Centro de Estudios Rurales Las Casas.

VIVEIROS DE CASTRO, Eduardo B.
1986   *Araweté: os deuses canibais*, Rio de Janeiro, Jorge Zahar Ed. / Anpocs.
1987   "Nimuendajú e os Guaraní" en Nimuendajú 1987, XVII-XXXVII.

VOGT, Evon Z.
1960   *Zinacantan*, Cambridge, Mass., Harvard University Press.

VOGT, Evon Z. edit.
1971   *Desarrollo cultural de los Mayas*, México, UNAM, Centro de Estudios Mayas.

WACHTEL, Nathan
1976   *Los vencidos: los indios del Perú frente a la conquista española (1530-1570)*, Madrid, Alianza Editorial.

WASSERSTROM, Robert
1735   *La lengua tzoltzil en Chiapas*, San Cristóbal Las Casas (traducción moderna de sermones tzotziles).

WEBER, Max
1966   *The Sociology of Religion*, London, Social Sciences Paperbacks.

XIMENEZ, Francisco
1720?   *Historia de la Provincia de San Vicente de Chiapas y Guatemala de la Orden de Predicadores*, Guatemala, Biblioteca Guatemala, 1929-1931.

Index

Boldface numbers indicate pages on which appear definitions of many Indian and/or Spanish words or phrases in the text.

Tembeta, **188**
Tesapyso, **190**
Thakhi, **138**
Tijwanej, **61**
Tinka, **82**
Tinku, **140**, 143
Tio, **156**
Ti'ti 'o'tantayel, **27**
Tiyusa, **135**
Toral, Fray Alfonso de, 54
Trinity: Quechuas and, 81; Tseltals
    and, 29
Tsaltalan, 23
Tseltals, 23-25; angels and, 33;
    baptism and, 36-37; Bible and,
    61-62; catechism and, 61; devils
    and, 33-34; eschatology and, 34-
    35; Eucharist and, 46; evil and,
    28; fear and, 60; festivals for
    saints and, 43-47, 57-59; God
    and, 29, 57; happiness and, 26-
    27; harmony and, 26-28; healing
    and, 40-42; Heaven and, 35-36;
    Hell and, 35-36; indigenous
    priesthood and, 62-63; Jesus and,
    29-31; liturgy and, 46, 62;
    marriage and, 37-39; Mary and,
    30, 31-33, 60; Mass and, 46;
    missionaires and, 48-59; original
    sin and, 30; priesthood and, 39-
    40; 48-56, 61-66; punishment
    and, 53-55, 60; rebellion of 1712,

55-56; saints and, 31-33, 648;
    Trinity and, 29
tut mahtanil, **37**
Twins, myth of the, 197-99, 201
Uinik, Halach, 57
Ukhupacha, 87
Uma Pureq, **83**
Urbanization: Aymaras and, 157-59;
    Quechuas and, 102-18
Urqu, Aymaras and, 145
Utel, **27**
Uywiri, **130**, **133**
Vara, **139**
Vega, Inca Garcilaso de la, **80**
Wak'a, **131**
Waloq, **92**
Wamanis, 81, **82**
Wamichakuy, 86
Waranq Ispilan Mallku, **133**
Warmipalabrakuy, **91**, 102
Wilancha, **141**, 142
Wirjina, **131**
Witchcraft: Tseltals and, 63
Yajwal Ahaw, 33
Yak-che, **31**
Yana, 86
Yanantin, **85**, 86
Yatiris, **131**, **134**, **141**, 146
Yporu, **213**
Yvy marane'y, **214**
Yvy okai, **213**
Yvypyte, **209**